Michael Moore, c.1639–1726

IRISH IN EUROPE MONOGRAPHS

Michael Moore, *c.*1639–1726

Provost of Trinity, Rector of Paris

Liam Chambers

FOUR COURTS PRESS

Set in 10.5 on 12.5 point Ehrhardt for
FOUR COURTS PRESS LTD
7 Malpas Street, Dublin 8, Ireland
e-mail: info@four-courts-press.ie
http://www.four-courts-press.ie
and in North America
FOUR COURTS PRESS
c/o ISBS, 920 N.E. 58th Avenue, Suite 300, Portland, OR 97213.

A catalogue record for this title
is available from the British Library.

ISBN 1–85182–809–5

Printed in Great Britain
by Antony Rowe Ltd, Chippenham, Wilts.

Contents

Abbreviations

Add. MS	Additional manuscripts
ACF	Archives du Collège de France
AN	Archives Nationales, Paris
ASV	Archivio Segreto Vaticano
AUP	Archives de l'Université de Paris
Anal. Hib.	*Analecta Hibernica*
Archiv. Hib.	*Archivium Hibernicum*
BHVP	Bibliothèque Historique de la Ville de Paris
BL	British Library
BN	Bibliothèque Nationale de France
BSG	Bibliothèque Sainte-Geneviève, Paris
Cal S.P. Dom	*Calendar of state papers preserved in the Public Record Office, domestic series* (81 vols, London, 1856–1972).
Cal. Treas. bks	*Calendar of treasury books 1660–[1718] preserved in the Public Record Office* (32 vols, London, 1904–69).
Collect. Hib.	*Collectanea Hibernica*
DED	Michael Moore, *De existentia Dei et humanae mentis immortalitate secundum Cartesii et Aristotelis doctrinam disputatio* (Paris, 1692).
DNB	*Dictionary of National Biography*
DPP	Michael Moore, *De principiis physicis, seu corporum naturalium disputatio* (Paris, 1726).
GO	Genealogical Office (National Library of Ireland)
HMC	Historical Manuscripts Commission
Hortatio	Michael Moore, *Hortatio ad studium linguae Graecae et Hebraicae, recitata coram eminentissimo D.D. Marco Antonio Barbadico* (Montefiascone, 1700).
IER	*Irish Ecclesiastical Record*
IHS	*Irish Historical Studies*
MC	Minutier Central (Archives Nationales, Paris)
NAI	National Archives, Ireland
NLI	National Library of Ireland
PRO	Public Record Office, London
Proc. RIA	*Proceedings of the Royal Irish Academy*
RCBL	Representative Church Body Library, Dublin

TCD	Trinity College, Dublin
UCD	University College Dublin
VSM	Michael Moore, *Vera sciendi methodus* (Paris, 1716).

A NOTE ON SPELLING

Original spellings (in English and other languages) have been retained in direct quotations from primary sources.

Acknowledgments

I am greatly indebted to Thomas O'Connor for his advice and friendship as I researched and wrote this book. He supervised the doctoral thesis on which the book is based and generously offered suggestions and criticism as I prepared the present text. I was fortunate to study at the Department of Modern History at NUI, Maynooth and benefited immensely from the expertise of the staff and my fellow postgraduate students. In particular, I would like to thank Vincent Comerford who encouraged my postgraduate studies from the beginning. Brendan Devlin suggested the topic and provided assistance. Bruno Neveu and Bernard Plongeron assisted me at an early stage in my research. My thanks to Joseph Bergin, Colm Lennon, John Cleary, Thomas Duddy, David Lederer, Hugh Fenning and Liam Irwin who kindly read earlier drafts of various chapters and made suggestions. I am also grateful to the many others who offered advice and encouragement, including Benignus Millet, Priscilla O'Connor, Niall McKenzie, Seamus Cullen, Graham Gargett, Éamon Ó Ciosáin, Michael Brown, Dáire Keogh, James Kelly, Pádraig Lenihan, David O'Shaughnessy, Ruán O'Donnell and Sean Patrick Donlan.

I would like to acknowledge the financial assistance without which this project would not have been possible: a Bourse d'Études awarded by La Fondation Irlandaise, which enabled me to stay at the Collège des Irlandais in Paris while undertaking initial research, a Daniel O'Connell Postgraduate Fellowship awarded by NUI, Maynooth and a Government of Ireland Scholarship. Special thanks to the rector and staff of the Seminario Diocesano Cardinale Marco Antonio Barbarigo in Montefiasone for their hospitality. I would also like to thank the many archivists and librarians in Ireland, France, Italy and the Vatican City who provided assistance, in particular the staff of the John Paul II and Russell Libraries, NUI, Maynooth and Mary Immaculate College Library.

I am grateful for the generous grants-in-aid of publication provided by Thomas O'Connor and the Irish in Europe Project, and John Hegarty, Provost of Trinity College, Dublin.

My thanks to Michael Adams and all the staff at Four Courts Press for their customary patience and efficiency. My colleagues in the Department of History at Mary Immaculate College – Liam Irwin, Maura Cronin, Úna Ní Bhroiméil and Deirdre McMahon – provided a congenial and supportive working environment over the past few years in which I was able to complete this project. My greatest debt, as always, is to my family and friends, especially Seamus Callagy and Siobhan McCarthy, Deirdre Wilson, my parents Kathleen and Jimmy, and my brother Paul.

Series editor's introduction

This series of historical monographs appears under the auspices of the Irish in Europe Project (*Tionscnamh na nÉireannach san Eoraip*) based in the history department, NUI Maynooth. The aim of the series is to present to the public new research on connections between Ireland and Europe in the early modern period. It is part of a larger research initiative to quantify and interpret the Irish European migration phenomenon between the Middle Ages and the modern era.

Thomas O'Connor
Dept of History
NUI, Maynooth

Introduction

Michael Moore, priest, philosopher and educationalist, was one of the thousands of Irish Catholics who migrated to continental Europe in the seventeenth and eighteenth centuries.[1] Born in Dublin around 1639, he went abroad to avail of the educational opportunities closed to Irish Catholics at home. Moore studied at Nantes and Paris, but rather than returning to Ireland after completing his studies, he settled into an academic life at the University of Paris in the 1660s. He maintained close Irish connections, however, and returned to Ireland in 1686 where he played a pivotal role in the Catholic revival under James II as vicar general of the archdiocese of Dublin. In 1689 he became the first Catholic provost of Trinity College Dublin, before falling foul of the king the following year, which resulted in his banishment. He returned to a successful career on the Continent, initially in Italy, before his election as rector of the University of Paris in 1701. He undertook extensive educational reform, at a seminary in Montefiascone in the 1690s and the Collège de Navarre in Paris, where he was appointed principal of arts students in 1702. Moore championed Aristotelian philosophy throughout his career, from his early years as a professor of philosophy at the Collège des Grassins in Paris until the first decades of eighteenth century when he taught at the high-profile Collège de France. He published three books defending Aristotle against the increasingly popular ideas of René Descartes and the Cartesians: *De existentia Dei et humanae mentis immortalitate secundum Cartesii et Aristotelis doctrinam disputatio* (Paris, 1692), *Vera sciendi methodus* (Paris, 1716) and *De principiis physicis, seu corporum naturalium disputatio* (Paris, 1726). By the time he retired in 1720 his career spanned six decades and therefore permits a revealing examination of Irish migrant engagement with education, ideas and Catholicism on the continent in the seventeenth and early eighteenth centuries.

Moore was one of the most prominent clerical migrants of the period and he was routinely included in Irish and French biographical dictionaries published in the eighteenth century, such as those by Pierre Nicholas Desmolets, Louis Moreri or Walter Harris.[2] By the end of the nineteenth century the *Dictionary of Nation-*

---

1 For recent work on the Irish abroad in the seventeenth and eighteenth centuries see: T. O'Connor (ed.), *The Irish in Europe, 1580–1815* (2001); T. O'Connor and M.A. Lyons (eds), *Irish migrants in Europe after Kinsale, 1602–1820* (2003). See also: J.J. Silke, 'The Irish abroad, 1534–1691' (1976); J.G. Simms, 'The Irish on the continent, 1691–1800' (1986). 2 P.N. Desmolets (contin. A.H. de Salengre), *Continuation des mémoires de littérature et d'histoire* (1726–31), ii (published 1727), pp 202–4; L. Moreri, *Le grand dictionnaire historique ou le mélange curieux de l'histoire sacrée et profane*, 18th edn

al Biography was making extravagant claims on his behalf, for example that 'He helped to remodel the University [of Paris] for Louis XIV, who founded for him the college of Cambray [*sic*].'³ Patrick Boyle, the rector of the Collège des Irlandais in Paris, published a more satisfactory account of Moore's life in 1916. It was based on an oration delivered by the rector of the University of Paris, M. Delaval, shortly after Moore's death in 1726 and Boyle's own investigations into the history of Irish clergy in France.⁴ Boyle's comment that Moore was 'the most distinguished Irish Catholic scholar of the seventeenth century' was over-enthusiastic, but it is significant that among the huge amount of material he uncovered and published, Michael Moore stood out enough to merit special treatment.⁵ John Brady added further information in two brief but significant articles published in 1958 and 1960, pointing out Moore's continued associations with Ireland during the 1670s and early 1680s.⁶

In the 1930s, Trinity College Dublin chose to resurrect their associations with Moore. On 2 July 1937, the day after the ratification of the new constitution by plebiscite, the President of the Executive Council of the Irish Free State, Eamon de Valera, opened a new reading room at the college.⁷ After invoking the memory of Thomas Davis, an illustrious former student, in the main library building, de Valera unveiled a memorial near the entrance to the Reading Room which read:

> This tablet is inscribed in memory of the Rev. Michael Moore, D.D., at one time head of this college, by whose exertions the Library and its manuscripts were saved from destruction when the College was occupied by military forces in 1689. Later he became Rector of the University of Paris. Died in Paris in the year 1726, and was buried in the chapel of the Irish College in Paris.⁸

(1740), vi, p. 467; Sir J. Ware, *The whole works of Sir James Ware concerning Ireland, revised and improved*, ed. W. Harris (1739–45), ii, pp 288–90.   3 *DNB*, xxxviii (1894), p. 336. The claim is also made in otherwise reliable sources, for example, A. Bellesheim, *Geschichte der Katholischen Kirche in Irland* (1890–1), iii, pp 713–14. It appears to be based on N[icholas] D[onnelly], 'The diocese of Dublin in the eighteenth century' (1888), p. 847, note 1.   4 P. Boyle, 'Dr Michael Moore, sometime Provost of Trinity College and Rector of the University of Paris (A.D. 1640–1726)' (1916). The oration was copied into the register of the Nation d'Allemagne, and published at the end of Boyle's article (ibid., pp 13–16).   5 Boyle, 'Dr Michael Moore', p. 7. Among his publications relevant to this study are: P. Boyle, *The Irish College in Paris from 1578–1901* (1901); idem, 'Irishmen in the University of Paris in the 17th and 18th centuries' (1903); idem, 'The Irish College in Paris 1578–1901' (1902); idem, 'Glimpses of Irish collegiate life in Paris in the seventeenth and eighteenth centuries' (1902). He also published article length studies of two prominent Irish priests in revolutionary France: idem, 'The Abbé John Baptist Walsh D.D., administrator of the Irish foundations in France from 1787–1815' (1905); idem, 'The Abbé Charles Kearney, D.D. (1762–1824): his life and sufferings during the French Revolution' (1908).   6 J. Brady, 'Dr Michael Moore' (1958); idem, 'Dr Michael Moore' (1960).   7 B. Grimes, 'The library buildings up to 1937' (2000), pp 82–4; 'Papers relating to the 1937 reading room and the planned war memorial' (TCD MUN/P/2/434/1–7).   8 1937 Reading Room, Trinity College, Dublin.

The memorial was the idea of the vice-chancellor, Sir Thomas Molony, who recorded his satisfaction that the state and college could come together 'in doing justice, perhaps belated justice, to the memory of a great man and a great scholar who died over two hundred years ago.'⁹ The *Irish Times* used the opportunity to encourage a rapprochement between the state and college, commenting that 'Trinity owes a duty to the nation, we ask the nation to recall that it owes a duty to Trinity.'¹⁰ Although anxieties had surfaced in the college when de Valera came to power in 1932, the authorities realised quickly that they had little to fear from the new government. In fact, de Valera was responsible for granting major funding to the college in 1947, which marked 'the first important step towards integration with the new Ireland and official recognition by the state as an institution of national importance'.¹¹

Not everyone welcomed de Valera's visit to Trinity College in 1937. The extreme *Catholic Bulletin* consistently opposed any rapprochement between the state and Trinity College during the 1930s, describing the college as an 'essentially anti-Catholic Academy'.¹² Predictably, the journal attacked de Valera's visit and castigated the memorial to Michael Moore as a cynical ploy.¹³ Sean Moran argued that Trinity College was part of a system that had forced Catholics like Moore to seek education overseas. The 'summer scheme' was nothing more, he complained, than an attempt to usurp Michael Moore's legacy for political purposes: 'it was a favourable opportunity for pushing forward [the] purpose of drawing Catholic students into the Elizabethan Fortress of Protestant England established, and maintained ever since, as a defiance of Catholic teaching concerning Catholic Education'.¹⁴ It was also a 'confessedly long-delayed and non-committal recognition of Dr Moore', for the college used the designation 'head' rather than 'provost' on the memorial tablet.¹⁵ 'His memory needs no such uncalled-for performance', concluded Moran, 'as that which has been planned and staged, this summer of 1937, as part of a persistent Touting Scheme for T.C.D.'¹⁶

In the 1990s Colm Connellan published an up-dated biography of Moore, amalgamating information supplied by Harris, Boyle and Brady, and adding some material on the history of Trinity College during the reign of James II.¹⁷ While Connellan made no systematic attempt to analyse Moore's writings, he did comment that *De existentia Dei* 'deserves to be edited and studied in detail'.¹⁸ Connellan also co-translated excerpts for publication in *The Field Day anthology of Irish*

9 *Irish Times*, 3 July 1937.   10 Ibid.   11 R.B. McDowell and D.A. Webb, *Trinity College, Dublin, 1592–1952: an academic history* (1982), p. 475. On de Valera's relationship with the college see: D. Fitzpatrick, 'Eamon de Valera at Trinity College' (1982); J. Lydon, 'The silent sister: Trinity College and Catholic Ireland' (1991), pp 42–3.   12 *Catholic Bulletin*, Oct. 1934. Other attacks were carried in Jan. 1934, Apr. 1934, Oct. 1934, Dec. 1934 and July 1935. See also: M. O'Callaghan, 'Language, nationality and cultural identity in the Irish Free State, 1922–27: the *Irish Statesman* and the *Catholic Bulletin* reappraised' (1984).   13 S. Moran, 'Michael Moore of Paris: commentary on a summer scheme staged within Trinity College' (1937).   14 Ibid., p. 614.   15 Ibid., p. 611, 614–15.   16 Ibid., p. 615. 17 C. Connellan, 'Michael Moore (1640–1726)' (1992).   18 Ibid, p. 268.

writing in 1991.[19] Moore has also featured in recent studies of Irish intellectual history by Thomas Duddy and the cultural history of the Collège des Irlandais in Paris by Proinsias Mac Cana.[20] Duddy has commented that:

> One of the most important of [the] exiled Irish scholars was Michael Moore (1640–1726), a passionate Aristotelian who was actively engaged in attacking the new philosophy of Cartesianism. In a trilogy of Latin texts Moore launched an impressive critique of Descartes' theory of knowledge, arguing that the Aristotelian conception of ideas and their relationship to the world was a more promising foundation for a truly 'scientific' knowledge of the world.[21]

As Duddy recognises, the crucial context to Moore's life and ideas was the Irish Catholic experience of migration and exile in the early modern period. As early as the sixteenth century soldiers, clergy, students and merchants sought more favourable conditions and political support on the Continent. The battle of Kinsale marked an important turning point and the defeat of Spanish and Irish troops resulted in the migration of thousands of Irish soldiers and their dependants to Spain. Later high points of migration in the 1650s and 1690s were also significant, but often deflect attention from the constant lower-level migration which occurred throughout the seventeenth and eighteenth centuries.[22] While the mass migration of the nineteenth century has loomed much larger in Irish historical consciousness, Louis Cullen has pointed out that early modern migration was actually proportionately larger than better known post-1800 movements of population.[23]

The diverse motives underlying migration, including religion, politics, social mobility and poverty among others, ensured the development of complex and dynamic Irish communities in European cities. The establishment of Irish brigades and colleges in foreign cities were only the most direct manifestations of the success of Irish Catholic communities abroad. After overcoming the initial hostility of host populations, Irish merchants were able to establish themselves in ports and cities and operated lucrative trade networks. Though soldiers, clergy and merchants were the most successful groups among the Irish, many poor migrants struggled to makes ends meet in their new surroundings. There is evidence that Irish communities sought to protect the weakest among them, but despite appeals on religious grounds the poor sometimes even found themselves deported back to Ireland, particularly during the early phases of migration in the sixteenth and early seventeenth centuries.[24]

19 S. Deane (ed.), *The Field Day anthology of Irish writing* (1991), i, pp 965–6. 20 T. Duddy, *A history of Irish thought* (2002), pp 78–81; P. Mac Cana, *Collège des Irlandais Paris and Irish Studies* (2001), pp 152–8. 21 Thomas Duddy (ed.), *Dictionary of Irish philosophers* (Bristol, 2004), p. xiii. 22 É. Ó Ciosáin, 'A hundred years of Irish migration to France, 1590–1688' (2001). 23 L. Cullen, 'The Irish diaspora of the seventeenth and eighteenth centuries' (1994), pp 139–40. Cullen's figures include pre-1800 migration to north America. 24 D. Bracken, 'Piracy and poverty: aspects of the Irish Jacobite experience in France, 1691–1720' (2001); M.A. Lyons, '"Vagabonds", "Mendicants", "Gueux":

Education became a fundamental impetus for migration from the mid sixteenth century. Restrictions on Catholic education in Ireland meant that thousands of students attended the colleges and universities of Catholic Europe. This
was accelerated by the demands of the Council of Trent (1545–63) that bishops
establish seminaries for the education of the clergy, clearly an impossibility in Ireland before the late eighteenth century. As numbers increased, Irish clerical and
student communities in foreign towns and cities established Irish Colleges with the
support of wealthy individuals, local churches and central governments. Most
Irish Colleges were established in the Low Countries, France and the Iberian
peninsula, though some could be found in other parts of Europe by the middle of
the eighteenth century. As the seventeenth century progressed, the universities
and Irish Colleges in France became the main destinations for Irish students and
colleges opened in Paris, Bordeaux, Lille, Nantes, Poitiers, Douai and Toulouse.[25]
The Irish in Paris belatedly acquired a permanent college in 1677, when Irish clergy were granted use of the old Italian Collège des Lombards, which remained the
main centre for Irish students until the establishment of the Collège des Irlandais
in the late eighteenth century. By the outbreak of the French Revolution, the
majority of Irish clerical students were educated in France and most passed
through the Irish Colleges in Paris.[26]

Though the establishment of the Irish Colleges helped to ensure the survival
and development of Catholicism in Ireland, foreign education naturally created
problems. For instance, it is clear that many students chose to remain on the Continent after completing their studies. Indeed, in his important analysis of Irish clerics in France, Laurence Brockliss has suggested that the intention of many families
who sent a son abroad to study for the priesthood was that the student would establish a career on the continent rather than returning home.[27] But establishing a
career in France or elsewhere was not easy. While Irish institutions naturally
required a limited supply of administrators, and sometimes teachers, and the
French and other churches absorbed many Irish clerics who were reluctant to
return home, promotion would always be more difficult for an unconnected foreigner than a native. Nevertheless, a considerable number found employment as
personal tutors, chaplains, educational administrators or university and college professors.

French reactions to Irish immigration in the early seventeenth century' (2000). **25** For general
accounts see: J. O'Boyle, *The Irish Colleges on the Continent* (1935); C. Giblin, 'Irish exiles in Catholic
Europe' (1971); idem, 'The Irish Colleges on the Continent' (1978); T.J. Walsh, *The Irish continental
college movement* (1973); D. Murphy, *A history of Irish emigrant and missionary education* (2000), pp
75–122. Douai and Lille were in the Spanish Netherlands when colleges were founded there in 1601
and 1610 respectively. The Poitiers college was established by the Irish Jesuits in 1674 and administered by them until the order's suppression in 1762. It was not a seminary, but educated young
Catholic lay students. **26** As well as the work of Patrick Boyle, see: R. Amadou, 'Saint-Ephrem des
Syriens: de Collège des Lombards à nos jours' (1986), pp 7–66; L. Swords, 'The Collège des Lombards' (1978). **27** L.W.B. Brockliss and P. Ferté, 'Irish clerics in France in the seventeenth and eighteenth centuries: a statistical study' (1987), p. 550.

Irish Catholic scholars who settled on continental Europe wrote and published on a remarkably wide range of subjects.[28] A flick through the pages of Walter Harris's updated *The Writers of Ireland*, published in the mid-eighteenth century, reveals dozens of Irishmen who published abroad and this is but the tip of the iceberg.[29] Recent studies of Peter Lombard, Thomas Messingham, David Rothe, Luke Joseph Hooke, Cornelius Nary, Sylvester Lloyd and Richard Creagh have shown that Irish Catholic writers based on the Continent, or who spent considerable time there, were neither isolated nor cut off from the mainstream of European intellectual developments.[30] They were not anachronistic in their academic tastes, but engaged with the defining intellectual debates of the seventeenth and eighteenth centuries. Émigré scholars who were fortunate enough to find employment at educational institutions which attracted Irish students are particularly interesting for they permit an examination of the educational experience of Irish students abroad. Brockliss noted that we must examine 'the cultural effect of study at Paris [or elsewhere], both on the students themselves and on the public they later served … Indeed until much more is known about the content of university teaching during the period and some attempt is made to study the philosophical, theological and political views of Scottish and Irish clerics, such an analysis is impossible.'[31]

Michael Moore provides an important opportunity to tackle the issues raised by Brockliss. Using his publications, institutional records, scattered letters and information drawn from many other sources, this book provides an intellectual biography and a case study of the experience of Irish clerical migrants in Europe. Moore's career illustrates the ways in which an Irish migrant could establish himself in France and Italy. He was involved in a wide range of educational institutions as a student, administrator and professor, and he helped reform educational programmes in Montefiascone and Paris. His life also underlines the significance of return migration to Ireland, in Moore's case during the reign of James II. Historians have largely neglected the impact of James's reign on the Irish Catholic church. Moore's short career in 1680s Ireland reveals that there was a far from harmonious relationship between church and state.[32]

---

28 B. Millet, 'Irish literature in Latin, 1550–1700' (1976). For Paris, see the recent work of P. Mac Cana, *Collège des Irlandais Paris and Irish Studies* (2001).   29 Sir J. Ware, *The whole works*, ed. Harris, ii, passim.   30 C. Lennon, *An Irish prisoner of conscience of the Tudor era: Archbishop Richard Creagh of Armagh, 1523–86* (2000); T. O'Connor, 'Towards the invention of the Irish Catholic *Natio*: Thomas Messingham's *Florilegium*' (1999); idem, 'Thomas Messingham (*c.*1575–1638?) and the seventeenth-century Irish church' (2000); idem, 'A justification for foreign intervention in early modern Ireland: Peter Lombard's Commentarius (1600)' (2003); C. Lennon, 'Political thought of Irish Counter-Reformation churchmen: the testimony of the "Analecta" of Bishop David Rothe' (1999); T. O'Connor, 'Custom, authority and tolerance in Irish political thought: David Rothe's *Analecta* 1616' (2000); P. Fagan, *Dublin's turbulent priest: Cornelius Nary, 1658–1738* (1991); idem, *An Irish bishop in penal times: the chequered career of Sylvester Lloyd OFM, 1680–1747* (1993); T. O'Connor, *An Irish theologian in Enlightenment France: Luke Joseph Hooke, 1714–96* (1995); idem, 'Surviving the civil constitution of the clergy: Luke Joseph Hooke's revolutionary experiences' (1996).   31 L.W.B. Brockliss, 'The University of Paris and the maintenance of Catholicism in the British Isles, 1426–1789: a study in clerical recruitment' (1986–9), ii, p. 605.   32 For a recent exception see: H. Fenning, 'Dominic Maguire,

Moore also provides an important opportunity to assess the reactions of Irish migrants to intellectual developments on the continent. It is clear that Irish Catholics engaged with European philosophical developments in the seventeenth and early eighteenth centuries. The Irish Jesuit Christopher Holywood wrote on Aristotelian natural philosophy and astronomy in the early 1600s. Mark Bagot, a Catholic member of the Dublin Philosophical Society, had the works of Galileo transcribed for his perusal. The physician Bernard Connor and another Jesuit, Joseph Ignatius O'Halloran, embraced mechanism, the latter being one of the first to teach Newtonianism in Bordeaux.³³ Moreover, Irish Franciscans across Europe championed the Scholasticism of John Duns Scotus in the seventeenth century. Under the supervision of Luke Wadding, the first collected edition of Scotus's writings was published in 1639, drawing heavily on the work of earlier Irish Scotists such as Hugh MacCaghwell. Dozens of commentaries and textbooks, many written by Irishmen, followed.³⁴ As a professor of philosophy in Paris, Moore witnessed the rise of the 'new philosophy' of Descartes and the Cartesians and participated in the intellectual upheavals of the seventeenth century. The battle between committed Aristotelians, like Moore, and the Cartesians was one of the pivotal intellectual contests of the period.³⁵ Indeed, historians have increasingly recognised the longevity and significance of late Aristotelianism in France, not least because it was the dominant philosophy against which Cartesianism and other new ideas emerged.³⁶

Moore provides a suitable prism through which to examine the impact of the Aristotelian-Cartesian contest on university politics and the attendant reverberations for an Irish Catholic and his world. Moreover, his Aristotelianism was representative of the philosophical education imparted to thousands of Irish Catholic students until well into the eighteenth century. Any student who wished to pursue a career in the church, law or medicine, had to undertake studies in languages and philosophy as a preliminary. The subject was, therefore, 'an integral part of [the student's] intellectual development'.³⁷ Moore's writings allow us to study an important aspect of the intellectual formation of Irish students in Catholic Europe.

O.P., archbishop of Armagh: 1684–1707' (1999–2000).   33 J.J. Pérez-Camacho, 'Late Renaissance humanism and the Dublin scientific tradition (1592–1641)' (2000); J. Corboy, 'Fr Christopher Holywood S.J. 1559–1626' (1944); 'Tractatus Galilei de motu locali, cum appendice de centro gravitatis. Transcriptus ex originali a Guliemo Dowell in gratiam Marci Bagoti in comitatu Catherlogiae viventis, Feb. 1687' (Marsh's Library, Dublin, MS 24.Z.8); D. Coakley, *Irish masters of medicine* (1992), pp 15–25; M.J. Counihan, 'Ireland and the scientific tradition' (1997); C. Preston, 'Le Collège des Irlandais de Bordeaux' (1971).   34 B. Millet, 'Irish Scotists at St Isodore's College, Rome in the seventeenth century' (1968); C. Giblin, 'Hugh MacCaghwell O.F.M. and Scotism at St Anthony's College, Louvain' (1968); C. Balic, 'Wadding, the Scotist' (1957).   35 Important studies include: R. Ariew, *Descartes and the last scholastics* (1999), which collects essays published by the author over the past decade; L. Cohen Rosenfield, 'Peripatetic adversaries of Cartesianism in 17th century France' (1957); C.A. Kors, *Atheism in France 1650–1729, volume 1: the orthodox sources of disbelief* (1990); L.W.B. Brockliss, *French higher education in the seventeenth and eighteenth centuries: a cultural history* (1989). The last three works briefly discuss Moore's philosophy.   36 See in particular: C. Mercer, 'The vitality and importance of early modern Aristotelianism' (1993).   37 L.W.B. Brockliss, 'Curricula' (1996), p. 565.

Through Moore, this study explores the survival and revival of Irish Catholicism in the early modern period. European centres of education provided refuges for Irish students, clerics and scholars, and increased Irish engagement with European educational methodologies and intellectual developments which helped to shape and strengthen the Irish Catholic church. Though Irish Catholicism was never fully reformed in the early modern period, it was heavily influenced by the European experience of so many of its leading figures. Assessing the significance of migration, exile, education and European thought will be central to the reassessment of the history of early modern Irish Catholicism.

Family, education and early career:
Ireland and France, 1639–86

The 1640s and 1650s were decades of crisis for Irish Catholics. Almost continuous warfare between 1641 and 1653 was quickly followed by massive land expropriation by the victorious Cromwellian government. By the time Charles II was restored to the throne in 1660, the social and political structures of the island had been irrevocably altered. While Catholics generally welcomed the Restoration, they could not undo the changes of the previous decades. During this period of instability and dislocation, Michael Moore was born and raised in Dublin, one of the few areas of the country to remain outside confederate control. A reconstruction of his family background reveals a multi-faceted and well connected social world, but one acutely affected by the insecurity and mobility of political life in early and mid seventeenth-century Ireland. Moore's early obituarists and biographers either knew little about his family or were content merely to affirm the importance of his Catholic parentage. In fact, he had extensive and influential connections to prominent families from the Pale region in Dublin and its hinterland.[1]

Moore's parental family was connected to the Gaelic Irish O'Moores of Laois. His maternal family, the Dowdalls, were prominent landowners in County Meath. Moore was also closely related to other Old English families, most importantly the Wogans and De La Hoydes of Kildare. These links help explain later connections with families like the Barnewalls, Talbots and Fleminges, as well as the prominent positions Moore occupied, particularly in Ireland during the 1680s. The genealogical evidence suggests that Moore straddled the worlds of the Old English and Gaelic Irish. The level of interaction between the two has been emphasised in recent historical writing. As one commentator puts it: 'the increased assimilation within the Catholic elite in the early decades of the seventeenth century blurred existing ethnic boundaries'.[2]

The most substantial information on Moore's background and family was provided by Walter Harris in the mid-eighteenth century: 'Michael Moor[e], a secular priest, and D.D. son of Patrick Moor, merchant, and Mary, daughter to Mr

1 William Smyth has commented that 'County Dublin was obviously part of a wider cultural region of the pale which actually constituted one single property, information and marriage field for the Old English.' 'Exploring the social and cultural topographies of sixteenth and seventeenth century County Dublin' (1992), p. 144; J. Kingson, 'Catholic families of the Pale' (1955, 1956, 1960). 2 M. Ó Siochrú, 'Introduction' in idem (ed.), *Kingdoms in crisis: Ireland in the 1640s* (2001), p. 15.

Dowdal of Mountown, was born in Bridge Street in the city of Dublin in 1640.'[3] According to a short account of Moore's life compiled by Pierre Nicholas Desmolets in 1727, Moore was eighty-seven when he died in August 1726, suggesting that he was born in 1639, not 1640. This is supported by a 1669 reference which noted that Moore was, at that point, over thirty years old.[4] Bridge Street in Dublin was relatively affluent in the early seventeenth century, at least if one is to judge by the residents listed by Sir John Gilbert. These included Sir Paul Davies, John Cheevers, Simon Luttrell, Sir Erasmus Burrowes, Sir John Read and Patrick D'Arcy.[5] In 1625 Luke Rochfort established a pre-seminary 'classical school' in Bridge Street, with the assistance of a prominent merchant and recusant, Thomas Plunkett.[6] This strengthens the impression that Michael Moore's family was a comfortable merchant household. Nicholas Donnelly noted that one Patrick Moore, whom he identified as Michael's father, was cessed for St Audoen's parish in 1643. One James Moore lived in Bridge Street in 1665.[7]

The Dowdalls of Mountown, Moore's maternal family, were relatively prominent at a local level. Mountown (alternatively Mounketowne or Monktown) was a parish in the barony of Skreen in County Meath. In 1640–1 Edward Dowdall, a Protestant, owned land in the parish of Mountown, some of it jointly with two Irish Catholics, Sir Christopher Bellew and a Mr Bellinge.[8] The head of the family after the death of his father in 1617, Edward Dowdall was registrar of the court of chancery in Ireland and died on 1 December 1665. He married Margaret, daughter of Sir Henry Piers of Tristernagh, County Westmeath. Edward Dowdall and Margaret Piers had nine recorded children, none of whom was called Mary. The only identifiable Mary Dowdall of Mountown was the granddaughter of Edward Dowdall, the child of his fourth son, Nicholas.[9] The closely related Dowdalls of Athlumney were also prominent in County Meath. Though Edward Dowdall of Athlumney, cousin of his Mountown namesake, was a Protestant, his children were raised as Catholics.[10]

3 Ware, *The whole works*, ed. W. Harris, ii, pp 288.   4 This appears in the register of the Nation d'Allemagne. Cited in L.W.B. Brockliss and P. Ferté, 'A prospography of Irish clerics who studied in France in the seventeenth and eighteenth centuries, in particular at the universities of Paris and Toulouse' (unpublished, 1987), p. 129.   5 J.T. Gilbert, *A history of the city of Dublin* (1854–9), i, pp 326–36.   6 J. Brady, 'Archdeacon Luke Rochfort and his circle' (1962), pp 113, 117.   7 N. Donnelly, *Short histories of Dublin parishes* (1904–17), part 9, p. 212; *The fifty-seventh report of the keeper of public records and keeper of the state papers in Ireland* (1936), appendix iv, p. 555.   8 *The civil survey A.D. 1654–1656, vol. v: County of Meath* (1940), pp 57–8. A collection of family papers does exist, but contains nothing relating to the pre-1674 period: Verschoyle-Campbell [Dowdall] Papers (NLI, P.C. 231, unsorted).   9 See: 'Dowdall formerly of Mountown' in Sir B. Burke, *A genealogical and heraldic history of the landed gentry of Ireland*, new edn (1912), p. 191; Pedigrees of the Dowdall family (GO MS 169, pp 356–61, MS 177, pp 105–12). A. Clarke, *The Old English in Ireland, 1625–42* (1966), pp 119, note 5, 203–5. Edward Dowdall was a major creditor on the Dublin Staple between 1627 and 1638, amounting to a total of £5,100, though he also borrowed £600 in 1632 (J. Ohlmeyer and É. Ó Ciardha (eds), *The Irish statute staple books, 1596–1687* (1998), pp 91, 210). Margaret Piers (or Pierce) was well connected. Her maternal grandfather was Thomas Jones, archbishop of Dublin. Her paternal great-grandfather was the antiquarian Sir James Ware: see C.T. Lambert (ed.), *Some funeral entries of Ireland* [1907–12], pp 92, 114.   10 J. Brady, 'Archdeacon Luke Rochfort and his circle' (1962), pp 113,

On the outbreak of the 1641 rebellion, the Dowdalls were swept up by events. Edward Dowdall of Mountown's brother, Nicholas Dowdall of Brownestowne, was sheriff of County Meath in 1641 and, at the instigation of Nicholas Preston, Viscount Gormanstown, he called the meeting of Meath gentry and landowners which resulted in the Crofty Hill negotiations with the Ulster rebels and Rory O'More in December 1641. Edward Dowdall also attended this and subsequent meetings at which the Old English Meath landowners and gentry finally agreed to participation in the rebellion and where they discussed military organisation and strategy. He later hosted secret meetings between Rory O'More and Gormanstown in his own home, and was involved in opening communications between the rebels and Catholic gentry in Connaught.[11] Nicholas Dowdall of Brownestowne later claimed under examination that he had been forced to assist the rebels 'through feare and terror ... he living in the barronie where they kept their camp, and through the threats of the nobilitie against anie who would not bee seene at theire meeteings, and not out of anie desire hee ... ever had to side or partake with them in this warr ...'[12] His brother, Edward, provided the government with information around the same time, in March 1642, though it is not clear if he shared similar opinions. Though Michael Moore's mother cannot be identified with any certainty, his maternal family were prominent local landowners with Catholic and Protestant connections and links to the government and the confederates.

Moore's father is also difficult to pin down and there are even discrepancies concerning his name. While Walter Harris named him as 'Patrick Moor[e]', Michael Moore stated in 1695 he was the 'son of the late Andrew Moore', a fact he was unlikely to forget.[13] In 1640 an Andrew Moore was a small landowner in County Dublin. The civil survey of the 1650s lists him as an 'Irish papist' who owned 10 acres of arable land 'in ye towne of ffinglas Elmers land', parish of Finglas in the barony of Nethercross. The land was valued at five pounds and described as follows:

> The p'risses pay a chiefe rent to ye Archbishop of ——. The tythes did belong to ye parson of ffinglass anno 1640 now to ye Colledge. Bounded on ye east with Sr Robert fforth his land; on ye north with Sr Edward Bagshaw his land in ffinglass. The house and improvement in ye south part of the land.[14]

117; T. O'Connor, 'Thomas Messingham (*c.*1575–1638?)', pp 96, 103, note 38. **11** Examination of Edward Dowdall of Moncketowne [*sic*], 13 March 1642 in J. Gilbert (ed.), *History of the Irish Confederation and the war in Ireland, 1641–1643* (1882–9), i, pp 268–78; Examination of Nicholas Dowdall of Brownestowne, 17 March 1641 in ibid., pp 278–85. For an interesting discussion of the early rebellion in Meath see: P. Lenihan, *Confederate Catholics at war 1641–49* (2001), p. 33–38. **12** Gilbert (ed.), *History of the Irish Confederation*, p. 285. **13** C. Giblin, 'The Processus Datariae and the appointment of Irish bishops in the seventeenth century' (1957), pp 606–9. **14** R.C. Simington (ed.), *The civil survey A.D. 1654–1656, vol. vii: County of Dublin* (1945), p. 134.

L.J. Arnold's study of the Restoration land settlement in Dublin notes an Old English Catholic landowner called Andrew Moore in possession of eight acres in 1640. During the 1660s his name disappeared but by this stage one Patrick Moore owned eight acres.[15] However, it is impossible to conclude that this was Michael Moore's family.

Nonetheless, it is possible to reconstruct something of Michael Moore's paternal family, through his Wogan connections. In his will, drawn up in 1721, Moore stated: 'J'ay laisse le bien que j'auris en Irlande *a mon beau frere Wogan* et a ses heritiers males a certaines conditions portees par le contrait entre nous, ayant [?] seulement une pension viagere de soissante livres sterling ma vie durant dont j'ay a peine recu deux annees ou quelque peu d'avantage.'[16] The will and related documents also mentioned a niece (who died between 1721 and 1723) and nephew called Wogan.[17] Dame Judith Wogan, wife of Stephen Browne ('Estienne Broown') appears on a later document.[18] To these can be added Anne Wogan, wife of Corneil O'Driscoll, lieutenant-colonel of Mahony's Irish regiment in Spain. On 21 February 1715 she acquired an annuity of 1,500 livres, which belonged to Michael Moore, and of which he had made a gift to the Collège des Lombards for an unspecified foundation. In 1707 one Anne De La Hoyde, widow of Jean (John) Wogan, had acted with power of attorney for the same Anne Wogan.[19]

Clearly there was a strong connection between Moore and the Wogans. In the aftermath of the defeat of Jacobite forces in Ireland in the late 1680s and early 1690s, Michael Moore was mentioned on a list of outlawed Irish Jacobites. The writer mistakenly identified him as a Jesuit, but more importantly gave his residence as Rathcoffey in County Kildare, the seat of the most important Wogan line in Ireland.[20] It is reasonable to assume that Moore's brother-in-law was John Wogan of Rathcoffey, who was in possession of the family's estate at Rathcoffey

---

15 L.J. Arnold, *The Restoration land settlement in County Dublin, 1660–1688* (1993), pp 153, 157. 16 'I left the property which I had in Ireland to my brother-in-law Wogan and to his male inheritors, on certain conditions carried by the contract between us, having [received?] a life pension of only sixty pounds during my life of which I have scarcely received two years [payment], or similar small advantage.' Michael Moore's will, 10 April 1721, codicil to the will, 1 May 1721, second codicil to the will, 7 December 1723 (AN, MC, ET XVII/632, Novembre–Decembre 1723). Summarized in Swords (ed.), 'Calendar of Irish material in the files of Jean Fromomt … part 2, 1716–1730', pp 111–13. My italics. 17 Michael Moore's will, 10 April 1721, codicil to the will, 1 May 1721, second codicil to the will, 7 December 1723 (AN, MC, ET XVII/632, Novembre–Decembre 1723). 18 'Inventaire, Aoust 1726' (AN, MC, ET XVII/647). 19 Untitled documents, 21 February 1715 (AN, MC, ET XVII/571); Swords (ed.), 'Calendar of Irish material in the files of Jean Fromomt, notary at Paris, May 1701–24 Jan. 1730, in the Archives Nationales, Paris: part 1, 1701–15' (1992–3), pp 84, 113. A further O'Driscoll-Moore connection was the marriage of John Driscoll and Mary Moore at St Germain-en-Laye in 1706. The couple had an illegitimate daughter who was baptised in the same parish seven years previously. John was the son of Corneille Driscoll, presumably the same man, though his wife was Hélène Driscoll in 1706. See: C.E. Lart (ed.), *The parochial registers of St Germain-en-Laye: Jacobite extracts of births, marriages and deaths* (1910–12), i, p. 68, ii, pp 8–9. 20 J.G. Simms (ed.), 'Irish Jacobites: lists from TCD MS N.1.3.' (1960), p. 89; R.C. Simington (ed.), *The civil survey A.D. 1654–1656*, vol.iii: *County of Kildare* (1952), p. 208.

during the late 1680s and well into the eighteenth century. In 1678 John Wogan married his second wife, Judith Moore.[21]

John Wogan was the second son of Nicholas Wogan of Rathcoffey and his wife Catherine Preston, daughter of Jenico, fifth Viscount Gormanstown. Colonel Nicholas Wogan participated in the 1641 rebellion and in consequence was outlawed for high treason the following year and seized of his property at Rathcoffey in 1643. John Wogan's mother, Catherine Preston petitioned the duke of Ormond in 1663 for the partial return of her husband's estate. She died in 1683, as did her eldest son, William Wogan.[22] The following year a 'small amount' of the original estate was regranted to John Wogan, who became increasingly influential during the reign of James II.[23] He was a captain in Fitzjames' infantry during this period, sheriff for County Kildare in 1687 and a representative of the county at the parliament of 1689. Following the defeat of Jacobite forces he was attainted in 1691 with his kinsman Patrick Wogan of Mainham.[24] Yet by the early eighteenth centuryq a Colonel John Wogan, presumably the same man, was granted a licence to carry arms on 30 March 1706.[25]

The identity of John Wogan's first wife is unknown. On 12 March 1678 a marriage settlement was drawn up between 'John Wogan of Rathcoffee, esq., and Judith Moore of St. Martins in the Fields, Middlesex, spinster'.[26] A further settlement was made by John Wogan and his wife, Judith Moore, on 18 June 1681. Hugh Law viewed the original document (now missing) while preparing a biogxrles Wogan in the 1930s and noted that Judith Moore was described as 'a lady of the Court of Charles II', which would explain her residence in London.[27] Indeed, the date of her marriage to John Wogan, and presumably her departure from court, overlaps with the beginnings of the Popish Plot when Catholic courtiers and servants were removed.[28] Further evidence seems to confirm the courtly connections held by Judith Moore. On 10 November 1675 the following was granted to Judith Moore:

> Warrant for a grant to Judith Moore of a pension of 150*l.* a year charged on the Irish revenue to be paid to her, her executors, administrators or

---

21 NLI Wogan Browne Papers, Reports on Private Collections, No. 354. This is the only identifiable marriage link between a Wogan of Rathcoffey and a Moore during the relevant period. 22 W.O. Cavenagh, 'The Wogans of Rathcoffey, Co. Kildare – a correction' (1906–8), pp 109–13; H. Law, 'Sir Charles Wogan' (1937), pp 256–7; M. Devitt, 'Rathcoffey' (1900), pp 81–3. 23 'The Wogans of Rathcoffey' (1890), p. 320. This short note was un-referenced and anonymous. 24 J. D'Alton, *Illustrations, historical and genealogical of King James' Irish army list, 1689,* 2nd edn (1801), i, pp 451–4. 25 Cavenagh, 'The Wogans of Rathcoffey, Co. Kildare – a correction', p. 112. 26 The location of the original document is unknown but the National Library prepared a report on the document, part of the Wogan Browne Papers, from which the quotation is taken. NLI Wogan Browne Papers, Reports on private collections, No. 354. The date was 12 March 1677 old style. 27 N.L.I., Wogan Browne Papers, Reports on private collections No. 354; Law, 'Sir Charles Wogan', p. 256. 28 Among them were two other Irish Catholics, Hannah Roche and Eleanor Wall, maidservants to Louise de Quérouailles, mistress to Charles II. See: H. McDonnell, *The wild geese of the Antrim MacDonnells* (1996), p. 64.

assigns, until the sum of 2,000*l.* be paid to her or them at one entire payment, the same being in lieu of a former grant of the King's right in the mills of Kilmainham, which was resumed on the Lord Lieutenant's information that the said mills were situate[d] within the King's deer park near Dublin and were proper to be kept therewith.[29]

This was an exceptional grant to an unmarried female Irish Catholic and confirms her rather intriguing status at court in England. In November 1675 the grant was approved, back-dated to 29 September, and 'entered in the present and future establishments of Ireland'.[30] At some point during the next twenty-six years the annuity was assigned to Major Walter Delamar, who petitioned for payment of the arrears in December 1701.[31] However, by 1711 the annuity was back in the hands of John and Judith Wogan who petitioned the lord lieutenant for 'payment of the arrears of an annuity of 150*l.* per ann. due out of the revenue of Ireland, and for placing the same on the establishment'.[32] Two years later the Wogans reassigned the annuity to one Richard Malone of Dublin, to whom they were in debt.[33]

   The close connections Judith Moore had with the English court belies the fact that she was a member of one of the best known Gaelic Irish families in Leinster, the O'Moore's of Laois and Kildare. Judith Moore was apparently the daughter of Anthony Moore of Balyna, County Kildare, and his wife Anne Hope, daughter of Alexander Hope of Mullingar.[34] As one of the seven septs of Laois, the O'Moore's owned extensive lands in the county until the 1550s when the area was planted and re-named Queen's County. In 1574, following a series of appeals, Elizabeth I granted Balyna, County Kildare, and Kilmainham Wood, County Meath, to the English-educated Charles or Callough O'Moore who died in 1618. Both his sons participated in the 1641 rebellion and confederate wars, most famously Rory O'Moore, who played a leading role in the early stages.[35] In compiling a history of the family, one of the last of the O'Moore's proper, James More (died 1779), noted that Rory O'Moore effected his escape at the start of the rebellion by lodging 'at Moore's a merchant in Bridge Street' before travelling north.[36] Combining this with his knowledge of Michael Moore, gleaned no doubt from Walter Harris, John Gilbert concluded that: 'The host of Roger O'More appears

29 *Cal. S.P. dom., 1675–1676,* p. 398.   **30** *Cal. treas. bks, 1672–1675,* p. 849.   **31** *Cal. treas. bks, 1697–1701/2,* p. 545.   **32** *Cal. treas. bks, 1708–1714,* p. 314.   **33** Deed dated 17 September 1713 (Registry of Deeds, Dublin, 11/166/4259).   **34** GO, MS 173, p. 142 (the detail appears as part of a Talbot of Malahide pedigree, pp 140–3).   **35** The Balyna lands were confiscated in 1641 when Rory O'Moore was charged with high treason, but restored to the family in 1686. See: Simington (ed.), *The civil survey A.D. 1654–1656, vol. iii: County of Kildare,* pp xix–xxi, 175–6, 185–6; N.M. Hickey, 'The Cromwellian settlement in Balyna parish, 1641–1688' (1985–6), pp 496–509.   **36** J. More, 'The O'More family of Balyna in the County Kildare, by James More of Balyna, circa 1774', ed. E. O'Leary and W. Fitzgerald (1918–21), p. 282. The land at Balyna had been forfeited by the De La Hoydes of Moyglare who were later related to Michael Moore (ibid., p. 279). For background on the O'Moore's see: V.P. Carey, 'Gaelic reaction to plantation: the case of the O'More and O'Connor Lordships of Laois and Offaly, 1570–1603' (1985).

to have been Patrick Moor, merchant, father of Dr. Michael Moore, who was born in Bridge Street in 1640'.[37] It has already been noted that O'More held secret meetings with Viscount Gormanstown in the home of Edward Dowdall of Mountown, possibly Michael Moore's maternal grandfather. Apparently, Judith Moore was the granddaughter of Rory O'Moore's brother, Colonel Lewis O'Moore who married Mary O'Reilly daughter of the chief of the Breffny-O'Reilly, Philip MacHugh O'Reilly, and daughter of their eldest son Anthony O'Moore and his wife Anne Hope.[38] However, on closer inspection Judith Moore does not fit into the existing genealogy of the O'Moore's of Balyna. She was too old in the 1670s to have actually been the daughter of Anthony Moore (who was born around 1653 or later) and Anne Hope. It is possible only to surmise that Michael and his sister Judith were the children of Andrew (or Patrick) Moore, a younger branch of the O'Moores of Balyna who had established themselves in Dublin.[39] Michael Moore's Gaelic Irish background is confirmed by a letter written to him in Irish in the aftermath of the defeat of the forces of James II in Ireland.[40] Indeed, the historian James MacGeoghegan, writing in the mid-eighteenth century, commented that Moore was 'of the celebrated tribe of the O'Morrus [*sic*] of Leix.'[41]

A number of Michael Moore's relations are noted on an inventory of his estate drawn up shortly after his death, which further underlines his Wogan connections. 'Dame Judith Wogan' was the daughter of John and Judith Wogan, and the second wife of Stephen Fitzwilliam Browne who died in 1767.[42] Nicholas Wogan was described as a captain in Berwick's regiment of Irish infantry. The eldest son of John and Judith Wogan was Colonel Nicholas Wogan of Rathcoffey. However, Nicholas Wogan of Berwick's regiment was the son of Patrick Wogan of Richardstown, another branch of the family. The latter Nicholas Wogan became a naturalised French subject in 1724 and was involved in the Jacobite rebellions of 1715 and 1745.[43] Through the Wogans, a successful migrant family, Moore acquired connections that stretched across western Europe in the seventeenth and eighteenth centuries.[44] Michael Moore was also related to the De La Hoydes, a once prominent Old English family, who had slipped into obscurity by the late seventeenth and early eighteenth centuries. In 1721 he willed an annuity to a niece

---

37 Gilbert, *A history of the city of Dublin*, i, p. 329. 38 More, 'The O'More family of Balyna in the County Kildare, by James More of Balyna, circa 1774', pp 284, 288, and the genealogical table inserted between pages 276–7; *Burke's Irish family records*, pp 908–9. For a brief biography of Rory O'Moore see: *DNB*, xlii (1895), pp 176–8. 39 For a fuller discussion of the genealogical permutations see: L. Chambers, 'The life and writings of Michael Moore (*c*.1639–1726)' (2001), pp 32–6. 40 'Cormac comharba Ciarain' to Mileadh O Morro, *c*.1691 (BL, Add. MS 34,727, ff 159–62). 41 J. MacGeoghegan, *History of Ireland, ancient and modern*, trans. P. O'Kelly (first published Paris, 1759–62, O'Kelly translation published 1844), p. 493. 42 The couple had six known sons: John, Thomas, Nicholas, Michael, Christopher and Anthony. 'Wogan-Browne of Castle Browne' in Burke, *A genealogical and heraldic history of the landed gentry of Ireland*, pp 76–7. 43 R. Hayes, *A biographical dictionary of Irishmen in France* (1949), pp 317–18. For an attempt to disentangle the two Nicholas Wogans see: Law, 'Sir Charles Wogan', pp 258–9.

called De La Hoyde, while four De La Hoydes appeared in the 1726 inventory. Marguerite De La Hoyde was the widow of Laurence De La Hoyde, another captain in Berwick's regiment, and was living in Paris at the 'cloistre de St Estienne … paroisse de St Benoist'. The other De La Hoydes were Michael, Melchior, both 'Irish gentlemen', and Mary, the wife of Mr Barrer.[45]

Moore's family network reveals urban and rural, Old English and Gaelic Irish, and indeed Catholic and Protestant dimensions. His youth overlapped with a period of sustained political and social crisis and insecurity in Ireland, something keenly felt by families like the O'Moores, Wogans and Dowdalls. For Moore's generation, the Cromwellian 1650s marked a watershed in Irish history.[46] Many of them chose migration as a survival strategy, a phenomenon that became more pronounced as the seventeenth century progressed. In fact, Moore would become involved with a number of prominent pale families while on the Continent, in particular the Barnewalls (Matthew and Barnabas), the Talbots (Richard and Peter) and the Fleminges. Moore's family background in Dublin and its hinterland provided access to a network of relations which stretched to continental Europe in the second half of the seventeenth century. Irish priests who were established in continental cities often provided legal and administrative fronts for other Irish exiles.[47] In Michael Moore's case, a network of family relations straddled Irish and French residences. A large proportion of those mentioned in his testamentary documents had taken up military careers in France in the late seventeenth-century.

As Éamon Ó Ciosáin has reminded us, large-scale Irish migration to France was well-established before the late seventeenth century. In the 1650s, when Moore left Dublin for the Continent, there were an estimated 30,000 Irish soldiers in the French army.[48] The early 1650s also witnessed a massive exodus of perhaps 1,000 Irish priests, many of them destined for the Continent. By July 1653 sixty Irish priests had taken up residence in the northern French port town of Nantes.[49] A 1666 report listed numerous Irish inhabitants in the province of Brittany, including many priests.[50] Bishop Robert Barry of Cork and Cloyne ministered in

44 See: F. D'Arcy, 'Exiles and strangers: the case of the Wogans' (1989), pp 171–85. 45 Michael Moore's will, 10 April 1721, codicil to the will, 1 May 1721, second codicil to the will, 7 December 1723 (AN, MC, ET XVII/632, Novembre-Decembre 1723); 'Inventaire, Aoust 1726' (AN, MC, ET XVII/647); D'Alton, *Illustrations, historical and genealogical of King James' Irish army list, 1689*, i, pp 477–8. This provides a very brief family history. 46 'Cormac comharba Ciarain' to Mileadh O Morro, *c.*1691 (BL, Add. MS 34,727, f. 161v). 47 See Liam Swords' comments at the beginning of 'Calendar of Irish material in the files of Jean Fromomt … part 1, 1701–15', pp 77–9; Priscilla O'Connor has recently explored this aspect of exile networks in 'Irish clerics and Jacobites in early eighteenth-century Paris (1700–30)' (2001). 48 É. Ó Ciosáin, 'A hundred years of Irish emigration to France, 1590–1688', p. 101. 49 B. Millet, 'Survival and reorganisation 1650–95' (1968), pp 4–5. It should be noted that the same decree of 6 January 1653 which banished 'Jesuits, seminary priests and other priests holding papal orders' also banned foreign education for Irish Catholics: S. Kavanagh (ed.), *Commentarius Rinuccinianus, de sedis apostolicae legatione ad foederatos Hiberniae catholicos per annos 1645–9* (1932–49), v, pp 85–8. 50 'Estat et roolle des Irlandais Catholiques habituez dans la

the region between 1652 and 1662.[51] Because of its geographical position, Nantes developed as a substantial centre of Irish exiles during the seventeenth century. Initial suspicion and hostility at the start of the century gave way to increasing acceptance and support of Irish exiles from the 1650s.[52] Despite the emergence of an Irish community in the area, there was no Irish College in Nantes until 1689.[53] There was an attempt to establish an independent Irish College in Nantes during the 1640s when Richard Gybbon began teaching a course of philosophy against the wishes of the university. A few years later he linked up with a fellow Irishman, Patrice Maubrouy, to teach grammar and rhetoric as well. The pair were finally ordered to leave the town in 1650.[54] It is possible that this premature attempt to establish an autonomous educational institution, having aroused the opposition of the existing establishment, retarded the development of a full Irish College in Nantes for decades.

Moore's early biographers were in agreement that he received his earliest education in Nantes. Harris noted that: 'Having laid a competent stock of grammar learning at home, he was sent to France, and had his first academick education in the College of Nantz' and according to Desmolets he 'étudia d'abord à Nantes sous les Peres de l'Oratoire'.[55] The Congrégation de l'Oratoire, founded by Pierre de Bérulle in 1611, quickly became an influential and reforming force in French education, establishing twelve schools by the time de Bérulle died in 1629. In 1625 the political authorities in Nantes accepted a proposal from the Oratorians to take over the previously secular Collège Saint-Clément, having refused, the previous year, to cede control to the Jesuits. During the 1650s the new administration expanded the curriculum, adding another professor of philosophy and initiating a course in theology.[56] By 1670 the Collège Saint-Clément had approximately 1,200 students, mostly drawn from Nantes and the surrounding area, and there was a strong Irish connection. The inquiry ordered by Colbert in 1669 noted the presence of five Irish theology students.[57] One P. LeBlanc 'un Irlandais' held a chair of theology for twenty years from 1658.[58]

province de Bretagne [1666]' (Les Archives du Ministère des Relations Extérieures, Les fonds anciens, Mémoires et Documents, France, 1508, ff. 329–337). This valuable document does not include details for Nantes.   51 A. Walsh, 'Irish exiles in Brittany' (1897), pp 125–38.   52 A. Walsh, 'Irish exiles in Brittany' (1897, 1898); J. Malthorez, 'Notes sur les prêtres Irlandais réfugiés à Nantes aux XVIIe et XVIIIe siècles' (1912); R. Hayes, 'Irish associations with Nantes' (1939); É. Ó Ciosáin, 'Les Irlandais en Bretagne 1603–1780: "invasion", accueil, intégration' (1994).   53 The college established in 1689 was essentially a student hostel, founded at a time when Nantes was full of Irish Jacobite refugees. The college gained official seminary status in 1765 when it was formally connected to the local university. A. Walsh, 'Irish exiles in Brittany' (1898), pp 323–45; O'Boyle, *The Irish colleges on the Continent*, pp 181–200.   54 A. Bachelier, *Essai sur l'Oratoire à Nantes au XVIIe et au XVIIIe siècles* (1934), p. 73.   55 Ware, *The whole works*, ed. Harris, ii, p. 288; Desmolets, *Continuation des mémoires*, ii, p. 202; Boyle, 'Dr Michael Moore', p. 14.   56 For a brief history of the college see: M.M. Compère et D. Julia, *Les collèges français, 16e-18e siècles* (1988), ii, pp 486–92. The college was granted permanently to the Oratorians in 1672.   57 Compère et Julia, *Les collèges français*, ii, p. 488.   58 Bachelier, *Essai*, p. 62. This was Revd John White, an Irish Oratorian, see: Hayes, 'Irish associations with Nantes', p. 120.

Since we know that Moore studied philosophy at the University of Paris, where he graduated in 1662 from what was usually a two-year course, it is reasonable to assume that Moore completed his grammar studies at Nantes in 1660.[59] The humanities course at French colleges was firmly focused on the study of Latin, thus Brockliss comments: 'the core curriculum of the six-year course consisted of the study of linguistic principles of Latin, illustrated by Latin texts and supported by practical exercises'.[60] The course began in sixth class and proceeded through to first class. During the final two years the student took a course in rhetoric and politics.[61] As Brockliss puts it: 'After six years studying the humanities in a collège de plein exercise, no one but the dullest scholar could have emerged from the rhetoric class who was not an extremely competent Latinist.'[62] Presumably Moore left Nantes for Paris in 1660 to expand his educational and social opportunities by connecting with the most important exiled community of Irish on the continent and seizing the opportunity to study at one of Europe's most acclaimed universities. He must have left Nantes as a highly proficient rhetorician for he was later to teach the subject at the Collège des Grassins. There may also have been a more practical consideration for the move to Paris. The pensionnat, that is the living quarters for students, was closed at Nantes, or at least partially closed, from 1660 until 1678 due to reconstruction.[63]

The University of Paris, like most seventeenth-century universities, continued to reflect its medieval heritage. There were four faculties, the three 'higher' faculties of theology, law and medicine, as well as the faculty of arts. All students wishing to pursue a course at one of the higher faculties had to pass through the faculty of arts. Therefore, all students studied philosophy. From the fifteenth century, the faculty of arts became a mere examining and awarding body, without actual teaching functions. The teaching of humanities and philosophy was undertaken at one of the collèges de plein exercise. As well as these teaching colleges, there were a large number of non-teaching colleges, which essentially functioned as student hostels. The Irish Collège des Lombards, established in the 1670s, was such a non-teaching college. When Moore arrived in Paris in 1660 there was no Irish College, and it is not entirely clear which college he attended, but it was probably the Collège de Grassins. Edward Browne, an English visitor, described the Collège des Grassins in the early 1660s: 'Within is a pretty faire Court. Those boyes that are in pension in the College dyne together in the hall. 5 or 6 severall Classes as appears by the writing over severall dores.'[64]

59 P. Lallemand, *Histoire de l'éducation dans l'ancien Oratoire de France* (1888). He discusses the Oratorian relationship with Cartesianism, pp 112–39. For recent analysis see: R. Ariew, 'Oratorians and the teaching of Cartesian philosophy in seventeenth-century France' (2002).   60 Brockliss, *French higher education*, p. 111. For his discussion of 'The Humanities' see: pp 111–81.   61 In fact, the lowest, sixth, class was apparently only instituted in the Collège Saint-Clément in 1656 following the sale of the Collège Saint-Jean. If this was the case Moore must have followed an unorthodox five-year course, beginning in 1655. This of course assumes that he took the full course, rather than entering a higher class. See: Compère et Julia, *Les collèges français*, ii, p. 488.   62 Brockliss, *French higher education*, p. 181.   63 Compère et Julia, *Les collèges français*, ii, p. 486.   64 Cited in J. Lough, *France*

The philosophy course was divided into four sections: logic, ethics, physics (natural philosophy) and metaphysics.[65] Logic was invariably taught first since it provided the analytical apparatus necessary not only for the study of other parts of the philosophy course, but more generally for the higher subjects as well. The 'science of right reasoning' remained focused on the *Organon* of Aristotle prefaced by Porphyry's *Universals*. The course in ethics was equally focused on Aristotle, or more accurately Thomas Aquinas's interpretation of Aristotle. The course was taught in two parts: general ethics dealing with man as an individual and particular ethics dealing with the individual as part of a family and state. The traditional order of the philosophy course, as described above, was never strictly followed after the mid-seventeenth century, so that the metaphysics course might be taught immediately after the logic section, but traditionally physics was the third component of the course. It too remained largely wedded to the relevant Aristotelian texts in the early 1660s. Beginning with a general study of the natural body, based on Aristotle's *Physics*, it moved on to particular aspects of the natural world, which included the soul, derived from Aristotle's *De anima*.[66] The final element of the course was a study of metaphysics. The first half of the course examined the 'principles of being'. The second part was perhaps the least truly Aristotelian element of the course. It studied 'being as a spiritual substance', that is God, angels, the soul and other topics.[67] Brockliss has noted that: 'There is certainly plenty of indirect evidence to suggest that novel discoveries and ideas were creeping into the university from the 1650s.'[68] Yet when Moore took his course at the university it is highly unlikely that he was exposed to ideas which reflected the 'new learning', at least in the classroom. Having completed the course, Moore was awarded a Master of Arts degree in 1662.[69]

Moore made at least one influential friend in the early 1660s, a young French nobleman called Alexis de Barjot, who was closely involved in university politics in the second half of the century. In 1663 Moore wrote two pieces of Latin verse to his friend. It also appears that de Barjot defended his philosophy thesis under Moore in 1663. While the relationship is not well documented, de Barjot, who was rector in 1670–1 and again in 1675–6, was an influential ally for Moore at the university.[70] When he died around 1705, de Barjot left Moore an annual pension of two

observed in the seventeenth century by British travellers (1985), p. 273.   65 Brockliss, *French higher education*, pp 185–6.   66 See, for example, Moore's own physics course at the Collège de France, *De principiis physicis*, published in 1726.   67 For discussion of the various branches of the philosophical curriculum see: Brockliss, *French higher education*, pp 185–227, 337–90; idem., 'Philosophy teaching in France 1600–1740' (1981). On the philosophy course at the University of Paris in particular see: L.W.B. Brockliss, 'The University of Paris in the sixteenth and seventeenth centuries' (1976), pp 146–71.   68 Brockliss, 'The University of Paris in the sixteenth and seventeenth centuries', p. 159.   69 This entitled him to membership of the Nation d'Allemagne, to which he was admitted on 11 November 1662. Liber procurationum Constantissimae Germanorum Nationis (1660–98) (AUP, registre 28, f. 19v). The significance of the Nation d'Allemagne for the Irish community in Paris is discussed below.   70 His full name was Alexis de Barjot de Moussy de Roncée. *Illustrissimo nobilissimoque adolescenti D.D. Alexio Barjot de Moussy de Roncée theses sustinenti carmen* [Offerebat Michael

hundred livres. However, Moore was forced to engage in a legal action with the guardian of Alexis de Barjot's heir to obtain the bequest. He won the case but later explained that: 'Je ne l'ay pas conclu faire par respect a la maison de Mons L'Abbe de Moussy.' A codicil to his will recommended that the judgment be enforced and the pension of about 1,600 livres bequeathed to the Collège des Lombards.[71]

De Barjot and Moore began their academic careers as professors of philosophy at the Collège des Grassins, founded by Pierre Grassin, a counsellor at parlement, in 1569.[72] Moore was professor of philosophy at the college from at least 1665, and probably from 1663.[73] Over the next few years he taught three of the four constituent parts of the philosophy course: logic, physics and metaphysics.[74] At an early stage in his career Moore was teaching the philosophical subjects on which he would later publish extensively. He also supervised the submission of philosophy theses by French and Irish students. In 1666 he sponsored five theses, including one by John (Joannes) Purcell from Kilkenny.[75] By 1669 Moore had acquired an administrative position and was described as: 'M. Michel Morus, sous p[rinci]pal des Grassins e[t] professeur en ph[ilosoph]ie'.[76] Around 1673 Moore began to teach rhetoric, the final class of the humanities course.[77] He continued to teach and hold his administrative position as vice-principal of the college during the 1670s and early 1680s.

It is clear then that Moore decided to make a career at the Collège des Grassins from the 1660s, rather than return to Ireland. This raises questions about the pur-

Morus Hibernus] (Paris, 1663); *Eminentissimo principi domino D. Antonio Barberino, sanctae Romanae ecclesiae cardinali camerario magno Franciae eleemosynario, Archepiscopi Duci Rhemensi designato Primo Franciae Pari etc. Dum sub eius auspiciis theses philosophicas sustineret illustrissimus ac nobilissimus adolescans Alexis Barjot de Moussy de Roncée* [Ita vouet et precatur Eminentiae tuae addictissimus et humillimus cliens Michael Morus Hibernus] (Paris, 1663). Two copies of each printed piece exist: Bibliothèque Sainte-Geneviève, Réserve, Y fol. 121 inv. 134, pièces 6, 25; Bibliothèque Mazarine, 274 A10 and 274 A 11. On the rectors of the university see: 'Liste chronologique des recteurs de l'Université de Paris, au XVIIe et au XVIIIe siècles' in C. Jourdain, *Histoire de l'Université de Paris au XVIIe et au XVIIIe siècles* (1862), pièces justificatives, cxxxxv.   **71** First codicil to the will of Michael Moore, 1 May 1721 (AN, MC, ET XVII/632, Novembre-Decembre 1723). It states that Alexis de Barjot died 'il y a quinze ou se[i]ze ans', that is, in 1705 or 1706.   **72** It is possible to trace the career of both men at the college from a surviving register for the years 1665–1673. Unfortunately neither the preceding nor subsequent registers have survived. De Barjot was a certainly a professor of philosophy at the college in July 1666, see: Collège des Grassins, Annales XVIIe siècle (*c.* 1665–72) (AN, MM 447 f. 104). On the college: G. Brice, *Description de la ville de Paris*, 6th edn (1713), ii, p. 297; J.B. Buzy, *Notice historique sur le Collège des Grassins* (1881); J. Delteil, 'Le Collège des Grassins à Paris' (1967). The college was situated on the modern rue Laplace (number 12), formerly rue des Amandiers.   **73** Collège des Grassins, Annales XVIIe siècle (*c.* 1665–72) (AN, MM 447, ff 11, 19).   **74** Physics (1665, 1666, 1668, 1669), Logic (1668, 1672), Metaphysics (1670). Moore's name is missing from the register in 1667 and 1671. Collège des Grassins, Annales XVIIe siècle (*c.*1665–72) (AN, MM 447, ff. 61, 84, 86, 99, 267, 276, 293, 297, 313, 314, 318).   **75** Ibid., ff. 16, 99, 102, 105, 109, 112, 297. A copy of Purcell's philosophy thesis is extant at the Bibliothèque de la Sorbonne, J. Purcell, *Conclusiones philosophicae* (Paris, 1666), as well as another thesis sponsored by Moore, Anian Boiscourion, *Conclusiones philosophicae* (Paris, 1666).   **76** Collège des Grassins, Annales XVIIe siècle (*c.*1665–72) (AN, MM 447, f. 293).

pose of his education in France. Was he sent abroad to study for the priesthood? There is no simple answer. However, in 1673 the register of the Collège des Grassins described Moore as 'hibernus baccalauraes theologes' and as a staunch and learned supporter of Aristotelian 'scientia'.[78] While some authors have arbitrarily described Moore as a 'doctor' of theology, his early biographers never mentioned such a distinguishing feature, nor did Moore have any direct connection with the Sorbonne.[79] The baccalaureate was a basic qualification bestowed on students after three years of study at the faculty of theology (following an examination known as the 'tentativa'), but was vastly inferior to the 'marketable' licence or doctorate.[80] This evidence for Moore's theological studies suggests that he had come to Paris to train for the priesthood, it was not something he decided on in the 1680s as suggested by Harris.[81]

The Collège des Grassins developed an intimate association with Irish students during the late seventeenth and early eighteenth centuries. Priest-students (those ordained before leaving Ireland to commence their studies) resident at the Collège des Lombards studied philosophy at the Collège des Grassins 'from time immemorial because of its proximity', according to a 1762 source.[82] The link was further enhanced by a series of bursaries (bourses) for Irish students which were established at the Collège des Grassins in the late seventeenth century, though this led to accusations and ultimately litigation against Irish students. The controversy had its roots in the provision of several bourses to students of Ulster extraction in the testament of an important member of the Irish community in France, Patrick Magin. Protracted legal wrangling dogged the provisions from the beginning. They were finally put in place in 1696, when the executor attached the

77 Delaval's 1726 oration, in Boyle, 'Dr Michael Moore', p. 14. In 1674 he was described as a professor of philosophy and eloquence (that is, rhetoric) Liber procurationum Constantissimae Germanorum Nationis (1660–98) (AUP, registre 28, f. 190). 78 Collège des Grassins, Annales XVIIᵉ siècle (*c.*1665–72) (AN, MM 447, f. 318). There is supporting evidence that Moore studied theology in Paris. In his 1715 *approbatio* penned for Cornelius Nary's translation of the New Testament, Moore stated that he had been 'sacrae theologiae lector et professor per annos septem cum in Gallia tum in Italia', suggesting two years study in France, before teaching theology for five years in Montefiascone. *The New Testament of our lord and saviour Jesus Christ newly translated out of the Latin vulgar and with the original Greek, and divers translations diligently compared and revised* (1718), unpaginated; Strangely, the theological qualification was not mentioned later. This is particularly noticeable in the lists of officers contained in the registers of the Nation d'Allemagne, which was quite pedantic in its recital of an individual's qualifications. Boyle, 'Irishmen in the University of Paris in the 17th and 18th centuries', pp 39–44. 79 The Irish letter sent to Moore in 1691 described him as 'dochtuir díadhachta a n-ardscolaimh Paríse'. (Cormac comharba Ciarain to Mileadh O Morro, *c.*1691 (BL, Add. MSS 34,727, f. 159)). 80 Brockliss and Ferté, 'Irish clerics in France in the seventeenth and eighteenth centuries', p. 532. 81 Ware, *The whole works*, ed. Harris, p. 288. 82 L. Swords (ed.), 'History of the Irish College, Paris, 1578–1800. Calendar of the papers of the Irish College, Paris' (1980), p. 105. Neal Carolan, a priest-student from County Meath, was sent to Paris in August 1662, where he studied philosophy at the Collège des Grassins and 'speculative divinity' at the Collège de Navarre. He returned to Ireland in 1667 and ministered in the diocese of Meath, but converted to the Church of Ireland in the 1680s, see: N. Carolan, *Motives of conversion to the catholick faith, as it is professed in the reformed church of England* (1688), 'the preface to the reader', unpaginated.

bourses to the Collège des Grassins, because the Irish residence at the Collège des Lombards was apparently full. Relations between the Irish community that established itself in the Collège des Grassins and the institution's authorities deteriorated rapidly. The Irish connection was dissolved on 4 May 1710 following the visit of university inspectors. Predictably, French sources blamed the Irish for the tension, arguing that the Irish students increased the college's financial difficulties. While Charles Magennis (Magin's successor as proviseur of the Collège des Lombards) appears to have worked for the establishment of an Irish group at the Collège des Grassins from 1682, there is no indication that Moore was involved in any significant way. In fact, the provincial bias of the bourses, though common during the period, may have put Moore off lobbying on his compatriots' behalf.[83]

The case neatly indicates the difficulties faced by the growing Irish community in Paris and the tensions caused by their relative poverty and insecurity. To overcome their insecurity, Irish students and graduates maximised any potential for the establishment of a corporate identity within the university. The best example is the Irish 'take-over' of the Nation d'Allemagne (German Nation) which provided a point of common interest and community support. As Laurence Brockliss puts it: 'For an Irish student before the establishment of the Collège des Lombards in the 1670s, the Nation was an obvious refuge: the only university institution where fellow exiles could gather for mutual support.'[84] Paris remained a 'master's' university, and the four nations that comprised the Faculty of Arts reflected this principle. The four nations governed the faculty, each nation representing a group of masters. These nations were the powerful Nation de France, the Nation de Picardie, the Nation de Normandie and the weak Nation d'Allemagne. The latter (until the fifteenth century, the Natio Anglicana) was the home of masters from the Continent, essentially the German states (the tribe of continentals), and Britain and Ireland (the tribe of islanders). By the seventeenth and eighteenth centuries it was effectively dominated by Irish members, for students from other regions had decreased in numbers. The Nation d'Allemagne was much smaller than the other three. While all qualified masters were admitted, senior membership, which entailed voting rights, was restricted to twenty.[85] Like the other nations, there were four basic officers: the procureur, the administrative head and representative; the censeur, who enforced discipline; the questeur, essentially the treasurer; the doyen or oldest member of the nation.[86]

83 On the controversy see: Delteil, 'Le Collège des Grassins à Paris', pp 255–66; Amadou, 'Saint-Ephrem des Syriens du Collège des Lombards à nos jours', pp 23–4; Boyle, 'Lord Iveagh and other Irish officers, students at the Collège des Grassins, in Paris, from 1684–1710', pp 385–94.   84 Brockliss, 'Irish clerics in France in the seventeenth and eighteenth centuries', p. 532.   85 M. Targe, *Professeurs et régents de collège dans l'ancienne université de Paris (XVIIᵉ et XVIIIᵉ siècles)* (1902), p. 32   86 For some background see: P. Perdrizet (ed.), *Le calendrier de la Nation d'Allemagne de l'ancienne Université de Paris* (1937); Targe, *Professeurs et régents*, pp 21–34; Brockliss, 'The University of Paris in the sixteenth and seventeenth centuries', pp 51–55; Boyle, 'Irishmen in the University of Paris in the 17th and 18th centuries', pp 26–45. For an interesting contemporary account see: J.B.L. Crevier (?), 'Estat de la faculté des arts' in Receuil des pièces concernant l'Université de Paris XVIᵉ–XVIIIᵉ siècles, n.d.

The nation was important for young migrants like Moore, who was admitted in November 1662. He continued to play a prominent role in the nation until 1720. He held the office of procureur four times (1671, 1673, 1708 and 1717) and doyen after 1685, or possibly 1684. As a member of the nation, Moore became part of the key group of Irish exiles within the University of Paris. In the early 1650s the Irish masters had encountered the wrath of the authorities following complaints concerning their attempts to band together too closely within the nation, but during Moore's membership it is clear that the Irish completely dominated the group.[87] Moore's first term as procureur does indicate a willingness to utilise the letter of the law to further his own standing within the university. In 1671 Moore was competing for the post with Edward O'Moloy, whom Moore claimed had not fulfilled all the formalities needed to become a member. Moore received the position and O'Moloy continued his complaints, though he was in turn appointed to the office shortly after.[88]

One event suggests that even during this early part of his career Moore had the capacity to extend himself beyond the limits usually accepted by his compatriots. Despite the fact that Irishmen dominated the Nation d'Allemagne during the seventeenth and early eighteenth centuries, only one Irishman was elected rector of the university in this period, Michael Moore himself in 1701. The honorific post of rector was in the hands of the arts faculty, and it was the responsibility of the nations to appoint a rector who was *always* from the lower faculty and simply 'approved' by the higher faculties.[89]

In fact, Moore was elected to the post in 1677, but turned down the appointment in a controversial and confusing episode. On 10 October 1676 Nicholas Pières was elected rector. While the post was technically held for three-month periods, invariably the incumbent continued in the position until he had completed one year of service. However, Michael Moore was elected to the post in the 'middle' of Pières term on 23 June 1677. The circumstances are quite hazy, but it appears the Nation de Picardie, not the Nation d'Allemagne as might be assumed, instigated the action. It was probably the result of one of many, often trivial, internation rivalries. In any case, Moore refused the appointment on the same day on the grounds that his acceptance would interfere with the work Pières was undertaking. The procureurs of the other three nations promptly confirmed Pières in his position for the remainder of the academic year. Moore, as will be seen, was not re-elected to the post until his return from Montefiascone in 1701. But his decision probably ensured that he did not make enemies in the university.[90]

[late 17th cent.] (BSG, MS 987, ff. 34–35). 87 Boyle, 'Irishmen in the University of Paris in the 17th and 18th centuries', pp 27–30. On Moore's position as Doyen: Liber procurationum Constantissimae Germanorum Nationis (1660–98) (AUP, registre 28, ff. 276–80). 88 Boyle, 'Irishmen in the University of Paris in the 17th and 18th centuries', pp 30–1; Liber procurationum Constantissimae Germanorum Nationis (1660–98) (AUP, registre 28, f. 134). 89 For further discussion of the post and its significance see chapter five, where Moore's 1701–2 incumbency will be dealt with. 90 'Liste chronologique des recteurs de l'Université de Paris, au XVIIᵉ et au XVIIIᵉ siècles' in Jourdain, *His-*

While Moore was embroiled in the rector controversy in 1677, his Irish colleagues in Paris were ensuring their control of the vacant Collège des Lombards.
It is surprising that Moore was not involved, though he would have a close relationship with the Collège des Lombards in the early eighteenth century. Nonetheless, Moore was in touch with events in Ireland, as two important incidents confirm. In 1678 one Edward Everard linked Michael Moore with the 'Popish Plot'.
The uncovering of an 'attempt' by leading English, Scottish and Irish Catholics
to subvert the established order and place a Catholic monarch on the throne was
initiated by the information supplied by Titus Oates in 1678. Oates had managed
to infiltrate English Colleges in Spain, and his evidence against leading Catholics
was followed by further incriminating, though equally unreliable, testimony of
others. The plot claimed a number of prominent victims until 1681 when the ultimate Irish scapegoat, Oliver Plunkett, the archbishop of Armagh, was executed
following a trial in London.[91]

One of the Irish-based accusers was Edmund Everard, a Catholic from Tipperary, who, in December 1678, made a number of allegations concerning the
activities of Irish and Scottish 'plotters' based in Paris during 1673.[92] Everard was
'employed as agent at the French court for the English Militia's concerns' in
1673.[93] His first set of accusations focused on the designs of a Scottish faction in
Paris based around Anne Gordon, the sister of the marquis of Huntley, and a
number of ecclesiastics who were 'conspiring' to place a new monarch on the
throne, possibly the duke of York or Charles II's illegitimate son, the duke of
Monmouth.[94] In the meantime Everard claimed that two Irish priests, Doctors
O'Brien and Molony, recommended him to the Talbots. Richard Talbot requested that Everard assist his brother Peter, the archbishop of Dublin, in his dealings
with the French court. When Everard agreed to have him introduced at court, he
reported that: 'the Bishop would have Mr Moore, a priest and philosophy professor at Paris, to accompany us thither on the next day.'[95] That evening Everard
managed to extract information concerning the plot from Peter Talbot. The basic

toire de l'Université de Paris, pièces justificatives, cxxxxv; Conclusions de l'Université, 1677–1682
(AUP, registre 33, ff. 11v-13).   **91** J. Brady, 'Oliver Plunkett and the popish plot' (1958). In the course
of his research Brady uncovered Moore's association with the plot: 'Dr Michael Moore' (1958).   **92**
E. Everard, *The depositions and examinations of Mr Edmund Everard (who was four years close prisoner
in the Tower of London) concerning the horrid popish plot* (1679); the information furnished by Everard
before the committee of the house of lords in London was printed in HMC, *Thirteenth report, appendix, part vi: The manuscripts of Sir William Fitzherbert, Bart., and others* (1893), pp 141–5. On Everard's life see: R.H.A.J. Everard, 'The family of Everard: part iii Everard of Fethard, Co. Tipperary'
(1991), pp 201–3.   **93** *Depositions*, p. 1; HMC, *Fitzherbert*, p. 141. The text of these sources do not
match exactly, the quotations have therefore been taken from Everard's contemporary pamphlet.   **94**
Depositions, pp 1–3; HMC, *Fitzherbert*, pp 141–2. The Collège des Ecossais later became an important centre of Jacobite activity, see: B.M. O'Halloran, *The Scots College Paris, 1603–1792* (1997), pp
80–98.   **95** *Depositions*, p. 4. The text in the Fitzherbert papers is significantly different since there is
no mention that Moore was a priest: 'The Bishop would have Mr Moore a philosophy professor in
Graslin [Grassins] Colledge to accompany us theither next day.' See: HMC, *Fitzherbert*, p. 142.

aim was to empower the Catholics of England and Ireland, and specifically: 'That he was to propose ways to the King of France whereby to relieve them in their present extremities and persecutions and for to undertake their protection, and some of his ways was [*sic*] to arm some Irish and to secure a sea-port town in Ireland for the French'.[96] Everard went on to describe Peter Talbot's arrival at the French court the following day:

> The Marshall [Bellefond, grand steward to Louis XVI, who acted as go between] knew him at first sight and imbraced him, and acquainted the king with his coming, his Majesty receiving him with great civility led him into a private room where Mr Moore and I following them he beck'ned to Mr Moore that had the papers to advance: but I from the doorward saw the Bishop present a letter to the King and other papers which I think were sealed. I overheard he spoke in Italian at first entrance, their conference lasted about half an hour, and though that king is somewhat of a grave and somewhat morose temper, yet he often smiled, as at propositions that pleased him.[97]

It is clear that Everard's prime targets were the Talbots and Huntleys, whom he blamed for his later confinement in London. According to Everard, he reported the conspiracy to Sir Robert Walsh, unaware that he was in league with the Talbots, which ensured that Everard was imprisoned only one week after his arrival in London. His evidence was promptly ignored for the next five years until the frenzy unleashed by Oates's testimony.[98] A rather different version of circumstances was proffered by Walsh himself who replied in a pamphlet of his own that Everard had in fact been confined for his part in a conspiracy to poison the duke of Monmouth.[99] Over the next decade he continued to play a shadowy role in the underworld of espionage.[1]

It is easy to imagine how someone like Everard might decide to drag the Talbots or Lady Huntley into his imaginary conspiracy.[2] But why would he give an apparently obscure Irish professor of philosophy such a high profile role? According to Everard, Moore was fully conversant with the plan and a kind of 'right hand man' to Peter Talbot. After their visit to the French court Everard failed to extract further information from Talbot, but he recorded: 'Yet note, that Mr Moore did also generally touch unto me the matters of the aforesaid articles and plot, having heard it from the said Bishop, Peter Talbot, and his papers.'[3] The evi-

---

96 *Depositions*, p. 4; HMC, *Fitzherbert*, p. 143. **97** Ibid. **98** *Depositions*, pp 5–16; HMC, *Fitzherbert*, pp 143–5. **99** R. Walsh, *A true narrative and manifest, set forth by Sir Robert Walsh* (1679). **1** Everard, 'The family of Everard: part iii Everard of Fethard, Co. Tipperary', pp 202–3. **2** On leaving Ireland in 1673 Peter Talbot procured letters of introduction to Louis XIV from Charles II and the duke of York. He used his contacts at court to help establish the Irish college at Poitiers in 1674. See: F. Finegan, 'The Jesuits in Dublin (1660–1760)' (1965–71), p. 53; idem, 'The Irish College at Poiters: 1674–1762' (1965), pp 19–23. For Talbot's statements while in prison see: W.P. Burke, *The Irish priests in the penal times (1660–1670)* (1914), pp 104–9. **3** *Depositions*, p. 5. This statement is completely

dence may not be sufficient to suggest that Moore was plotting a French invasion of Ireland, but it indicates that Everard knew him in Paris, probably as a close contact of Talbot's. Peter Talbot, a controversial character throughout his career, was consecrated archbishop of Dublin in Antwerp in 1669, and landed in Dublin the following year. By 1673 he had been forced to leave Ireland and was known to have been in France. He was arrested in October 1678, the chief accusation against him being involvement in a conspiracy to assassinate Ormond. He died in prison two years later, no doubt depriving Moore of an important patron.[4]

The link between Michael Moore and the powerful Talbots is further illustrated, not only by Moore's prominent position in Jacobite Ireland, but by his role in another Irish related affair revolving around the Fleminge family, lords of Slane.[5] During the late 1670s and 1680s Michael Moore was charged with the education of Christopher Fleminge, the young lord baron of Slane, and his siblings. Christopher Fleminge was the son and heir of Randall Fleminge, sixteenth Lord Slane by his second wife Penelope Moore, daughter of Henry Moore, first earl of Drogheda by his wife Alice, who was to play and important role in the affair, and had a influential brother in the first earl of Sunderland. Following the Restoration, Randall Fleminge had his lands restored through the court of claims. Interestingly, during the Popish Plot period it was claimed that in 1672 he was involved in a conspiracy of 'bringing over a French army to Ireland to settle the Catholic religion'.[6] He was murdered in October 1676, and his wife died in the same year.[7] This placed Randall Fleminge's children in a rather precarious position, since their legal guardian was declared to be their maternal grandmother, Alice, the dowager countess of Drogheda, a Protestant.[8] The Catholic upbringing of the family was now in doubt. It was decided therefore to place Christopher (born 1669) and his siblings, Henry and Alice, in the care of a Catholic tutor on the Continent. The prime mover of this plan was Father Barnabas Barnwall, vice-commissary of the Capuchins in Ireland. In a 1678 joint testimonial addressed to Rome, Oliver Plunkett and his close colleague, John Brenan, the archbishop of Cashel, requested the promotion of Barnewall to the rank of commissary:

missing from HMC, *Fitzherbert*. The Ormond papers contains a list of persons 'that were listed as undertakers to bring in so many men and so much money', including one 'Dr Moore', see: HMC, *Calendar of the manuscripts of the marquess of Ormonde K.P. preserved at Kilkenny Castle*, new series (1902–20), iv, p. 475.   **4** D. McCarthy (ed.), *Collections on Irish church history from the MSS of the late V. Rev. Laurence Renehan D.D.* (1861), i, pp 202–28; P.W. Sergeant, *Little Jennings and fighting Dick Talbot: a life of the duke and duchess of Tyrconnel* (1913), especially volume one, pp 227–74. 'Peter Talbot's alleged scheme for Ireland', found among his papers in July 1671, is included in appendix C, pp 646–8. Article eleven states: 'That they [Irish Catholics] have a good correspondence abroad, for that great numbers of their nation are soldiers, priests and merchants, in esteem with several great princes and their ministers.'   **5** Brady also first noted this episode, see his: 'Dr Michael Moore' (1960).   **6** HMC, *Eleventh report, appendix, part 1: The manuscripts of the house of lords 1678–88* (1887), p. 194.   **7** For genealogical details see: G.C. Cockayne, *The complete peerage* (1887–98), 5 (xii/i), pp 17–21; W. Betham, *Historical and genealogical memoir of the family of Slane in the county palatine of Meath, Ireland*, ed. G.A. Birdsall (published by Betham in 1829; revised edn, 1969), pp 12–16.   **8** See for instance: *Cal S.P. dom., 1677–1678*, pp 196–8.

He deserves every commendation for having converted to the faith a noble lady, the wife of mylord of Slane, while also arranging to have mylord's children taken to France, with the result that they were freed from serious dangers to their faith. Thus that noble family which never professed any other than the true faith was preserved spiritually and temporally.[9]

It is not clear why the children were delivered into the care of Michael Moore, who seems to have acted as a legal guardian, as well as taking responsibility for their education. But it seems to confirm that Michael Moore was well connected with a wide circle of Catholic Pale families. In fact the Fleminges, Barnewalls and Dowdalls were all inter-related.[10]

To the children's guardian, Alice Moore, their whereabouts were of both religious and financial concern, and she made strenuous efforts to have them returned into her care. The affair came to a head in 1683, when the full force of English diplomacy was applied to the matter.[11] In April 1683, it was reported to Lord Preston, Charles II's envoy in Paris:

I should not have troubled your lordship this night *but the Countess of Drogheda presses it very much*: it is to signify to your lordship that you should get the privy seal that is gone out to be served upon the Lord Baron Slane of Ireland, and his brother and sister, who are now in the hand of one Morus, an Irishman in the College de[s] Grassins at Paris.[12]

On 31 August 1677 the English court ordered the Fleminges, then in the care of 'Michael Moore, Gent., and some Popish Priests', to return to Ireland to the care of their legal guardian, Alice Moore. By 1683, an English official wrote: 'but that the said Michael Moore still detains the said children, and as we are further informed is about disposing the said Christopher Lord Slane in marriage, without the knowledge and consent of the said countess of Drogheda'. The letter repeated the request that Moore return the children to their grandmother and guardian, and refrain from arranging a marriage for Christopher Fleminge, adding: 'as he will answer the contrary at his peril'.[13] Moore not only disregarded the instructions to return the children to Ireland; he must have been responsible for the marriage of Christopher Fleminge the following year. On 19 September 1684 the fifteen-year-old Lord Slane married Ann, the daughter of Sir Patrick Trant. If Moore hoped that the youthful nobleman would become a protégé, he was to be disappointed. While Christopher Fleminge participated in the Jacobite parliament of 1689 and fought at the Boyne, he was outlawed following his cap-

9 J. Hanly (ed.), *The letters of Saint Oliver Plunkett, 1625–1681* (1979), pp 502–3. 10 Cockayne, *The complete peerage,* 5 (xii/i), pp 17–21; *Burke's peerage and baronetage,* 105th edn (1970), pp 184–5. 11 See the summary of a petition of March 1683 (new style) in *Cal. treas. bks, 1681–1685,* p. 738. 12 L. Jenkins, Whitehall, to Lord Preston, 21 April 1683 in HMC, *Seventh report, part 1* (1879), p. 363. My italics. 13 Charles R to Viscount Preston, 4 June 1683 in HMC, *Seventh report, part 1* (1879), p. 263.

ture at Aughrim. After release, he joined the Jacobite exodus to France, but later entered the service of Queen Anne in Portugal. In 1707 his title was restored but not his estates, and in 1713 he was created Viscount Longford. He died landless in the same year as his former guardian and educator, Michael Moore, in 1726.[14]

His care and education of the Fleminge children brought Moore to the attention of Peter Talbot's brother, Richard. In a codicil to his will, dated 24 April 1683, Richard Talbot recorded that his trustees 'shall satisfy and pay unto Michael Moore of Dublin, gentleman, Vice-provost of the College of Grassine [*sic*] in Paris, and ancient professor of philosophy in the university of the said city, the sum of £1,000 sterling, for his care taken in the education of the children of the late Lord of Slane'.[15] The extraordinarily large sum indicates the importance attached to the issue by Talbot, especially given the impending marriage of Christopher Fleminge. It also shows a clear relationship between Michael Moore and the leading Irish Catholic, who would become the most important political figure in Ireland within a few years. It is against this backdrop of continued involvement in Irish political and religious affairs and connection with the Talbots that Moore's role in Ireland during the late 1680s must be placed.

---

14 Cockayne, *The complete peerage*, 5 (xii/i), pp 19–21; D'Alton, *King James Irish Army list (1689)*, i, pp 342–3; HMC, *Report on the manuscripts of his grace the duke of Portland K.G., preserved at Welbeck Abbey*, viii (1907), pp 245, 369; *Séamus Dall MacCuarta dánta*, ed. S. Ó Gallchóir (1971), pp 70–1, 91–3. 15 Cited in D'Alton, *King James Irish Army list (1689)*, i, p. 66.

2

'A dangerous subject': the Catholic revival in Dublin, 1686–90[1]

The accession of James II in February 1685 raised Irish Catholic expectations for sweeping change in their favour, and the Irish Catholic clergy greeted the new regime with enthusiasm.[2] James supported religious toleration though he had no intention of creating an established Catholic church. However, he recognised the influence of the Catholic clerical elite and provided them with modest state incomes as early as 1686.[3] Under the lord lieutenant, Clarendon, the rate of change was relatively slow and the Catholic episcopacy lobbied hard for the appointment of Richard Talbot, created earl of Tyrconnell in 1685, as viceroy.[4] Bishop Patrick Tyrrell of Clogher, a strong supporter of Tyrconnell, advised James in August 1686 that 'in order to replant Religion in your dominions, you ought to begin with Ireland, where the work is more than half done to your hand … It is plain that the reality of the danger lies in your delay of making your Catholick [sic] subjects considerable.'[5] The rate of change quickened after Tyrconnell's appointment as lord deputy in January 1687, and within a few years Catholics dominated the army and judiciary, and were admitted to local and national government.

The church underwent a considerable revival in Ireland. John Brenan, the experienced archbishop of Cashel, reported the changes to Rome in November 1687:

> This long tempest of persecution has at length come to an end, and the Divine Mercy has been pleased to comfort the faithful in these parts by the coming to the royal throne of our most pious King James who publicly professes the Catholic and Apostolic faith, and in an exemplary manner exercises the Christian virtues. Soon after his coronation he appointed as Viceroy of this kingdom the Earl of Tirconnell, a native of the land and brother of the late Archbishop of Dublin, of happy memory. He is a sincere and zealous Catholic, very desirous to promote the glory of God and

---

1 Ware, *The whole works*, ed. Harris, ii, p. 289. 2 J.G. Simms, *Jacobite Ireland, 1685–91* (1969); J. Miller, 'The earl of Tyrconnell and James II's Irish policy' (1977); J. McGuire, 'Richard Talbot, earl of Tyrconnell (1630–91) and the Catholic counter-revolution' (1989); idem, 'James II and Ireland 1685–90' (1990). 3 Simms, *Jacobite Ireland*, pp 27–8. 4 H. Fenning, 'Dominic Maguire, OP. Archbishop of Armagh: 1684–1707' (1999–2000), pp 39–40; J.G. Simms, 'Dublin in 1685' (1965), p. 225. 5 Cited in W. King, *The state of the Protestants of Ireland under the late King James's government* (1691), pp 303, 305; Simms, *Jacobite Ireland*, p. 28.

the splendour of the true religion, and to advance the Catholic nobility and gentry to the public offices and wealth.[6]

The Catholic revival also created problems, in particular, open toleration of the clergy exposed divisions between secular and regular priests.[7] The problems faced by the church during the reign of James II have not yet been fully explored by historians. Moore's case underlines the double-edged nature of the Catholic revival, as struggles emerged for control of valuable institutions like Trinity College Dublin or Christ Church Cathedral. Beneath these conflicts lay a more deep-seated set of problems concerning the rate of change in favour of Catholics and the role of the monarch in the affairs of the church. Moore's strong line on these questions would ultimately lead to his downfall and return to France.

The Catholic revival naturally encouraged Irish clerics to return from the Continent. The exodus of senior Irish clergy from Paris was so great that the Irish-dominated Nation d'Allemagne ceased meeting between July 1685 and June 1691.[8] Michael Moore was in a particularly strong position to take advantage of the new religious and political climate in Ireland. According to some sources, he returned in 1684, but this could not have been the case.[9] Moore participated in the business of the Nation d'Allemagne, until 17 July 1685.[10] After the Nation ceased functioning, Moore continued to participate in meetings of the faculty of arts, as doyen of the Nation d'Allemagne, until October 1686, when his name disappears from the records.[11] Moore took a rather curious legal step before leaving for Ireland. In August 1686 he became a naturalised French subject.[12] This granted a foreigner equal rights to ordinary French subjects but also stipulated that the holder should remain in France (which explains Moore's need for a second letter of naturalisation, granted in 1702). Since French naturalisation afforded Moore no legal protection in Ireland, it is difficult to understand his actions.[13] In any case, Moore left France for Ireland in October 1686 or shortly after.[14]

6 P. Power (ed.), *A bishop of the penal times being the letters and reports of John Brenan bishop of Waterford (1671–93) and archbishop of Cashel (1677–93)* (1932), p. 88.   7 Simms, *Jacobite Ireland*, pp 27–8; Fenning, 'Dominic Maguire, O.P., Archbishop of Armagh: 1684–1707', pp 40–3.   8 There is no study at present of the number of clergy who returned during 1685–91, but the suspension of the nation's activities is suggestive. See: Liber procurationum Constantissimae Germanorum Nationis (1660–98), (AUP, registre 28, ff 280–1).   9 *DNB*, xxxviii, p. 336.   10 Liber procurationum Constantissimae Germanorum Nationis (1660–98) (AUP, registre 28, f. 280).   11 Conclusions de l'Universite, 1683–1689 (AUP, registre 35, ff 34v, 38, 54, 54v, 55, 56).   12 'Lettre de naturalité … pour Michael Morus natif de Dublin en Irlande, a Versailles au mois d'Aout 1686' (AN, Le secretariat d'état de la maison du Roi, O1 30, f. 298). The original letter is not extant at the Archives Nationales in Paris, indicating that Moore received it. It is listed in the inventory of his belongings: 'Inventaire', 27 August 1726 (AN, M.C. ET/XVII/647, f. 14–5).   13 On letters of naturalisation see: Archives Nationales, *Les étrangers en France XVIIᵉ siècle-1789. Guide des recherches aux Archives Nationales* (1998) pp 25–43.   14 It should be noted that in September 1695 Moore stated that he lived in Dublin 'about ten years ago': C. Giblin, 'The *Processus Datariae* and the appointment of Irish bishops in the seventeenth century', p. 607. Sir John Percival's diary entry for 6 February 1686, that he went to Trinity College to meet 'Mr Moor' cannot possibly be our subject (HMC, *Manuscripts of the earl of Egmont*, iii (1893), p. 336).

Walter Harris provides the most detailed account of Moore's return:

> ... but at length returning home [he] was with reluctance prevailed on to enter into priest orders, and was ordained by Luke Wadding the titular bishop of Ferns. Patrick Russell at that time titular Archbishop of Dublin, advanced Moor[e] to the Prebend of Tymothan in St Patrick's Church, and committed the care of the whole diocese to him as his titular vice-general.[15]

Why did Harris suggest that he was 'with reluctance prevailed on' to become a priest? John Brady has already noted that Edmund Everard's *Depositions* described Moore as a priest, though all other Irish references from the 1670s and 1680s simply label him 'gentleman'. Indeed, the 1677 reference to Moore's care of the Fleminge children mentions 'Michael Moore, Gent., and some Popish Priests' which appears to distinguish Moore from the ordained clergy. However, we know that Moore studied theology, so it appears that Everard was correct in thinking he was a priest in 1673. Whether or not Luke Wadding was the man who ordained Michael Moore, which seems unlikely, Harris's comments suggest a connection between them. In 1668 Luke Wadding was asked to return from Paris (where he may have known Moore) by his cousin, Bishop Nicholas French of Ferns, to become vicar-general of the diocese. In 1672 he was appointed coadjutor, but the consecration was deferred to protect him. When French died in 1678, Wadding became bishop-elect and vicar-capitular, but ceased even to act as vicar-general to save himself from banishment. He was finally consecrated bishop in 1683 or 1684.[16] A few fleeting references in Wadding's notebook, to a Doctor Moore, are the only tangible evidence that Moore and Wadding were connected.[17]

On Moore's return to Dublin, Archbishop Patrick Russell appointed him parish priest of St Catherine's and vicar-general of the archdiocese.[18] Moore played a significant part in the diocesan synod that met on 9 May 1688.[19] It recognised the importance of the new regime, asking that masses be said for the 'prosperity, health and preserving of our most serene King James ... and Richard, earl of Tyrconnell'.[20] Moore was also appointed to the prebandry of Tymothan and appears on three lists of Dublin canons during the Jacobite period, the last dated July 1689.[21] He may also have been appointed a court chaplain after James II's arrival in Ireland in March 1689.[22] Moore's high profile is partly explained by his

15 Ware, *The whole works*, ed. Harris, ii, pp 288–9. 'Titular' in this quotation means Catholic. 16 L. Wadding, *A pious garland being the December letter and Christmas carols of Luke Wadding, bishop of Ferns, 1683–1688* (1684, new edn, 1960), pp 1–10. 17 P. Corish (ed.), 'Bishop Wadding's notebook' (1970), pp 99, 106. 18 Donnelly, *Short histories of Dublin parishes*, part 9, pp 213–15. 19 W.M. O'Riordan, 'On two documents in the *Liber Decanatus I*, in the Dublin Diocesan Archives' (1956), pp 369–73. For a brief summary of the synodal decrees see: E. Rogan, *Synods and catechesis in Ireland, c.445–1962* (1987), pp 48–9; J. D'Alton, *The memoirs of the archbishops of Dublin* (1838), pp 449–56. 20 Cited in A. Forrestal, *Catholic synods in Ireland, 1600–1690* (1998), pp 101–2. This request had also been made in the synodal decrees of 1686. 21 O'Riordan, 'On two documents in the *Liber Decanatus I*, in the Dublin Diocesan Archives' pp 373–80. 22 Connellan, 'Michael Moore (1640–1726)', p. 263.

family relationship with the archbishop, Patrick Russell. Moore's brother-in-law, John Wogan, presented an altar stone to James Russell, the archbishop's step-brother, in 1689, in recognition of his consecration as dean of the archdiocese and apostolic protonotary. Later, James Russell willed the bulk of his estate to Stephen Brown of Castle Brown before his death in 1728. Browne was married to Moore's niece, Judith Wogan, the daughter of John Wogan.[23]

The Catholic revival presented an opportunity to re-establish educational centres in Ireland. The most obvious target for those who wished to promote third-level Catholic education in Dublin was Ireland's sole university: Trinity College. But James was reluctant to make rapid changes at the college. The evidence suggests that Tyrconnell, in line with his policy for the promotion of Irish Catholics to senior positions in other areas of public life, favoured a re-organisation of Trinity College and the admission of Catholics. Michael Moore's educational experience in France, and his connections with Richard Talbot, made him a prime candidate for the position of provost. However, the gradual opening of the college to Catholics resulted in competition between secular and regular interests for control. At the same time, the existing Church of Ireland administration attempted to retain their authority.

For much of the period, the college authorities continued to profess their loyalty to James II and maintain a functioning Protestant institution, but signs of unease slowly emerged. When the college attempted to send plate to England for sale, Tyrconnell's suspicions were aroused, though his predecessor Clarendon had been unconcerned. In the end, the plate was sold in Dublin rather than London.[24] All attempts to install Catholics at Trinity College were firmly resisted. In 1686 the fellows opposed James II's order for the admission of Arthur Greene (a Catholic) as a lecturer in the Irish language. They later refused to acknowledge the president elected by the College of Physicians, because he was a Catholic.[25] A well-documented case involved the attempts of another Catholic, Bernard Doyle of Drogheda, to occupy a fellowship granted by a mandamus from James. Doyle refused to take the fellow's oath, which contained the oath of supremacy, and appealed his case to the king in 1687 and 1688. However, the college authorities shrewdly based their opposition to Doyle, not on the grounds of his religion, but, as the title of one

---

23 Donnelly suggested that James Russell was 'probably' a stepbrother of Patrick Russell. This is confirmed by Patrick Russell's will. See: Donnelly, *Short histories of Dublin parishes*, part 6, pp 31–4, part 8, p. 192; W. Carrigan 'Catholic episcopal wills' (1915), pp 66–7; P.J. Breen and N.E. McKeith, *St Patrick's College Maynooth Museum of Ecclesiology: a catalogue of ecclesiastical items spanning two centuries of the history of the college* (1995), p. 72. John Wogan was appointed high sheriff of Kildare in October 1686 and represented the county in the Jacobite parliament in 1689: C. McNeill (ed.), 'Reports on the Rawlinson collection of manuscripts preserved in the Bodleian Library, Oxford' (1930), p. 37; J.G. Simms, *The Jacobite parliament of 1689* (1974), p. 23. See also chapter one for Moore's relationship with the Wogan and Browne families. 24 John Hely Hutchinson, 'An essay towards a history of Trinity College Dublin' n.d. [he was provost between 1774 and 1794] (TCD, MSS 1774, 1774a; the present study has used the typescript version, 1774b), pp 208–12. 'Plate' was presented to the college by incoming students to be used by the authorities. 25 Hutchinson, 'An essay towards a history of Trinity College Dublin', pp 207, 215. 26 Report dated 1687 (TCD,

report put it: 'some instances of ye lewd, debauched and scandalous behaviour'.[26] Doyle fought to clear his name, but claimed in 1688 that the fellowship had been granted to 'one Hassett'.[27] In reality, the provost, Robert Huntington, and the fellows successfully resisted these minor challenges before 1688. But when the chancellor of the college, the duke of Ormond, died and his grandson, the second duke, was chosen to replace him, Huntington took the opportunity of a private investiture in London to depart on 26 September 1688. He remained in England until after the battle of the Boyne.[28] This placed effective control in the hands of the vice-provost, Dr Acton, who died in December 1689.[29] There was a continuous flow of fellows from Ireland, particularly during 1688 and 1689. On 1 March 1689, as the college register put it 'most of the fellows embark't for England' leaving only Acton and four others.[30] Nonetheless, when James arrived in Dublin, the college presented an address of welcome on 24 March 1689.[31]

The successful resistance to the appointment of Catholics at Trinity College contrasted strongly with events at Cambridge and Oxford in 1687 and 1688. James's attitude to the universities in England must have been deeply worrying for the fellows in Dublin. The conversion to Catholicism of Obadiah Walker, master of University College, Oxford, turned the institution into a focal point for Catholic hopes. But it was the death of the president of Magdalen College in March 1687 that signalled the start of the real battle over James's educational policy. The fellows of the college ignored James's order to elect Anthony Farmer, 'a reputed Catholic', as president and after much debate elected and installed one of their own, John Hough. They defended their actions by claiming that Farmer was completely unsuitable and therefore they could not elect him without breaking the oaths they swore when admitted as fellows. After protracted wrangling, Hough's election was declared void, Farmer's candidature was dropped, and the fellows reluctantly accepted James's second nominee, Samuel Parker, the bishop of Oxford. Continued resistance led to the expulsion of almost all the fellows by

MUN/P/1/534). **27** 'Petition of Bernard Doyle' (1688?) (TCD, MUN/P/1/542). The case can be followed through the following series of muniment documents: TCD, MUN/P/1/532–542a. The 'one Hassett' might be the fellow who fled on 1 March 1689 (new style) [Hutchinson, 'An essay towards a history of Trinity College Dublin', 218]. It is also possible he was Arthur Blennerhassett whom the king granted admission as a fellow on 9 April 1688. He later renounced his claim and seems to have been a Catholic see: TCD, MUN/P/1/555, 555a. H.L. Murphy suggests that he accepted the vacancy: *A history of Trinity College Dublin from its foundation to 1702* (1951), pp 166–8. **28** Hutchinson, 'An essay towards a istory of Trinity College, Dublin, pp 213–14. James II overruled Tyrconnell's objections to the new chancellor, Sunderland to Tyrconnell, 8 September 1688 (PRO, State Papers, Ireland 63/340, f. 299). **29** See the relevant excerpts from the register cited in Connellan, 'Michael Moore (1640–1726)', pp 264–5. The original is held in TCD: 'General registry from 1640' [1640–1740] (Muniments/V/5/2). **30** College register cited in Connellan, 'Michael Moore', p. 264; Hutchinson, 'An essay towards a history of Trinity College Dublin', pp 217–19. In February 1689 (new style) the authorities ordered that £200 be sent to England for the support of those who had been forced to flee (ibid., p. 217). **31** Hutchinson, 'An essay towards a history of Trinity College Dublin', p. 219; College register cited in Connellan, 'Michael Moore', p. 264. Acton and the remaining fellows met the king on 17 June 1689 (ibid.).

November 1687 and the admission of Catholic replacements began in earnest. Parker's death, in March 1688, raised the stakes still further. The prominent English Catholic priest, Bonaventure Giffard, replaced him, offering the prospect of a complete Catholic take-over. This was clearly what the papal nuncio had in mind when he commented that a Catholic president could 'establish there with authority a place, where the true doctrine should be publickly taught, and thence spread consecutively to the other parts of the realm'.[32] Though there were Anglican and Catholic fellows in the college during Giffard's presidency, clearly the Catholics dominated despite student and local resistance. However, James was forced to back down in the mounting crisis during the autumn of 1688, and in October he restored John Hough and the 'excluded' fellows to the college. Their spirited resistance had become a major embarrassment to the regime.[33] What did the Magdalen College saga mean for the future of Trinity College Dublin? Possibly that the admission of Catholics was inevitable, though James may have been unwilling to rouse the antagonism of the Protestant administration.

By 25 October 1688 Oxford was in the hands of Williamite troops. James's arrival in Ireland the following year, and the decision of so many of the fellows at Trinity College to remove themselves to England, must have encouraged Tyrconnell to install a Catholic provost. Walter Harris believed that Tyrconnell recommended Michael Moore to James II, and that he was appointed provost 'by the unanimous recommendation of the then prevailing Roman Catholick Bishops'.[34] An alleged petition written by the Irish Catholic bishops in 1689 requested permission to 'make use of the University of Dublin'. The bishops argued that they were the best group to present candidates for employment as 'directors or teachers (whether secular, or regular clergymen)' and that the college should be a 'general seminary for the clergy of this kingdom'.[35] Recommendation by the bishops and Tyrconnell would have strengthened Moore's claims to the post. The college statutes introduced by Archbishop William Laud in 1637 had transferred the right to appoint the provost from the fellows of the college to the crown.[36] However, if James did appoint Moore, he does not feature in extant college records.[37]

32 Cited in J.R. Bloxam (ed.), *Magdalen College and King James II 1686–1688* (1886), p. 242.   33 A. Macintyre, 'The college, King James II and the revolution, 1687–1688' in L. Brockliss et al. (eds), *Magdalen College and the crown: essays for the tercentenary of the restoration of the college 1688* (1988); L. Brockliss, 'The 'intruded' president and fellows' (1988). Events can also be followed in: Bloxam (ed), *Magdalen College and King James II, 1686–1688.*   34 Ware, *The whole works*, ed. Harris, ii, p. 289.   35 *Dublin Magazine* (Sept 1762), pp 514–15. Internal evidence suggests that the document was composed after the mass exodus of fellows from the College on 1 March 1689, but the publisher provided no indication of the provenance of the document.   36 William Laud, the controversial archbishop of Canterbury, was chancellor from 1633 until his execution in 1645. See: McDowell and Webb, *Trinity College, Dublin, 1592–1952*, pp 14–15, 517 note 27; C. Maxwell, *A history of Trinity College Dublin, 1591–1892* (1946), pp 39–40; Connellan, 'Michael Moore (1640–1726)', pp 264–5.   37 According to the college register, William ordered the College to seize Catholic books after his victory, but when the order was executed after six months, many had already been lost, those that survived 'were placed in the countess of Bath's library' (J.W. Stubbs, *The history of the University of Dublin from its foundation to the end of the eighteenth century* (1889), p. 133). Moore does not appear in the unpublished eighteenth

Various French sources asserted that Moore was appointed provost of Trinity College, including Delaval's 1726 oration, which also identified Tyrconnell as the main sponsor.[38] It is nonetheless difficult to provide firm evidence. Connellan speculated that the following passage in the college register probably indicated the date when Moore was placed in charge. The college had already been subject to searches for arms, and on 16 September 1689 was seized as a garrison by Sir John Fitzgerald and 'the scholars were all turned out by souldiers'.[39] On 21 October 1689, the register recorded:

> Several persons by order of the government, seized upon the chapel and broke open the Library. The Chapel was sprinkled and new consecrated and mass was said in it; but afterwards being turned into a storehouse for powder, it escaped all further damage. The Library and the gardens and the provost's lodgings were committed to the care of Macarty, a priest and Chaplain to ye king, who preserved 'em from the violence of the souldiers …[40]

According to Harris, Moore was also responsible for the preservation of the library: 'To his special care is owing the conservation of the valuable collection of manuscripts and other books, which now adorn the college library; at a time when that house was turned into a popish garrison, the chappel into a magazine, and many of the chambers into prisons for Protestants.'[41] William King, then imprisoned in the college, recorded that on 22 October, perhaps when he was given the news,

> Mass was s[ai]d in the College Chapel & the College & Library delivered to Dr Moore, & some fryers & priests ye scholars beds & other conveniencys and furniture were refused to ye owners. & twas sd 500lb worth of

century history of the college by John Hely-Hutchinson, which was closely based on surviving muniment records: 'An essay towards a history of Trinity College Dublin'. (TCD MS 1774b) **38** French biographies of Moore claimed that he had been placed in charge of the 'University of Dublin': Desmolets, *Continuation des mémoires*, ii, p. 202; Morieri, *Le grand dictionnaire*, p. 467; Boyle, 'Dr Michael Moore', p. 14. **39** College register cited in Connellan, 'Michael Moore' (1640–1726), p. 264. Sir John Fitzgerald studied in Nantes in the early 1660s and may well have known Moore. He was almost certainly responsible for removing the Leabhair mór Leacáin from the library of Trinity College. He later lodged the manuscript at the Collège des Lombards in Paris. See: P. MacCana, *Collège des Irlandais Paris and Irish Studies*, pp 140–60; The Marquis McSwiney of Mashanaglass, 'Notes on the history of the Book of Lecan' (1928–9), pp 31–50. If the manuscript was removed in 1689–90 Moore was probably in charge of the college, though there is no direct evidence to associate him with its 'disappearance'. **40** Cited in Connellan, 'Michael Moore (1640–1726)', p. 264. The anonymous diarist whose account appears in the *Ormonde MSS* stated that the college had been 'seized on' during a search on 25 February and that prisoners were held at the college from 9 September: 'A diary of events in Ireland from 1685 to 1690' in HMC, *Ormonde MSS*, new series, viii, pp 360, 371–2. **41** Ware, *The whole works*, ed. Harris, ii, p. 289. Also, Murphy, *A history*, pp 174–6; W. Macneile Dixon, *Trinity College Dublin* (1902), pp 66–8; Maxwell, *A history of Trinity College Dublin*, pp 84–5.

books already imbeziled [*sic*] & to ye valu[e] of 3,000lb damage done to ye place.[42]

King later stated that 'One Moore, a popish priest, was nominated provost; one Macarty library keeper, and the whole designated for them and others of their fraternity.'[43] This supports Connellan's suggestion that Moore received the post by nomination or royal mandamus. Indeed, King noted that the monarch could legally 'dispense' with the college statutes.[44]

There is another version of the events surrounding Moore's provostship, presented in the narrative of the period by Thomas Sheridan. His *Historical account* needs to be approached with caution, since Sheridan had been a secretary to Tyrconnell before falling out of favour.[45] Sheridan argued that as early as 1687 Tyrconnell favoured Moore for the stewardship of Trinity College and lobbied accordingly. He wrote:

> He was also crossed[46] in his designs of making Dublin College presently popish, in order to which, as soon as he was sure of the Government of that kingdom, he sent for Mr Moor[e] from Paris to be provost, a person suspected for Jansenism, and twice forced to abjure that heresy; and for a beginning he recommended one Jordan, a convert, to be made a fellow by mandamus, against which Sheridan advised him, assuring him nothing could more startle the Protestants than that, and was confident the King would not yet at least think it proper. However he wrote and was also in this denied. Soon after he got the Catholic bishops of Dublin, Meath, Clogher and others to recommend Mr Moor[e] to the King and pray that the management and conduct of that house might be put into the hands of seculars; which the King refused, either as unreasonable, or else persuaded the Jesuits were fitter for that function.[47]

According to Harris, then, Moore was never appointed provost. James's educational policy in Ireland was, theoretically at least, Jesuit-driven.[48] In June 1688

---

42 H.J. Lawlor (ed.), 'Diary of William King, D.D., Archbishop of Dublin, during his imprisonment in Dublin Castle' (1903), p. 397. On King's imprisonment see: P. O'Regan, *Archbishop William King of Dublin (1650–1729) and the constitution in church and state* (2000), pp 30–1.   43 King, *The state of the Protestants of Ireland*, p. 194.   44 Ibid., p. 184. For King's commentary on James's relationship with Trinity College, pp 184–97.   45 On Sheridan's reliability see: J. Miller, 'Thomas Sheridan and his "Narrative"' (1976), pp 105–28. For a recent discussion of Sheridan's politics: V. Geoghegan, 'Thomas Sheridan: toleration and royalism' (2001).   46 Sheridan had been discussing what he claimed were Tyrconnell's failed attempts to ensure that he could alter newly granted corporation charters. This suggests the events described may have occurred around 1687 (Simms, *Jacobite Ireland*, pp 55–6).   47 T. Sheridan, *An historical account of some remarkable matters concerning King James the second's succession* [1702] in HMC, *Calendar of the Stuart papers belonging to his majesty the king preserved at Windsor Castle* (1904–23) vi, pp 26–7. The question of Michael Moore's links with Jansenism will be dealt with in chapter five.   48 One of his closest advisors was the Jesuit, Edward Petre. From

Sunderland informed Tyrconnell that when places became available at government-controlled schools in Ireland they were to be filled by Jesuit appointments.[49] The society quickly responded to the decision and an appointment was made in Cashel in August.[50] However, not all James's educational changes were connected with the Society of Jesus. The monarch supported the establishment of a third-level college in Kilkenny that was spearheaded by the secular clergy of the diocese of Ossory. The idea was first mooted in 1686, but the statutes establishing the Royal College of St Canice, with many Irish priests who had been resident on the continent on the staff, were produced only in February 1690. The institution lasted a mere six months before the change of regime returned it to a Protestant secondary school patronised by the duke of Ormonde.[51]

The evidence suggests that James considered granting control of Trinity College to the Jesuits in spring 1690. By this stage, Moore had already fallen out of favour with the king. It is probable that the monarch then had a re-think and decided that the Jesuits were more fitting appointees. In spring 1690, the Jesuit general, Thyrsus Gonzalez, informed the recently appointed Irish superior, Patrick Lynch, that James had come to such a decision. Moreover, he noted that several English Jesuits would be sent to Dublin to staff the college.[52] However, Tyrconnell commented in April 1690:

> As to the affair of the King's putting the Jesuits into the colledge [sic] here, I doe not believe he ever had any such thoughts, for it's that would not only give great offence to all the world, I mean to England and Scotland, but very much discompose the whole clergy of this kingdome, and, madam, you know this age will not bear being too fond of the Jesuits.[53]

as early as 1686 James pressed Petre's case for a cardinalate. He was already a privy councillor: J.S. Clarke, *The life of James II* (1816), ii, pp 76–7; J. Miller, *Popery and politics in England, 1660–1688* (1973), pp 233–8. **49** Sunderland to Tyrconnell, 18 June 1688 (PRO, State Papers, Ireland 63/340, ff 287–8). Simms described this as a 'sensational piece of educational policy' (*Jacobite Ireland*, p. 43). **50** Simms, *Jacobite Ireland*, p. 43. The Jesuits were dispensed from taking the Oath of Supremacy which had been a stipulation attached to the positions: Sunderland to Tyrconnell, 31 August 1688 (PRO, State Papers, Ireland 63/340, ff 294–5). On early seventeenth-century attempts to establish a Jesuit 'university' in Dublin see: E. Boran, 'The foundation of Jesuit colleges in seventeenth-century Ireland' (1998). **51** J. Leonard, ' Kilkenny's short-lived university (Feb–July 1690)' (1988); idem, *A university for Kilkenny: plans for a royal college in the seventeenth century* (1996). The involvement of Irish clergy based in Paris is particularly noteworthy in this case, especially that of Donat O'Leary, like Moore a member of the Nation d'Allemagne in Paris. He was sent to Ireland by William Bailly to assist in the foundation of the college in Kilkenny. His account, from the register of the Nation d'Allemagne, is reproduced in Leonard, *A university for Kilkenny*, pp 57–9. Tyrconnell had initially rejected O'Leary's request for support because of the order granting educational institutions in Ireland to the Jesuits. **52** F. Finegan, 'The Jesuits in Dublin, 1660–1760' (1965–71), pp 59–60, 96. **53** L. Tate (ed.), 'Letter-book of Richard Talbot' (1932), p. 119. On Edward Petre see: *DNB*, xlv, pp 91–3.

In April 1690 James II instructed the lord chancellor, Alexander Fitton, to 'visit' the college and at that point ordered the two remaining fellows, George Thules and John Hall, to hand over the keys, which duly occurred. Hely Hutchinson noted solemnly that no such visitation actually happened: 'There were none to be visited but those two unfortunate gentlemen, the sad remains of a once flourishing university.'[54]

The college was bound to be the cause of controversy between the competing educational interest groups in Ireland. It is likely that when the military forces decided in October 1689 that the college was required for its plans, Tyrconnell used an opportune moment to install his candidate, Moore, as provost. Indeed, James II was not in Dublin at that point.[55] But it is clear that Moore never had the opportunity to exercise the functions of provost before his involvement in the college ended abruptly in early 1690. Events at Magdalen College offer a glimpse of what might have unfolded in Dublin. Brockliss has concluded that James was not trying to create a Catholic seminary in the Oxford college: 'Arguably he was attempting to create a confessionally-mixed community whose members were united by a common loyalty to a divinely appointed monarch.'[56] But, as Brockliss recognises, such a policy could not survive in the seventeenth century and in reality these were the first steps towards full Catholic control. In the end, the Irish bishops may have realised their wish to turn Trinity College into a Catholic institution. But Moore was no puppet of the king and his loyalty to James was conditional. His banishment (discussed below) precipitated a change in the government's policy concerning the future of a Catholic Trinity College. The collapse of Jacobite forces in Dublin in July 1690 rendered any such debate academic. The guard was lifted from the college in early July 1690, and the prisoners released, just before Dublin changed hands.[57]

Walter Harris argued that the conflict between the Jesuits and seculars concerning the control of Trinity College directly contributed to Michael Moore's banishment from Ireland shortly after his appointment as provost. The Dublin Jesuits, suggested Harris, 'laid hold' of a sermon preached by Moore at Christ Church Cathedral, before James II, on the gospel text: 'If the blind lead the blind, both shall fall into the ditch.'[58]

> In this discourse he laid the miscarriages of the king's affairs to his following too closely the councils [*sic*] of the Jesuits, and insinuated that they would be the king's utter ruin. Father Peters [*sic*] who had a defect in his

---

54 Hutchinson, 'An essay towards a history of Trinity College Dublin', pp 222–3; College register cited in Connellan, 'Michael Moore (1640–1726)', p. 266.   55 'A diary of events in Ireland from 1685 to 1690', pp 372–3.   56 L. Brockliss, 'The "intruded" president and fellows', p. 103. Brockliss goes on to argue that: 'It is much more probable that James and his advisors had no consistent religious policy with regard to Magdalen at all.' (p. 104)   57 Simms, *Jacobite Ireland*, pp 115–16. Some prisoners were removed in late June: 'A diary of events in Ireland from 1685 to 1690', p. 386.   58 Ware, *The whole works*, ed. Harris, ii, p. 289. The gospel text is from Matthew 15:15.

eyes, represented to the king the evil tendency of Dr Moor's sermon, and persuaded him that the text was levelled at his majesty through his confessors, and shewed him that Moor[e] was a dangerous subject and endeavoured to stir up sedition among the people. This weak prince was highly offended at the preacher, and ordered him immediately to quit the kingdom.[59]

Petre's charge that Moore was fomenting 'sedition among the people' indicates a more deeply rooted problem. This is also suggested by the version of events recorded by William King. In his Williamite apologia, *The state of the Protestants of Ireland,* King argued that James II was unable to keep promises made to his Protestant subjects on account of the alleged power of the Catholic clergy over their monarchs. In doing so, he cited Moore's case to support his point.

One Mr Moore preached before the King in Christs [*sic*] Church, in the beginning of the year 1690, his sermon gave great offence: he told his majesty that he did no justice to the church and churchmen, and amongst other things said that *Kings ought to consult clergymen in their temporal affairs, the clergy having a temporal as well as a spiritual right in the kingdom; but kings had nothing to do with the managing of spiritual affairs, but were to obey the orders of the church.* It is true King James highly resented this, and the preacher was banished, or voluntarily withdrew from court, but in this he spake the general sense of the clergy.[60]

The accounts of Harris and King suggest a rift, both between the secular and regular clergy in Dublin, and also between the church and the king. But neither satisfactorily explains the reasons for Moore's banishment.

The banishment resulted from a struggle between church and state concerning the right of nomination to vacant benefices at Christ Church Cathedral and the consequences for Catholic church administration. The revival of Catholic hopes and fortunes opened the way for claims to property which had been in the possession of the Church of Ireland since the reformation. Even before he left England, Tyrconnell reportedly planned to take 'Christ Church in Dublin from the Protestants for his own use'.[61] Christ Church Cathedral was transformed from an Augustinian priory to a secular cathedral between 1539 and 1544.[62] In 1689, an

---

59 Ware, *The whole works*, ed. Harris, ii, p. 289.   **60** King, *The state of the Protestants of Ireland*, p. 18. In King's text the italics indicated an apparent direct quotation. David Hayton has pointed out that anti-Catholic propaganda stressed this alleged link between Catholicism, absolutism and persecution, see: 'The propaganda war' (1990), p. 115.   **61** Sheridan, *An historical account*, p. 17   **62** Lorcán Ua Tuathail had established the Augustinians at Christ Church in the 1160s. By 1544 Christ Church's new status as a secular cathedral was ensured. There was no attempt to reverse the change in status during the brief reign of Mary (1553–8). See: S. Kinsella, 'From Hiberno-Norse to Anglo-Norman, *c.*1030–1300' (2000), pp 44–5; R. Gillespie, 'The coming of reform, 1500–58' (2000), pp 165–6; 171–3.

Irish Augustinian, P.D. Ryane, made strenuous efforts to re-establish his order's claims to Christ Church. Ryane appealed to the abbés of Sainte-Geneviève in Paris and other senior Catholic authorities in Europe for support. In 1689 he enlisted Michael Moore's assistance.[63] Three letters written in July and August 1689 mentioned Moore. On 14 July 1689, writing to Abbé Morin in Paris, Ryane presented the intended bearer of the letter:

> … mon bon amy Monsieur Morus grand vicaire de cette ville qui s'en vas à Paris de la part du Roy. Il a regenté autrefois au College des Grassins. [Il est] un tres habil hom[m]e et qui est dans seul ce pays dans un tres grand estime et haut reputation. S'il a du temps il se donnera la peine d'informer … de ce qui passe ici.[64]

No indication of Moore's royal mission is given, but this is hardly surprising given the possibility that he could have been intercepted en route to France. In a letter dated the following day, Ryane noted that: 'Jay mise entre les mains de Mons[ieu]r Morus grande vicaire de cette metropolis mon bon amy un pacquet … ou il y a la copie des lettres du roy hen. 8 et Jacques roy d'angl[eterre] et le bull obtenir par [?] p[ou]r possede[r] la prieure de Christ Church.' He also suggested that Moore would be able to present the case to the French and Roman courts.[65] By August, Ryane was expressing doubts about Moore's ability to cross the Channel undetected, and it seems he was seriously considering sending the relevant documentation to Paris by other means.[66]

The fact that Moore was considered a prime candidate for a royal (or vicere-gal) mission to France in the dangerous summer of 1689 ably illustrates how influential he was in the Jacobite regime. But he never undertook the mission, for Ryane did not mention him in correspondence compiled in the early months of 1690.[67] Augustinian hopes that they would re-establish a priory at Christ Church were not realised. Nevertheless, by the summer of 1689 Moore supported the Catholic take-over of Protestant churches. James was much more circumspect on the issue, and the bills presented to the 'patriot parliament' in May 1689 made it clear that James did not favour the 'restoration' of church property to Catholics, though he left vacancies in Protestant churches unfilled.[68] During the autumn of

63 Recueil des lettres originales relatives aux affaires religieuses de l'Irlande et plus particulièrement au prieuré de Christ Church, à Dublin; 1542–1689 (BSG, MS 2566).   64 '… my good friend Michael Moore, vicar-general of this city, who is going to Paris on behalf of the king. In the past he was regent of the Collège des Grassins. He is a very clever man and alone in this country is held in very high respect and reputation. If he has the time, he will take the trouble to inform you … of what is happening here': Ryane to Morin, 14 July 1689 (BSG, MS 2566, ff 7–8).   65 'I have put in the hands of Michael Moore, vicar-general of this city, my good friend, a packet which contains the letters of King Henry VIII and James, king of England, and the bull obtained by [?] for possession of the priory of Christ Church': Ryane to Morin, 15 July 1689 (BSG, MS 2566, ff 9–10). Ryane was counting on the support of the French queen and Cardinal Howard of Norfolk.   66 Ryane to Morin, 7 August 1689 (BSG, MS 2566, ff 2–3).   67 Ryane to Morin, 25 January, 3 February, 20 March 1690 (all dated 1689 old style) (BSG, MS 2566).   68 This was a source of income for the state. On the discussion of reli-

1689, the opportunity for the take-over of Protestant churches presented itself. Catholics eventually seized Christ Church Cathedral, while James was away from Dublin, on 27 October 1689.[69] Anthony Dopping, the Church of Ireland bishop of Meath and effective leader of the Anglican interest, requested the church's return. James apparently responded that he would not have sanctioned the seizure but was virtually powerless to reverse the events, though the following month he attended mass in the chapel.[70] The seizure of Christ Church created a new set of problems for the church and state authorities. While it was now possible to appoint Catholic members to the chapter, the question of jurisdiction was far from certain.[71] In fact, Alexius Stafford, a priest from the diocese of Ferns, had been appointed dean of Christ Church by papal provision as early as August 1686. Stafford was a high-profile cleric at the Jacobite court; he received an annual pension from the government in March 1686 (largely the reserve of the episcopacy), obtained an appointment as 'chaplain to the regiment of guards' in September and was appointed master of chancery in February 1688.[72] He later sat for the barony of Bannow, County Wexford, in parliament and was subsequently killed at the battle of Aughrim.[73] Despite Stafford's appointment by papal provision, there was opposition when he took up the post in 1689. His case probably mirrored one dealt with by Archbishop Brenan of Cashel. In 1691 he explained:

> Thaddeus Crowley obtained four years ago by Papal Bull the appointment to the Deanery of the Cathedral of Lismore. Arrived in Dublin *he found that the King did not allow any appointment except of those nominated by himself* and so Crowley surrendered the Papal Bull into the royal hand and subsequently obtained the royal appointment. I opposed this manner of procedure and I forbade the clergy or people of this district to receive Crowley as Dean.[74]

It is likely that James II appointed Stafford to the seized cathedral in Dublin and, despite his having a papal nomination, Archbishop Russell may have opposed Stafford's appointment in the same way that Brenan had opposed Crowley's. The

gion at the 1689 parliament see: Simms, *Jacobite Ireland*, pp 86–9.   69 It was still in Catholic hands the following February: King, *The state of the Protestants of Ireland*, p. 215; P.F. Moran, *Spicilegium Ossoriense* (1874–84), ii, p. 295; 'A diary of events in Ireland from 1685 to 1690', p. 372. The keys were taken on the previous day (26 August): D. Murphy, 'Christ Church Cathedral, Dublin: 1660–1760' (1995), p. 67.   70 'A diary of events in Ireland from 1685 to 1690', p. 373.   71 From the 1580s appointments to Christ Church were made by royal nomination, in contrast to St Patrick's where the dean was elected by the cathedral chapter, a tradition that was upheld with some difficulty during the reign of James II: R. Gillespie, 'The Shaping of Reform, 1558–1625' (2000), p. 183. On St Patrick's in 1689 see below, note 75.   72 Cogan, *The diocese of Meath: ancient and modern*, ii, p. 150; earl of Longford to Ormond, 6 September 1686, *Ormonde MSS*, n.s., viii, p. 452; 'A diary of events in Ireland from 1685 to 1690', p. 352; Richard Roche, 'Alexius Stafford: "the popish dean of Christ's Church"' (2000).   73 Roche, 'Alexius Stafford', pp 33–4.   74 Power (ed.), *A bishop of the penal times*, p. 98. (My italics.)

problem was jurisdiction. Both James and Rome claimed the right to nominate clergy to vacant positions; Crowley and Stafford had recognised James's prior authority.[75]

The chapter of Christ Church led by Alexius Stafford may have been in conflict with their Church of Ireland predecessors, but Stafford was also in conflict with a competing Catholic group of claimants.[76] Rome regularly appointed nominal deans of Christ Church during the seventeenth century. Stafford was appointed in accordance with this practice on 24 August 1686.[77] In February 1687 a change of policy was initiated when the papacy made appointments to other posts in the cathedral chapter: Matthew Barnewall (precentor), James Meara (treasurer) and John Gernon (chancellor).[78] The king was infuriated by these appointments, and apparent later ones, as is clear from the following unsigned draft of a letter sent to Cardinal Howard in Rome, in November 1687:

> The King has been informed that Mr Michael FitzHenry, Mr John Dempsy and Mr Edmund Dunne have been promoted by the pope to three benefices in Christ Church, Dublin, without his nomination or knowledge, and that your Eminency was acquainted therewith; and his Majesty expecting *that no person should be promoted to any benefice in his dominions but at his own nomination*, or the recommendation of some of his ministers in his name, which my Lord Castlemaine did let his holiness and his ministers know, his Majesty has commanded me to signify the same to you, that nothing of the like kind may happen for some time to come.[79]

In May 1688 John Dempsy was still a member of the chapter, as was one Patrick Skerrett. They had been appointed to the positions originally filled by Barnewall and Gernon respectively.[80] Among Stafford's fragmentary notes is a list of priests,

---

75 The deanery of St Patrick's Cathedral became vacant on the death of the incumbent in May 1688. Tyrconnell opposed the appointment of a Protestant replacement. Instead he favoured the post remaining vacant (to the benefit of the Irish revenue) or the appointment of a Catholic. In fact the Protestant chapter also apparently opposed a royal appointment and succeeded in electing their own dean, William King, in January 1689. The cathedral was later seized by Catholics but subsequently returned: Tyrconnell to the lord president, Dublin, 9 May 1688 in McNeill (ed.), 'Reports on the Rawlinson collection', p. 39; Simms, *Jacobite Ireland*, pp 42, note 82, 88.   76 On Stafford's Catholic chapter see: Murphy, 'Christ Church Cathedral, Dublin: 1660–1760', pp 67–74; K. Milne, 'Restoration and reorganisation, 1660–1830' (2000), pp 271–5; 'Some papers of Stafford, pretended Dean of this church and his chapter in 1689' (RCBL, C6.1.26.6.32).   77 N. Donnelly, 'The "per obitum" volumes in the Vatican Archivio' (1912), pp 34, 37. Appointments were made in 1644 and 1660. The practice may have been triggered by hopes raised during the confederate wars. Some Irish cathedrals were taken over by Catholics in the early 1640s: R. Gillespie, 'The crisis of reform, 1625–60' (2000), pp 205–6.   78 Donnelly, 'The "per obitum" volumes in the Vatican Archivio', p. 38. See also: O'Riordan, 'On two documents in the *Liber Decanatus I*, in the Dubin Diocesan Archives', pp 376–7, 379. The latter provides three contemporary lists of secular Dublin priests in the late 1680s.   79 McNeill (ed.), 'Reports on the Rawlinson collection', pp 57–8.   80 O'Riordan, 'On two documents in the *Liber Decanatus I*, in the Dubin Diocesan Archives', pp 376, 379.

possibly members of the cathedral chapter, Fathers Maguire, Lery, Darcy, Stafford, Mahony, Dournay and Grace.[81] None of these were papal appointees (except Stafford) nor do they feature in contemporary lists of the clergy of the archdiocese.[82] This suggests that there was a conflict between two competing Catholic chapters.

In 1685 Pope Innocent XI granted James II an indult permitting him to nominate bishops to vacant sees, a power the king continued to exercise in exile. But James clearly wanted more wide-ranging powers to appoint priests to benefices all over the country.[83] It was on this issue of royal interference in the affairs of the church that Michael Moore took his stand in early 1690. Though a strong proponent of the Catholic take-over of Protestant churches, he was deeply concerned by James's actions. In a hitherto unnoticed letter, apparently written in January 1691, Moore described his attempts to deal with this problem. His correspondent lived in France and was described as someone who had shown 'la charité toutte extraordinaire' for the Irish church.[84] Both Moore's support for P.D. Ryane, and his position at Trinity College, suggests that he was a vocal advocate of a far-reaching Catholic counter-revolution. However, his letter illustrates the difficulties encountered by proponents of such a project. James was cautious about promoting an overt policy in favour of Irish Catholics. Moreover, he was determined that new sources of church patronage remained within his sphere of authority. The increasingly powerful position of the Catholic church in Dublin brought it into conflict with the Jacobite court. This led to the accusations, reported by Harris, that Moore 'was a dangerous subject and endeavoured to stir up sedition among the people'.[85]

Moore's letter expressed support for James II, but his purpose in writing was 'de vous decouvrir les playes qui cette Eglise a recu durant le peu de temps que sa majesté a esté en ce pais cy'.[86] The cause was a 'pretendu chapitre' set up by James II in Dublin, which was granted the authority to nominate clergy to vacancies. This undermined the rights of the archbishop of Dublin, Patrick Russell, and led to threats against him and even the possibility that he would be replaced. Moore blamed James's council, rather than the king, but he warned that the dispute caused deep divisions in the archdiocese and had the capacity to extend throughout the country:

81 'Some papers of Stafford, pretended Dean of this church and his chapter in 1689' (RBCL, C6.1.26.6.32). 82 O'Riordan, 'On two documents in the *Liber Decanatus I*, in the Dubin Diocesan Archives', pp 369–80. 83 Giblin, 'The *Processus Datariae* and the appointment of Irish bishops in the seventeenth century', p. 35. Giblin briefly discusses James's nomination to benefices, pp 35–6. 84 'Letter of a Catholick priest in Ireland containing the grevences [sic] of the Irish clergy of the Romish faith under James II 1691', a copy in 'Collection of papers relative to Great Britain and Ireland copied from Pieresch's MSS in the hands of the President Mazauges at Aix in Provence (*c.*1736)' (TCD, MS 1184). The letter makes no mention of the Williamite occupation of Dublin, which suggests it was written at the start of 1690, when Moore's fateful sermon occurred, rather than 1691. Delaval's oration in 1726 claimed that Moore had remained in Dublin until after the Williamite occupation of the city: see Boyle, 'Dr Michael Moore', p. 14. 85 Cited in Ware, *The whole works*, ed. Harris, ii, p. 289. 86 '... to reveal to you the wounds which this church has received during the short time in which his majesty has been in this country': 'Letter of a Catholick priest in Ireland' (TCD, MS 1184, f. 1).

La seule eglise principalle de Dublin qui estoit la seule que possedoient les Catholiques [i.e., Christ Church Cathedral], s'est veue partagée par un schisme fineste qui selon touttes les apparences – *devoit partager touttes les Eglises du pais*, puisque les memes causes c'y sont, ou s'y seroient infailliblement trouvées.[87]

The right of royal nomination to vacant positions apparently rested on a parallel with the French church. Moore therefore argued at length that this was not the case. For example, he pointed out that in France, Louis XIV did not dispose of benefices without consultation with the church. Nor did the monarchy in Ireland enjoy a similar right. Indeed, Queen Mary had granted Catholic chapters the right to elect their own deans, without monarchical interference.[88] Under the system inaugurated by James II, Moore's own position as vicar-general was not only usurped, but Moore made it clear that the Jacobite chapter wanted to elect a vicar-general from among themselves.[89]

Moore spearheaded the opposition to James's 'pretendu chapitre'. His downfall was a direct result of this opposition. William King's report of Moore's sermon makes sense in this context. The letter outlines Moore's campaign and its consequences, though he does not mention himself by name:

Il y a eu un ecclesiastique qui prit la liberté d'en parle a S[a].M[ajesté]. en particulier et de la p[r]ier tres humblement de vouloir bien nommer quelque personne a qui on peut representer ces choses: mais n'ayant pas reussi, et croyant que Sa M. pouvoir estre prevenue contre luy, il s'addressa a Mr l'Ev[eque]. de Meath grand aumonier de Sa M. ce que ce prelat a eu la bonté de faire dans une tres scavante requette qui contenoit une partie de ces choses. Mais ce prelat ne peut alors rien obtenir, et on luy dit meme qu'on s'etonnoit, que luy qui estoit de la maison de Sa M. voulut s'opposer a ses droits. Alors cet ecclesiastique erut[?] estre obligé en conscience de protester contre des desordres si publics de la seul maniere qui luy restoit, et d'en toucher quelque chose dans un serment qu'il fis devant S.M. dans cette eglise meme ou des desordres se commettoient, et en presence de ceux qui en estoient ses autheurs: il a esté pour la recompense, a quoy il devoit s'attendre, traitté de seditieux, de turbulent et chassé de la ville qui estoit sa patrie, et le lieu de sa naissance, et dont il estoit grand vicaire sans aucune form de procès ou connoissance de cause choses sans examples jusques alors.[90]

87 'The only principal church in Dublin, which was the only one that the Catholics owned, was divided by a subtle schism, which according to all appearances would have divided all the churches in the country, since the same causes exist there, or would inevitably be found there' (my italics): 'Letter of a Catholick priest in Ireland' (TCD, MS 1184, f. 2). 88 'Letter of a Catholick priest in Ireland' (TCD, MS 1184, ff 2–9). The writer also deplored the lack of Catholic ecclesiastics in the privy council (f. 12). 89 Ibid., f. 12. 90 'There was an ecclesiastic who took the liberty of talking to his majesty

The unnamed ecclesiastic was obviously Moore, as is evident from the comment that he was vicar-general in Dublin. He requested at the end of the letter that his correspondent pass on the contents to 'des personnes plus eclairées que moy' to garner their opinion on the matter.[91]

Little is known about the 'pretended chapter' set up by James II. Certainly Patrick Tyrell and Patrick Russell were strenuously opposed to it, despite the fact that both men received payments from the royal exchequer.[92] Russell was a celebrant at royal ecclesiastical functions. Tyrrell was even closer to the regime; when Thomas Sheridan was removed from office in January 1688, Tyrrell filled his place as secretary of state to Tyrconnell.[93] An alleged address to the king, prepared by Patrick Russell on behalf of the Irish episcopacy in 1689, urged that 'the prelates and clergy ... be restored to their livings, churches, and full exercise of their ecclesiastical jurisdiction without which it is not to be expected that they can prevail to repress the vices most swaying in this age'.[94] James's chancery clearly infringed on this request. John Brenan, the archbishop of Cashel, also firmly opposed the new institution. He believed that Richard Piers and Thaddeus Crowley, 'with other few ambitious priests', had been behind 'the erection in Dublin of a new chancery (dataria) through which the King would confer absolutely all ecclesiastical benefices according to the old system of investiture and regalia that prevailed in France.'[95] Brenan opposed the new chancery's nomination of Richard Piers to the deanery of Waterford, insinuating that he had signed Gallican propositions in

in particular, and of begging him very humbly to be willing to name someone to which one could portray these things: but not having received [a reply], and believing that his majesty could be warned against him, he addressed himself to the bishop of Meath, chief chaplain to his majesty, which is what the prelate had the kindness to do in a very learned request which contained part of these things. But the prelate could obtain nothing, and he [the king] also told him that he was surprised, that he, who was in his majesty's court, would oppose his rights. Then this ecclesiastic had been obliged in conscience to protest against the disorders in public in the only way remaining to him, and to touch on something in a sermon which he made before his majesty in the church where the disorders were committed, and in the presence of those who were their authors: he was, as a reward, which he should have expected, treated as seditious, as turbulent, and dismissed from the city which was his 'homeland', and the place of his birth, and of which he was vicar-general, without any form of process or knowledge of the cause, apart from the examples until here': 'Letter of a Catholick priest in Ireland' (TCD, MS 1184, ff 12–13.   91 Ibid., f. 14.   92 On 22 January 1690 a meeting of the Catholic chapter of Christ Church recorded: 'Ordered that next Friday a petition be given in to the King and council for preserving the rights of the church unless uppon urgent reasons the Dean tell why fitt to give more time to the Archbishop': 'Some papers of Stafford, pretended Dean of this church and his chapter in 1689' (RBCL, C6.1.26.6.32). No context was given, but this was probably a reference to the dispute caused by Moore's inflammatory sermon.   93 D'Alton, *The memoirs of the archbishops of Dublin*, p. 450; Cogan, *The diocese of Meath*, ii, pp 140–51; 'A diary of events in Ireland from 1685 to 1690', p. 352; Simms, *Jacobite Ireland*, p. 28. Tyrrell was no stranger to clerical infighting: see T. Ó Fiaich, 'The appointment of Bishop Tyrrell and its consequences' (1955).   94 [P. Russell?], *An address given in to the late King James, by the titular archbishop of Dublin: from the general meeting of the Romish bishops and clergy of Ireland, held in May last, by that King's order* (1690), pp 8–9.   95 Power (ed.), *A bishop of the penal times*, p. 98. Power noted, in 1932, that 'The Erastian policy which dictated the erection of James's ecclesiastical chancery in Dublin has all but escaped the notice of Irish writers' (ibid.).

France. Piers and Crowley appealed to 'the King in Dublin and to the court and to the bishops resident there'. They later went to Rome to press their case, forcing Brenan to defend himself. Brenan, like Moore, noted that Tyrrell had given 'proof of great zeal on the instituting of this chancery.'[96] Clearly the chancery, or 'pretended chapter', was the source of widespread opposition within the Irish church. Moore had become the focus of this opposition in the diocese of Dublin, where Christ Church Cathedral had become the unlikely battleground.

It is possible that Moore travelled around the country in an attempt to gather support for his opposition to the chancery. When he provided evidence at the Processus Datariae hearings for three prospective Irish bishops between September 1695 and January 1696 in Rome, he showed a remarkably detailed knowledge of parts of Ireland outside Dublin. He could only have visited the regions in the late 1680s, but he supplies no information concerning the reasons for what was a virtual tour of parts of the country. At the hearing for Maurice Donnellan for Clonfert it was recorded: 'The diocese is extensive but the town of Clonfert has only a small number of inhabitants. Moore says he knows these things as he was in the diocese …'[97] Moore was equally knowledgeable about the dioceses of Cashel where he had 'visited various places' and Ossory which he had also seen first hand.[98] This tour of Ireland for support was possible since Moore was banished from Dublin, effectively removing him from court, rather than Ireland.[99]

By January 1690 Catholic clergy in Dublin were well aware of the slight hold on power of James II's administration. Moore's friend Ryane added a hysterical note to a letter to Morin in Paris at this time: 'Nous sommes ici en grand danger d'etre massacrés, ici tous les Protestants sont pour la Prince d'Orange.'[1] The collapse of the Jacobite regime in Ireland during 1690–1 ended the brief hopes of the Catholic church in Ireland and ushered in a new period of repression for Catholics in Dublin. Patrick Russell died in prison in 1692.[2] Moore had effectively removed himself from Jacobite sources of patronage. It is not clear if his opposition to James's short-lived chancery was related solely to benefices within the diocese or to episcopal appointments as well. The question of James's right of nomination was raised in Rome in 1693 after the monarch nominated Piers Creagh for the see of Dublin. It was pointed out that James was granted the right by Innocent XI, and he continued to nominate to vacant Irish sees until his death in 1701.[3]

96 Power (ed.), *A bishop of the penal times*, p. 98. The letter is dated 2 February 1691. On the wider context see: C. Giblin, 'The Stuart nomination of Irish bishops, 1687–1765' (1966), especially pp 35–6 for comments based on Brenan's letter. **97** C. Giblin, 'The *Processus Datariae* and the appointment of Irish bishops in the seventeenth century', p. 607. **98** Ibid., pp 609, 611. **99** 'Letter of a Catholick priest in Ireland' (TCD, MS 1184, f. 13). **1** D. Ryane to Morin, Dublin, 25 Jan 1690 (new style) (BSG, MS 2566, ff 36–7). **2** H. Fenning, 'The archbishops of Dublin, 1693–1786' (2000), p. 175; Valentine Rivers, Lisbon, to R. Eustace, Rome, 1692, in Donnelly, *Short histories of Dublin parishes*, part 9, pp 215–18. **3** Giblin, 'The Stuart nomination of Irish bishops, 1687–1765', p. 37. The most outspoken critic of the policy was John O'Molony, bishop of Limerick (translated from Killaloe on James's nomination in January 1689) who feared that James would use the prerogative to fill Irish sees with English clerics.

Harris recorded that on his departure from Ireland Moore 'complied as a faithful subject, but hinted at his departure, "that he only went as the King's precursor, who would soon be obliged to follow him"'.[4] In fact, Moore was banished twice over, for he was later outlawed by the incoming Williamite administration when he was, ironically, described as a Jesuit priest. He was among those outlawed for 'foreign treason', rather than domestic 'high treason'.[5] Moore returned to Paris by April 1691, but kept in touch with the course of the war in Ireland by correspondence. One letter has survived, which provides a lengthy account of the failed assault on Limerick by Williamite forces in August 1690. The author ultimately laid the blame for Irish problems with the Cromwellians. He also mentioned that Moore was contemplating writing a history of Ireland and promised to send more material concerning the war in Ireland.[6] Very few Catholics published histories of events in Ireland in the late 1680s. Hugh O'Reilly's *Ireland's case briefly stated* (1695), though it dealt only with events to 1685, angered James II and resulted in O'Reilly's dismissal from the Jacobite court-in-exile.[7] Rather than producing a damaging critique of James II's regime in Ireland, Moore turned to philosophy. In 1691–2 he wrote and published his first major work, partly in an attempt to reintegrate himself at the University of Paris.[8]

Moore was a strong supporter of a wide-ranging Catholic counter-revolution, but the monarch's support was crucial to the success of this enterprise and his insistence on control of church patronage ultimately weakened the Catholic revival. Problems were exacerbated by other conflicts involving members of the episcopacy. Moore may have been part of a group of senior Irish Catholic clerics composed of Tyrrell, Russell and Brenan, who strongly supported Tyrconnell's hasty promotion of Irish Catholics. It is noteworthy that Sheridan claimed that Tyrrell, Russell and Tyrconnell were the key supporters of Moore's appointment to Trinity College. Others, such as Maguire and Sheridan may have favoured a slower rate of change.[9] Clarendon believed that there was a rift between Dominic

---

4 Ware, *The whole works*, ed. Harris, ii, p. 289.   5 J.G. Simms (ed.), 'Irish Jacobites, lists from TCD MS N.1.3' (1960), p. 89   6 'Cormac comharba Ciaráin', Dublin, to Michael Moore, Paris, 24 April 1690 [*sic* – 1691] (BL, Add MSS 34,727, ff 159–62). The author was probably Gregory Fallon, bishop of Clonmacnoise, who was in Paris by February 1692: see J. Monahan (ed.), *Records relating to the dioceses of Ardagh and Clonmacnoise* (1886), pp 37, 115–21. For some comments and a partial transcription see: S. O'Grady and R. Flower, *Catalogue of Irish manuscripts in the British Museum* (1926–53), ii, pp 624–7. Flower argues that Fallon could not have been the author. The letter was in Irish with a Latin translation provided by Thomas O'Sullivan. He presented the letter to the English antiquarian collector Humphrey Wanley, the librarian for Lord Harlay in London, in 1718. It is not clear how O'Sullivan came into possession of the letter in the first place. O'Sullivan is best known for his *Dissertation ... prefix'd to the memoirs of the marquis of Clanricarde* (1722). See: Ann de Valera, 'Antiquarian and historical investigations in Ireland in the eighteenth-century' (1978), pp 25–7; Deane (ed.), *Field Day anthology of Irish writing*, i, pp 972–3, 1007–8.   7 P. Kelly, '"A light to the blind": the voice of the dispossessed élite in the generation after the defeat at Limerick' (1985); idem, 'Nationalism and the contemporary historians of the Jacobite war in Ireland' (1995).   8 The subject of chapter three.   9 Fenning rejects the idea of a rift between Maguire and Tyrconnell, but suggests that the archbishop may have 'tried to slow down the lord deputy's headlong rush towards total change'. See:

Maguire, the archbishop of Armagh, and Patrick Russell as early as 1687.[10] Maguire allegedly sided with Thomas Sheridan, after his removal from office, in an attempt to damage Tyrconnell. This stood in marked contrast to Patrick Tyrrell, Moore's first supporter in his campaign against James's chancery, who occupied Sheridan's vacant post. Sheridan's derogatory comments about Moore's alleged Jansenism have already been noted. The anonymous author of *The secret consults* suggested that Tyrconnell later revived a disagreement between John Brenan and Dominic Maguire, and that Petre, Moore's would-be foe in the dispute concerning Trinity College, had reprimanded Tyrconnell for doing so.[11]

The Catholic clergy were an important pillar of the Jacobite regime in Ireland, and played a key role during moments of tension, but this did not mean unquestioning, universal, church support.[12] Clearly the church had major expectations of the new regime, but as Moore discovered, the corollary of the state promotion of Catholicism involved both an increased competition within the church for places and the likelihood that the state would seek to interfere in these often-lucrative nominations.[13] Indeed, a similar debate had arisen in the 1640s when some Catholic bishops and lay supporters argued that the confederate supreme council had the right to nominate Irish bishops (as the 'king's proxies'), though the papal nuncio, Rinuccini, was strong enough to resist the pressure.[14] The collapse of the Catholic revival in 1690–1 overshadowed the problems inherent within it. It is not surprising that there was little open discussion of the topic in later years. Nonetheless, as Simms put it: 'In Ireland, no less than in continental Europe, a Catholic dynasty would certainly have sought to influence the policy and personnel of the Catholic church, which would thus be deprived of that freedom which was an unintended benefit of the penal laws.'[15] Moore was determined to resist encroachments on the church's freedom. But his support for a wholesale policy for the promotion of Catholic claims in Ireland ultimately contributed to the disintegration of the Jacobite cause in 1689–91. He had no choice but to re-build his career on the Continent.

'Dominic Maguire O.P., archbishop of Armagh: 1684–1707', p. 45. **10** D'Alton, *Memoirs of the archbishops of Dublin*, p. 449. This tension was probably a result of the dispute concerning the role of regular clergy in the new tolerant atmosphere of the late 1680s. The potential appointment of regular bishops was a particular source of strain. See: Fenning, 'Dominic Maguire O.P., archbishop of Armagh: 1684–1707', pp 40–3. **11** *A full and impartial account of all the secret consults, negotiations, stratagems, and intriegues of the Romish party in Ireland* (1689), pp 99–107; Miller, 'Thomas Sheridan (1646–1712) and his "Narrative"', p. 122. The reliability of the *Secret consults* pamphlet is particularly suspect. The author claimed that Sheridan married Petre's niece, which appears not to have been the case (ibid., pp 106, note 4, 108, note 8). **12** É. Ó Ciardha, *Ireland and the Jacobite cause, 1685–1766: a fatal attachment* (Dublin, 2002), pp 65–6. **13** In general see: Simms, *Jacobite Ireland*, pp 27–8, 42–3, 86–9, 93–4; J. Miller, 'The earl of Tyrconnell and James II's Irish policy' (1977); S.J. Connolly, *Religion, law and power: the making of Protestant Ireland, 1660–1760* (1992), p. 35. **14** T. Ó hAnnracháin, *Catholic reformation in Ireland: the mission of Rinuccini, 1645–1649* (2002), pp 234–5. **15** Simms, *Jacobite Ireland*, p. 94.

3

'Imperturbable as a rock in the midst of storms': battling the Cartesians, 1692[1]

The gradual collapse of the Jacobite regime in Ireland resulted in the arrival of huge numbers of Irish migrants in France in the early 1690s. Over 5,000 Irish troops were dispatched in 1690 as part of an exchange between Louis XIV and James II. After the Treaty of Limerick, during winter 1691, a further 15,000 soldiers and 4,000 dependants arrived in France.[2] Though the soldiers were not posted in the capital, many refugees must have made their way to Paris, where there was a well-established migrant network. Many of the senior Catholic clergy also crossed over to France, where some accepted local appointments. By 1692 six bishops were at James II's court in exile, at St Germain-en-Laye outside Paris, working for papal support on behalf of the exiled monarch.[3] Though out of favour with the Jacobite regime, Moore also made his way back to Paris, and he was certainly there by April 1691.[4] His main pre-occupation was to re-establish his contacts in Paris and, hopefully, find employment at the university. As Irish priests returned to the city, the Nation d'Allemagne began meeting for the first time since 1685 and Moore took part in business in 1691.[5] But obtaining a permanent university appointment would be a much more difficult prospect.

The Irish refugee crisis of the 1690s coincided with a major struggle for control of the philosophy curriculum at the University of Paris, between professors attracted to the 'new philosophy' of René Descartes and those who adhered to the 'old philosophy' which was based on Aristotle and the great thinkers of medieval Scholasticism. To stress his intellectual credentials, Moore set about preparing a major contribution to the Aristotelian-Cartesian debate. *De existentia Dei et humanae mentis immortalitate secundum Cartesii et Aristotelis docrinam disputatio* was published in Paris in 1692.[6] No doubt he hoped that his book would open

---

1 The title quote is taken from a description of Moore recorded at a meeting of the Nation d'Allemagne in 1708. The full description is quoted at the end of chapter five. Cited in Boyle, 'Dr Michael Moore', p. 12. 2 Figures are taken from the recent assessment by G. Rowlands, 'An army in exile: Louis XIV and the Irish forces of James II in France, 1691–1698' (2001), pp 2–3. This is an increase on the figures provided by Simms, *Jacobite Ireland*, pp 259–60. 3 Simms, *Jacobite Ireland*, p. 261. 4 If the date of his letter to an anonymous French correspondent is correct, then he arrived in Paris after January 1691. An Irish correspondent wrote to him in Paris in April 1691. For details see chapter two. 5 Meetings re-commenced in April 1691. Liber procurationum Constantissimae Germanorum Nationis (1660–98), (AUP, registre 28, f. 281); Boyle, 'Dr Michael Moore', p. 8. 6 On the existence of God and the immortality of the human soul, disputed according to the doctrine of

doors and enable him to settle down once again at the university. *De existentia Dei* is revealing about the philosophical ideas of a prominent Irish Catholic migrant; it also indicates the kind of ideas to which Irish students were exposed in Paris at an important junction for the development of the Irish student network in France.[7]

The writings of the ancient Greek philosopher, Aristotle, provided the framework for the university philosophy curriculum during the Middle Ages and, in most parts of Europe, continued to do so until the second half of the seventeenth century. The great medieval Scholastic writers, like Thomas Aquinas, effectively Christianised Aristotle, and despite some reservations, including the 1277 condemnation issued by the University of Paris, the Christianised Aristotle became the mainstay of philosophy courses in European universities. As Edward Grant puts it:

> Aristotelianism extended much beyond the works of Aristotle and became the dominant, and, for some centuries, the sole intellectual system in Western Europe. It was, as we all know, the basis of the curriculum of the medieval university, where it remained entrenched for centuries. From the time the works of Aristotle entered western Europe in the late twelfth century until perhaps 1600, or 1650, Aristotelianism provided not only the mechanisms of explanation for natural phenomena, but served as a gigantic filter through which the world was viewed and pictured.[8]

The Scientific Revolution of the sixteenth and seventeenth centuries provided the most serious threat to Aristotelianism, by challenging fundamental aspects of traditional natural philosophy. The new astronomical theories and discoveries of the early Scientific Revolution, particularly in the hands of Galileo, shook the Aristotelian establishment in the university to its core. However, the sheer eclecticism of late Aristotelianism, and its ability to absorb new ideas, was one reason for its ability to survive well into the seventeenth century.[9] Another was the fact that Galileo and other pioneers failed to provide a coherent alternative which could be taught in the universities. This changed as the century progressed and viable alternatives to Aristotelianism emerged. The French mathematician and philosopher René Descartes constructed one such alternative.[10] Floris Cohen has noted that 'To Descartes the traditional ideal of aiming for the totality of knowl-

Descartes and Aristotle.   7 At least eleven Irishmen taught philosophy at the University of Paris in the seventeenth or eighteenth centuries, but only Moore is known to have published on the subject. See: Brockliss and Ferté, 'Irish clerics in France', p. 547, note 74.   8 E. Grant, 'Aristotelianism and the longevity of the medieval world view' (1978), p. 94.   9 Ibid., pp 93–106; R. Ariew, 'Theory of comets at Paris during the seventeenth century' (1992). Copernican (and Tyconic) ideas were seriously discussed by French professors only after 1640: L.W.B. Brockliss, 'Copernicus in the university: the French experience' (1990).   10 S. Gaukroger, *Descartes: an intellectual biography* (1995); P. Dear, *Revolutionizing the sciences: European knowledge and its ambitions, 1500–1700* (2001), pp 80–100, 149–58.

edge was as alive as it had been for Aristotle, his principal quarrel with the Aristotelians and rival natural philosophers being that they had happened to totalize knowledge in the wrong manner, whereas Descartes ... knew how to do the job better.'[11] Born in 1596, Descartes received a classical education but became disillusioned by Aristotelian philosophy. In the late 1620s he set about constructing an alternative system of knowledge, rooted in the presumed certainty provided by mathematics. He suppressed his major scientific treatise, *The world*, in 1633, on hearing of the condemnation of Galileo in Rome. In subsequent years he created a 'metaphysical foundation' for his project, outlined in the *Discourse on method* (1637) and *Meditations on first philosophy* (1641). His most mature attempt to present his ideas as a complete textbook was the *Principles of philosophy* (1644). In 1649 Descartes moved to the court of Queen Christina of Sweden, where he died of pneumonia in 1650.[12] It is now clear from the work of historians that Aristotelianism did not succumb easily to the work of Descartes or others. Indeed, the reaction to Descartes' *Discourse* was surprisingly muted.[13] Nonetheless, Cartesianism increasingly challenged Aristotelianism in France during the second half of the seventeenth century by offering quantitative, mathematical and mechanical explanations of natural phenomena. Informal correspondence networks and more formalised scientific societies, such as the Académie des Sciences, established in 1666, meant that the new learning gained a hearing and attracted supporters.[14] But university professors were resistant to the new philosophy, setting the scene for a lengthy struggle, in which Michael Moore would become involved.[15] As Charles Alan Kors comments: 'If Aristotelian scholasticism were dead or dying, someone forgot to inform the publishers, reading public, students and authorities of France.'[16]

As a professor of philosophy at the Collège des Grassins from the mid-1660s, Michael Moore was in an ideal position from which to view the gradual advance of Cartesianism at the University of Paris. Brockliss has contended that Cartesian and other variants of the new learning began to creep into philosophy classes at the university from the 1650s. It was a decade later before these encroachments were taken seriously enough for some professors to begin discussing and attacking Descartes.[17] The natural philosophy (or physics) part of the philosophy course

11 H. Floris Cohen, *The scientific revolution: a historiographical inquiry* (1994), p. 168. See also: G. Hatfield, 'Metaphysics and the new science' (1991), p. 111; D. Garber, *Descartes' metaphysical physics* (1992), pp 1–4. For an argument that Cartesianism succeeded in France because of its *incomplete*, and therefore less threatening, nature see: Brockliss, 'Descartes, Gassendi and the reception of the mechanical philosophy in the French Collèges de plein exercise, 1640–1730', pp 466–8. 12 S. Gaukroger, *Descartes: an intellectual biography*. 13 D. Garber, 'Descartes, the Aristotelians and the revolution that did not happen in 1637' (1988), pp 47–86. For a recent statement of the argument that Descartes' metaphysical project must be placed firmly within late scholasticism see: J. Secada, *Cartesian metaphysics: the late scholastic origins of modern philosophy* (2000). 14 T. McLoughlin, 'Censorship and defenders of the Cartesian faith in mid-seventeenth-century France' (1979), p. 565. 15 Brockliss, *French higher education*, pp 185–227, 337–90. 16 C.A. Kors, 'Theology and atheism in early modern France' (1990), p. 246. 17 Brockliss, 'The University of Paris in the sixteenth and

was most radically overhauled by Cartesianism, a process which was not completed until the final decade of the seventeenth century. The metaphysics part of the course discussed existence and what amounted to natural theology, that is, the existence of God, the angels and the human soul. This part of the course was challenged by Cartesianism but not substantially altered even by the end of the seventeenth century. As Brockliss puts it: 'Aristotle weathered the rationalist storm with relative ease.'[18]

The increasing influence of Descartes in the university was most openly manifested from the early 1670s, when the authorities responded with a number of attempts to ban Cartesianism. Earlier in the seventeenth century, in 1624, the university had underscored the pre-eminence of Aristotle.[19] In 1663 Descartes' works were placed on the Index Librorum Prohibitorum with the note 'until they are corrected', which encouraged a series of French condemnations.[20] The first attempt to censor Cartesianism was a result of royal pressure. In 1671 the archbishop of Paris, François de Harlay, convened a meeting of university officials, including the rector, the deans of the faculties of theology, medicine and law, the procureurs of the four nations which comprised the faculty of arts and the principals of the colleges. The archbishop instructed them to abide by the 'rules and statutes of the University' and thereby uphold the authority of Aristotle.[21] The 1671 meeting must have involved Moore directly, since he was serving his first period as procurator of the Nation d'Allemagne at this time.[22] By 1673 Moore had already become known as an ardent defender of Aristotelianism.[23]

The 1671 censorship was not entirely successful. While the faculties of theology (1671) and medicine (1673) duly condemned Cartesianism, the faculty of arts remained silent, as did the Parlement of Paris. One reason was the popularity of Nicholas Boileau's anonymous *L'arrêt burlesque* which viciously satirised the

seventeenth centuries', p. 159; idem, 'Aristotle, Descartes and the new sciences: natural philosophy at the University of Paris, 1600–1740' (1981), pp 38–52.   18 Except in the natural philosophy part of the course: Brockliss, 'Philosophy teaching in France 1600–1740', p. 134. In general: ibid., pp 134–52; idem, *French higher education*, pp 205–16.   19 L. Thorndike, 'Censorship by the Sorbonne of science and superstition in the first half of the seventeenth century' (1955), pp 119–25.   20 The condemnations were gathered in one volume by J. du Hamel, *Quaedam recentiorum philosophorum ac praesertim Cartesii propositiones damnates ac prohibitatae* (1705). Du Hamel even made use of condemnations stretching back to the anti-Aristotelian censures of 1277. A summary can be found in Kors, *Atheism in France, 1650–1729*, pp 217–22. On the censorship of Cartesianism in early-modern France see: McLoughlin, 'Censorship and defenders of the Cartesian faith in mid-seventeenth century France'; R. Ariew, 'Damned if you do: Cartesians and censorship, 1663–1706' (1994), pp 255–74; idem, *Descartes and the last scholastics* (1999), pp 155–71; F. Azouvi, *Descartes et la France: histoire d'une passion nationale* (2002), pp 15–47. On the links between Cartesianism and Jansenism see: T.M. Schmaltz, 'What has Cartesianism to do with Jansenism?' (1999); S. Nadler, 'Arnauld, Descartes, and transubstantiation: reconciling Cartesian metaphysics and the real presence' (1988). 21 Jourdain, *Histoire de l'Universite de Paris*, pp 233–4; C. du Plessis D'Argentré, *Collectio judiciorum de novis erroribus* (1728–36), iii, p. 138.   22 Liber procurationem constantissimae Germanorum Nationis (1660–98) (AUP, registre 28, f. 118).   23 Collège des Grassins, Annales XVIIe siècle (1665–72) (AN, MM 447, f. 318).

attempts of the scholastics and their supporters to reverse new discoveries and theories by decree.[24] The important role played by the spurious *Arrêt* is well known, but the Irish dimension has only recently been underlined by Éamon Ó Ciosáin.[25] Boileau's piece had ordered 'all professors and masters to give assistance to the application of the present decree … and all Irish tutors and other subordinates of the University to lend them their arms and to round on all those who disobey. And bans Reason from the University for ever'.[26] Moreover, it asserted the restoration of the 'children of Duns Scotus' who had been forced to take refuge in 'Hibernia', and were now able to return to the university.[27] Ó Ciosáin argues that this text 'sowed the seeds of some of the eighteenth-century satirical lore about Irish clerics disputing furiously in the streets of Paris.'[28] Ó Ciosáin proposes a number of explanations. First, Nicholas Boileau linked the pro-Aristotelians, the Irish among them, with the thought of the medieval Franciscan thinker John Duns Scotus. As Ó Ciosáin points out, a number of Irish Franciscan writers were at the forefront of the rehabilitation of Scotus in the seventeenth century, allied to their claim that Scotus was Irish. Moreover, recent work by Roger Ariew indicates that Scotist philosophy was much more influential in seventeenth-century France than is often assumed, though Parisian professors were overwhelmingly Thomist in the second half of the seventeenth century.[29] Second, as immigrants the Irish provided a soft target. Third, financial hardship meant that Irish students were 'forced to live on their wits, their theological training being one of their few marketable skills'.[30] In other words, opportunism played its part in shaping the philosophical outlook of Irish students and clerics. Perhaps there was also a more specific reason for the inclusion of these scathing comments about the Irish and their identification with the Scholastic viewpoint. Michael Moore was the one Irish figure involved in the censorship of Cartesianism in 1671. It is therefore possible that Boileau's attack was aimed at both Moore and the Irish dominated Nation d'Allemagne, which he represented.[31] In any case, well before 1692 Moore had closely allied himself to the cause of Aristotelianism in the university.

Indeed, through his teaching at the Collège des Grassins, Moore must have become keenly aware of the way in which Cartesianism was seeping into the philosophy curriculum. Charles Jourdain noted that: 'Au Collège des Grassins, un autre Cartesien … Edme Pourchot, nommé regent de philosophie en 1677, professa ouvertement les nouvelles opinions.'[32] Roughly contemporaneous with

24 N. Boileau, *Oeuvres complètes*, ed. A. Adam (1966), pp 326–30; Ariew, 'Damned if you do: Cartesians and censorship, 1663–1706', pp 257–61; McLoughlin, 'Censorship and defenders of the Cartesian faith in mid-seventeenth century France', pp 566–7; Jourdain, *Histoire de l'Université de Paris*, pp 234–6. **25** É. Ó Ciosáin, 'Attitudes towards Ireland and the Irish in Enlightenment France' (1999), pp 142–3. **26** Cited in ibid., p. 142. **27** Ibid., p. 142. **28** Ibid., p. 143. **29** Brockliss, 'Philosophy teaching in France, 1600–1740', pp 138–42; Ariew, *Descartes and the last Scholastics*, pp 39–57. **30** Ó Ciosáin, 'Attitudes towards Ireland and the Irish in Enlightenment France', pp 145–6. **31** The failure of the faculty of arts to publicly condemn Cartesianism in the early 1670s suggests that Moore and the Nation d'Allemagne were in a vocal, but minority, pro-Aristotelian position. **32** Jourdain, *Histoire de l'Université de Paris*, p. 236.

Moore, Pourchot taught philosophy at the Collège des Grassins from 1677 to 1690, when he moved to the Collège de Mazarin.[33] Back in 1671 Boileau identified the enemies of Aristotle as 'Gassendistes, Cartésiens, Malebranchistes et *Pourchotistes'*.[34] This proximity of Cartesianism must have had an important effect on Moore. Besides, as noted already, Irish priest-students resident at the Collège des Lombards took their philosophy course at the nearby Collège des Grassins 'from time immemorial because of its proximity'.[35] Irish students may have been better acquainted with Cartesianism than many of their colleagues.

The divergent opinions of Pourchot and Moore who taught at the same collège de plein exercise exemplify the contrasting reactions to Cartesianism among the Parisian professors. As the new learning gained a foothold within the university, so censorship increased and the attacks on Cartesianism in print became more numerous.[36] In 1685 the faculty of arts received a formal order from the king banning the teaching of either Gassendist or Cartesian philosophy.[37] Kors has commented that:

> Textbooks and historians of philosophy focus, on the whole, on the sets of objections and replies concerning [Cartesian] proofs published in the very first edition of the *Meditations*. In fact, however, it was the two generations that followed Descartes' death that the *historically* most significant contestations occurred.'[38]

Anti-Cartesian publications took a variety of forms. Some continued to present the standard Aristotelian framework with little mention of Descartes. By the 1680s this was becoming increasingly uncommon. In the 1680s and 1690s books and pamphlets poured from the printers around the university, including satires, condemnations, textbooks, attacks and counter-attacks. Publications by Edmond Pourchot, Jean Baptiste DuHamel, Gabriel Daniel, Pierre Daniel Huet, Jean DuHamel and Sylvian Régis indicate that there was a vigorous debate in progress during the latter decades of the century.[39]

---

33 Brockliss, *French higher education*, p. 465.   34 Boileau, *Oeuvres complètes*, p. 327. On Pourchot see: Brockliss, *French higher education*, pp 299, 350, 352; Kors, *Atheism in France*, pp 276–7. Kors points out that Pourchot's Aristotelian veneer was so successful that the *Dictionnaire de théologie Catholique* mistook him for a straightforward Aristotelian!   35 Swords (ed.), 'History of the Irish College, Paris, 1578–1800. Calendar of the papers of the Irish College, Paris', p. 105; P. Boyle, 'Glimpses of Irish collegiate life in Paris in the seventeenth and eighteenth centuries' (1902), p. 443; idem, 'Lord Iveagh, and other Irish students, students at the Collège des Grassins in Paris, from 1684 to 1710', (1901). 36 Bouillier identified the period 1675 to 1690 as the most difficult for supporters of Descartes, see: Francisque Bouillier, *Histoire de la philosophie Cartésienne*, 3rd edn (1868), i, p. 483, more generally, pp 466–85.   37 Jourdain, *Histoire de l'Université de Paris*, p. 234; Kors, *Atheism in France*, p. 273.   38 Kors, *Atheism in France*, pp 301–2.   39 L.C. Rosenfield, 'Peripatetic adversaries of Cartesianism in 17th century France' (1957); Kors, *Atheism in France*, pp 265–322; Brockliss, 'Philosophy teaching in France 1600–1740'; Ariew, *Descartes and the last Scholastics*, passim. J.S. Spink lists ten works devoted to the Aristotelian-Cartesian debate which were published in Paris alone between 1685 and 1694, *French free-thought from Gassendi to Voltaire* (1960), p. 188. His list is by no means exhaustive.

In 1691, the year before the publication of Moore's *De existentia Dei,* eleven Cartesian and Jansenist propositions purportedly taught at the University of Paris were condemned outright and a promise extracted from the professors of philosophy not to teach any Cartesian doctrines.[40] The propositions pertinent to Cartesianism condemned the method of universal doubt as a path to knowledge, particularly that: 'One must doubt if there is a God until one has a clear and certain knowledge of it by long and serious examination.'[41] The third proposition suggested that where examination produced knowledge (or sentiment) contrary to the faith, it should nonetheless be followed if it 'appears evident'.[42] The fifth held that: 'One must reject all the arguments which theologians and philosophers have utilised until now with St Thomas to determine that there is a God'.[43] Descartes' natural philosophy, which was perceived to have serious consequences for the philosophical and theological explanation of transubstantiation, was criticised in the form: 'The matter of bodies is only their extension, and one cannot be without the other.'[44] The suggestion was that Cartesian ideas were not only false philosophically but dangerously heterodox and therefore a threat to the Catholic faith. Indeed, the perceived relationship between Cartesianism and Jansenism was one reason for the state's censorship of the former, especially from the early 1670s when Boileau had noted that Aristotle should be followed in the university 'à la peine d'estre declarée Janseniste et amie des nouveautez'.[45] Interestingly, Roger Ariew has suggested that the 1691 condemnation was specifically aimed at the Cartesianism of Moore's former colleague Edmond Pourchot.[46] There is no evidence that Moore was involved in drawing up the eleven propositions. But the fact that he was well acquainted with Pourchot's work and writing *De existentia Dei* at the time, suggests he was part of a group within the faculty of arts which supported the fresh condemnation. In this context Moore's publication was an unofficial underpinning of the vocal opposition of the university to Cartesianism.[47] Indeed, the following year, 1693, the influential Société de la Sorbonne restated its opposition to the new anti-Aristotelian doctrines.[48]

Moore addressed his book to the dean and doctors of the faculty of theology at the University of Paris, as the best possible judges of his work, noting that

---

40 Jourdain, *Histoire de l'Université de Paris,* pp 269–70, propositions eight to eleven are evidently 'Jansenist'.   41 Ibid., p. 269, proposition two.   42 Ibid.   43 Ibid., translated by Kors, *Atheism in France,* p. 273.   44 Jourdain, *Histoire de l'Université de Paris,* p. 269   45 Boileau, *Oeuvres complètes,* p. 330; Schmaltz, 'What has Cartesianism to do with Jansenism?', pp 44–5, 47–53, which identifies Robert Desgabets as the key figure in the association of Jansenism with Cartesianism, and both as potentially dangerous. Jansenism is discussed in chapter five.   46 Ariew, 'Damned if you do: Cartesians and censorship, 1663–1706', p. 265, note 10.   47 It should be pointed out that Moore does not refer explicitly to the various censures of non-Aristotelian philosophy produced by the University of Paris during the course of the seventeenth-century. At the end of *DED* he simply pointed out that the reformed statutes of the University of 1601 had established Aristotelianism as the basis of the philosophy course (ibid., pp 458–9).   48 Kors, *Atheism in France,* p. 272.

Descartes had addressed his *Meditations* to the same body just over fifty years previously. The well-known *Journal des Scavans*, usually regarded as a prominent disseminator of the new learning, announced the publication of *De existentia Dei* in December 1691[49], and the following month carried a brief review:

> Lorsque M. Descartes publia ses meditations touchant la premiere philosophie, et qu'il y entreprit de démonstrer l'existence de Dieu, et l'immortalité de l'ame, il jugea à propos de dédier son ouvrage à la faculte de theologie de Paris, pour munir de l'autorité de ce corps celebre contre les attaques de ses ennemis.
>
> L'auteur de ce traité a eu des semblences motifs pour l'addresser à la mesme compagnie et pour le soumettre à son jugement, dans l'esperance que quand elle l'aura examiné, elle reconnoitra que les raisons que M. Descartes a voulu faire passer pour les raisons invincibles, n'ont rien de l'evidence ni de la certitude de la démonstration; et que celles dont les Anciens Philosophes se sont servis sont incomparablement plus fortes et plus solides.
>
> Comme tout le sistême de M. Descartes semble fondé sur la connoissance distincte qu'il a prétendu avoir de sa pensée, l'auteur de ce traité l'a commencé par l'examen de la définition que M. Descartes donne de la pensée, est a tâche de prouver que jamais il n'en avoit bien connu la nature, non plus celle de l'ame, que celle du corps que la matiere et l'etendue. C'est ce que l'auteur se propose de faire voir dans le reste de son ouvrage, où il se sert d'une methode tres facile et tres claire.[50]

Moore's work was much more than a re-statement of standard Scholastics theories as taught at the University of Paris. Instead, he directly compared the metaphysics of Aristotle and Descartes in an attempt to show that Descartes' 'first philosophy' was deeply flawed, and that only Aristotle could provide the basis for a coherent metaphysics, consistent with Christianity. Consistency with Christianity was the standard against which all philosophers measured their work; hence the

49 *Le Journal des Sçavans*, 1692, p. 468. The book was granted 'Privilege du Roy' in October 1692.
50 *Le Journal des Sçavans*, 1693, pp 10–11. 'When Descartes published his meditations concerning first philosophy, and there undertook to demonstrate the existence of God and the immortality of the soul, he saw fit to dedicate his work to the faculty of theology in Paris, to provide the authority of that famous body against the attacks of his enemies. The author of this treatise had similar motives for addressing the same company and submitting to their judgement, in the hope that when they have examined it, they will recognise that the reasons Descartes wanted to pass as invincible reasons, have no evidence or certitude of demonstration and that those which the old philosophers used are incomparably more solid and strong. Since Descartes' whole system seems founded on distinct knowledge, which he claimed to have of his thought, the author of this treatise begins it by examining Descartes' definition of thought and has tried to prove that he did not understand its nature, nor that of the soul, that of the body, matter or extension. This is what the author proposes to look at in the rest of his work where he himself uses a very easy and clear method.'

dedication of *De existentia Dei* to the Paris faculty of theology. Moore's work therefore contrasts strongly with the attempts by Jean Baptisite DuHamel in *Philosophia vetus et nova ad usum scholae accomodata* (Paris, 1677) and later Edmond Pourchot in *Institutio philosophica ad faciliorem veterem ac recentiorum philosophorum lectionem comparata* (Paris, 1695) to reconcile Cartesianism and Aristotelianism. Moore's purpose was not just to undermine Cartesian mechanism, but also to derail the project of a number of Parisian academics who sought to accommodate the 'old' and 'new' philosophies. In *De existentia Dei* Moore argued that Aristotelianism and Cartesianism conflicted on a huge range of concepts and were therefore de facto incompatible.

In the dedicatory letter Moore stated that: 'There has arisen a controversy among us which is not to be totally despised nor is it unworthy of your most serious consideration immediately, even though our dispute was begun *not so much about the truth of things as about the weight and significance of arguments.*'[51] In other words, neither God's existence nor the immortality of the human soul was at issue; rather, the quarrel centred on *how* these precepts could be known. Descartes' demonstrations, claimed Moore, were untenable and therefore damaged the 'truths' which they supposed to support.[52] Furthermore, Moore questioned the purpose behind Descartes' metaphysics. In common with other late Scholastics Moore charged Descartes with resurrecting a version of ancient atomism, and attacked him on that basis:

> There is no lack of people who say, therefore, that these (tasks) [i.e. Descartes' metaphysics] were undertaken by him in order that a certain sinister suspicion should be dispelled about the new philosophy which he was then contemplating. Since this appears to be developed from almost unchanged principles of Epicurus or Democritus, it can justifiably be seen to be the same (as their philosophy).[53]

The problem with ancient atomism, for Moore, was the lack of room for divine agency in a universe where atoms interacted by chance.[54] Descartes' metaphysics was the justification of a much larger project, and by challenging it Moore was attacking the entire system at its foundations.

In the second set of objections appended to the *Meditations on first philosophy*, Marin Mersenne suggested that Descartes should set out his ideas carefully along geometric lines, not only to clarify his argument, but also to provide a suitable model of his method of demonstration.[55] The resulting 'Arguments proving the

---

51 *DED*, dedicatory letter (unpaginated), my italics. Translations from the letter and epistle have been provided by Dr John Cleary. *DED* is divided into two 'books'. Book one deals with the theories of Descartes, book two presents the Aristotelian case (pages 1–331 and 331–464 respectively). Book two also considers the philosophy of the Italian Renaissance thinker Pietro Pomponazzi on the soul. 52 *DED*, dedicatory letter (unpaginated). 53 Ibid., preface (unpaginated). 54 Ibid., preface (unpaginated). 55 R. Descartes, *The philosophical writings of Descartes*, trans. J. Cottingham, R.

existence of God and the distinction between the soul and the body arranged in geometric fashion' provided a succinct summary of the *Meditations*.[56] The 'Arguments' comprise ten definitions (e.g. thought, idea and substance), seven 'postulates'[57] (e.g. concerning the method of doubting or the fact that the idea of God contains necessary existence), ten axioms (e.g. it is impossible for nothing to cause the existence of something) and finally four demonstrations proving that God exists and that the body and mind are distinct.[58] Moore chose to concentrate his attack on this particularly refined statement of the Cartesian system. He noted that: 'there is no place where he [Descartes] worked harder than at the end of the second objections against his *Meditations*. In fact, here he tried to accomplish what he was proposing in a geometrical manner through definitions, postulates, axioms and demonstrations.'[59]

Moore's declared intention was 'to examine the truth of his [Descartes'] proposals, not according to the criterion of faith but rather according to what appears true and clearly proven to us: a criterion which Descartes himself is sometimes wont to recommend'.[60] In fact, Moore accused Descartes of a retreat into fideism on the question of the soul, and included a discussion of the Renaissance humanist Pietro Pomponazzi for this reason. When Moore stressed the importance of the doctrine of previous philosophers and appealed to their authority in the dedicatory letter, he was careful to stress that this 'owes the origin, certitude and self-evidence of its demonstrations to the constant and perpetual perceptions and experiments of the senses'.[61] Thus Moore was affected by the criticisms of Scholasticism made by various proponents of the new learning. There was no uncritical appeal to the authority of Aristotle in *De existentia Dei*, nor was Descartes overtly accused of heterodoxy.

Moore spent much of his time in *De existentia Dei* undertaking detailed critiques of each of Descartes' definitions, postulates, axioms, and finally the demonstrations.[62] For example, Descartes' definition of idea as 'the form of any

Stoothoff and D. Murdoch (1985), ii, p. 92.   **56** Descartes, *The philosophical writings*, ii, pp 113–20. It should be noted that Descartes himself warned his readers: 'that I do not intend to include such material as I put in the *Meditations*, for if I did so I should have to go on much longer that I did there. And even the items I do include will not be given a fully precise explanation. This is partly to achieve brevity and partly to prevent anyone supposing what follows is adequate on its own.' (Ibid., p. 113). Against this should be balanced the fact that Moore was well aware of the content of the *Meditations*, as well as the *Discourse on method* and *The principles of philosophy*, see: *DED*, preface (unpaginated). **57** Cottingham notes that: 'Descartes is here playing on words, since what follows is not a set of postulates in the Euclidian sense, but a number of informal requests.' See: Descartes, *The philosophical writings*, ii, p. 114, note 3. Hence Moore initially calls them petitions (petitiones) but later postulates (postulata), see: *DED*, pp 5, 222–79. **58** Descartes, *The philosophical writings*, ii, pp 113–20. **59** *DED*, preface (unpaginated). **60** Ibid. **61** *DED*, dedicatory letter (unpaginated). **62** My analysis of Moore's text has concentrated on selected sections: Descartes' definitions of idea (pp 47–86), soul (pp 101–29) and God (pp 196–208); postulate concerning perception (pp 224–31); demonstrations of God from the idea of his existence (pp 297–300) and the distinction of mind and body (pp 313–31); Aristotles' demonstrations of God's existence (pp 340–3); difficulties with the 'Aristotelian' soul (pp 345–60); Moore's demonstration of the immortality of the human soul (pp 376–81,

given thought' played a fundamental role in his system.[63] Moore argued, in what would become a constant refrain, that such a definition was open to multiple interpretations, in other words it was neither clear nor distinct. Even if one accepted that Descartes meant that an idea showed us only the thought of a thing, one was still left with the problem of discerning which was prior to the mind, the thought or the idea. According to Descartes, we seem to have a thought first, and then formulate an idea. Moore argued that, in fact, we first perceive a thing, after which an idea follows and then our thought.[64] In another attack which Moore repeated frequently, he argued that even 'the followers of Descartes' could not agree on what he meant in this definition.[65] Moore then considered other interpretations of 'idea' drawn from the work of Aquinas, Augustine, Plato and Aristotle, resulting in the description of idea as the definition of a thing.[66] For example, 'the idea of a circle is nothing (other) than the definition of a circle itself'.[67] Drawing on Aquinas, Moore argued further that an idea is 'the sensible form of the thing itself abstracted from the thing itself and subsisting in the mind'.[68] The ideas and the subject are clearly different in terms of matter, but they are the same 'in a formal sense'.[69] We are able to know the truth, therefore, when we conclude that there is no contradiction between our idea and the object, since the idea is derived from the form of the object and is not merely a construct of our imagination. Crucially, ideas are not innate but result from our interaction with external objects, which restores the Aristotelian position that all knowledge comes by way of the senses.[70] Indeed, it has been argued that Descartes employed a very similar conception of ideas, retaining the position that 'the objective existence of things in the mind is constituted by the presence in the mind of the essence [or form] of the thing', though Descartes' followers disagreed about the means by which this occurs.[71]

One of the most difficult problems for late Aristotelians was the charge that their over reliance on sense experience led them into error. Therefore Descartes' first postulate, which asked readers to realise the uncertainty of judgement based on the senses, a key component of Cartesian metaphysics, is particularly note-

396–403); Pomponazzi, Aristotle and the soul (pp 411–52); conclusion (pp 452–63). **63** Descartes full definition in the 'Arguments' was: 'I understand this term to mean the form of any given thought, immediate perception of which makes me aware of the thought. Hence, whenever I express something in words, and understand what I am saying, this very fact makes it certain that there is within me an idea of what is signified by the words in question. Thus it is not only the images depicted in the imagination which I call 'ideas'. Indeed in so far as these images are in the corporeal imagination, that is, are depicted in some part of the brain, I do not call them 'ideas' at all; I call them 'ideas' insofar as they give form to the mind itself, when it is directed towards that part of the brain.' (Descartes, *The philosophical writings*, ii, p. 113; cited in *DED*, pp 47–8). See: J.M. Beyssade, 'The idea of God and the proofs of his existence' (1992); Ariew, *Descartes and the last scholastics*, pp 58–76; Secada, *Cartesian metaphysics*, pp 77–114. **64** *DED*, pp 50–1. **65** Ibid., pp 51–2; For analysis of another scholastic on Cartesian ideas see: N. Wells, 'Jean DuHamel, the Cartesians and Arnauld on idea' (1999). **66** *DED*, pp 54–6. **67** Ibid., pp 63–4. **68** Ibid., p. 57. **69** Ibid., pp 57–8. **70** Ibid., pp 59–60. **71** F. Wilson, 'The rationalist response to Aristotle in Descartes and Arnauld' (1994), p. 58.

worthy.[72] If Descartes' request was accepted, much of Moore's Scholastic edifice was open to assault. Moreover, this request was the crucial first step in constructing a 'new' first philosophy. Moore argued that 'after long consideration and frequent reading of Descartes' *Meditations*', he had concluded that it was false to suggest that the senses were always fallible.[73] To Moore it was *obvious* that there were problems with deriving knowledge from sense experience. We could, for instance, have only a 'probable opinion' of some things. Sometimes sense experience allows us to form opinions that could not be taken as absolute truths; our knowledge is at best imperfect. Hence, Moore pointed out, Aristotle did not comment on everything but only on those things which could be investigated through the senses, or through the investigation of causes. But the guarantor of our knowledge, as derived through the senses, was the correct application of method or 'scientia'. Correctly applied this allowed us to gain knowledge about geometry, God, the mind and truth. If our sense experience was not certain, neither was our judgement; to put it another way, if we cannot trust our senses, we cannot trust our reason for which they are the foundation. If this was the case, 'scientia' would be impossible.[74]

By examining and refuting the building blocks of Descartes' 'Arguments', Moore was in a position to attack his demonstrations. For example, the second demonstration stated: 'That the existence of God can be demonstrated a posteriori merely from the fact that we have an idea of God within us.'[75] This could not be accepted because, as Moore had already argued, the idea of a thing is nothing more than a definition, and this cannot provide a demonstration of necessary existence. A demonstration of the existence of God cannot be based on our idea of Him; rather it had to based on our observation of nature.[76]

The demonstration of the immortality of the human soul was a much more intricate and intricate issue, involving as it did difficulties arising from the writings of both Descartes and Aristotle. Aristotle was at best ambiguous on the question of immortality and at worst rejected it.[77] Descartes' fourth demonstration asserted that: 'There is a real distinction between the mind and the body.'[78] But he made no mention of the immortality of the mind or soul. Moore therefore pointed out that even if he accepted that Descartes proved the distinction of mind and body (which he rejected in any case) it would not follow from the soul's immateriality that it was immortal. Indeed, he pointed out that Scholastics accepted the

---

72 Descartes, *The philosophical writings*, ii, pp 114–15.   73 *DED*, pp 224–5.   74 Ibid., pp 225–31. 75 Descartes, *The philosophical writings*, ii, p. 118.   76 *DED*, pp 297–300. Kors picks up on this criticism made by Moore in *Atheism in France*, pp 312–13, 315–16, 320. More generally on the various positions adopted on the debate about God's existence see: ibid., pp 265–322; M. J. Buckley, *At the origins of modern atheism* (1987), pp 68–99   77 These problems run through Moore's first discussion of the subject, *DED*, pp 313–30; Garber, 'Soul and mind: life and thought in the seventeenth century', pp 759–69; Fowler, *Descartes on the human soul*; T.L. Prendergast, 'Descartes: immortality, human bodies, and God's absolute freedom' (1993); Secada, *Cartesian metaphysics*, pp 236–63.   78 Descartes, *The philosophical writings*, ii, pp 118–19.

distinction between the souls and bodies of animals, but did not suppose that they were immortal.[79]

In the second set of objections to the *Meditations*, Mersenne had stressed the criticism Moore was later to make: 'Seventhly, you [Descartes] do not say one word about the immortality of the human mind ... it does not seem to follow from the fact that the mind is distinct from the body that it is incorruptible or immortal.'[80] Since Descartes said nothing about the subject in the course of the 'Arguments', Moore turned to Descartes' answer to Mersenne in the second set of replies.[81] Descartes admitted that if, as Mesenne suggested, God had given man a nature which ended 'simultaneously' with the body, he could not refute the point since it depended on God's free will.[82] Moore seized on this admission and claimed it was based less on a concern with the free exercise of God's will than on a misunderstanding of the nature of the soul.[83] The crucial point was that Descartes was unable to provide a rational demonstration of the immortality of the human soul, *'despite his disciples' assertions'*.[84] In the battle between Aristotelians and Cartesians the provision of such a demonstration was crucial, especially on such a fiercely contested subject.

Descartes argued that the mind was a distinct substance and that the death of the body was predicated only on change of shape; therefore the mind could not perish (unlike the body). Moore pointed out that the souls of animals perish at the same time as their bodies. Animals seem to sense and imagine, and according to Descartes these are thoughts; therefore animals would have a thinking substance (the mind for Cartesians), which perishes at death. In any case, since God was able to create us from nothing, clearly God could return us to nothing.[85] In response to this point (as made by Mersenne) Descartes had commented, 'then it is for God alone to give the answer. And since God himself has revealed to us that this will not occur, there remains not even the slightest room for doubt on this point.'[86] This assertion allowed Moore to underline his claim that Cartesianism relied on revelation and was unable to demonstrate the immortality of the human soul through reason. As Moore pointed out, the debate was not one about God's omnipotence but about what we could know through the exercise of natural reason.[87] He wrote: 'The service of the philosopher is to investigate the nature of a thing, to declare the proper attributes concerning one's subject through proper cause, to demonstrate for example that the body is mortal, that the soul is immor-

---

79 *DED*, p. 321. He deals with the demonstration in detail on pages 313–20. 80 Descartes, *The philosophical writings*, ii, p. 91. On completion of the *Mediations*, Descartes sent the text to selected correspondents for comments. As a result six sets of 'objections' and Descartes' 'replies' were appended to the first edition of the *Meditations*. A seventh set of objections composed by the Jesuit Pierre Bourdain, with Descartes' replies, was published in the second edition of the *Meditations* (ibid., pp 63–5). 81 Descartes, *The philosophical writings*, pp 108–9. The reply is cited by Moore point by point, *DED*, pp 321–6. References to the section below are to Descartes' text. 82 Descartes, *The philosophical writings*, ii, pp 108–9. 83 *DED*, p. 322. 84 Ibid., p. 322. My italics. 85 Ibid., p. 322–5. 86 Descartes, *The philosophical writings*, ii, p. 109. 87 *DED*, pp 326–7.

tal ...'[88] Moore was satisfied that he had exposed Descartes' inability to provide demonstrations of the soul's immortality, or God's existence, *through the exercise of reason*.[89]

Moore's critique of Descartes on the soul illustrates the way in which the debate was conducted in the late seventeenth century. It was not a straightforward conflict between ecclesiastical authority and rational philosophy. These were, in fact, compatible. It was a debate about how truths accepted at the level of revelation could be known and demonstrated through the exercise of reason; in other words, about how the compatibility could be illustrated philosophically. Therefore, the danger of Cartesianism stemmed in part from its rejection of the fundamental precepts of Scholastic philosophy and its perceived inability to provide competent alternatives. For instance, Moore's demonstrations of the existence of God were, in this context, relatively straightforward and based firmly in sense experience. He repeated the 'five ways' provided by Aquinas (though he attributed them to Aristotle). They were based on the assertion that it is necessary that there is a first being, truth, good, efficient cause and motion.[90] However, the question of the soul was arguably more significant because of the difficulties with the Aristotelian concept of 'anima', which engendered a range of competing interpretations. Moore was therefore forced to examine the 'difficulties' of the Aristotelian soul, or more precisely the difficulties faced by Scholastic philosophers who inherited a 'Christianised' Aristotle.[91]

Moore outlined three central problems. First, while God's existence can be demonstrated 'a posteriori', the mind's immortality must be shown 'a priori', that is, it can only be perceived by examination of the mind's own operations.[92] Second, the immortality of the soul was recognised as a complex philosophical issue, leading some thinkers to adopt a fideist position. Moore claimed that Descartes ultimately occupied such a fideist standpoint.[93] Third, Aristotle allegedly stated that the human mind is mortal.[94] In answer to this contention Moore tried to show that Aristotle never claimed that the soul was mortal, he was at least ambiguous on the question.[95] Moore continued: 'Therefore the human soul, as Aristotle says ... is the form, ratio and essence of the living thing, or man, which is not a certain simple form, as some suspect, but complex, containing form of various parts'.[96] The basic philosophical issue concerned the separability of matter and form. Moore argued that for Aristotle, the vegetative and sensitive parts of the soul were clearly inseparable from the body, since their operations are inconceivable without the body; for example, nutrition, growth and generation or sight, hearing and imagination. The intellective part of the soul, which resides in humans alone, however, is separable from the body because it has operations

---

88 *DED*, p. 327.   89 Ibid., pp 328–9, general criticism follows on pages 329–31.   90 Ibid., pp 340–3.
91 Especially, *DED*, pp 345–60.   92 The rational soul was properly called the mind (mens). There were also the non-human 'minds' of God and the angels (*DED*, pp 104–16). For discussion of terminology see: C.F. Fowler, *Descartes and the human soul: philosophy and the demands of Christian doctrine* (2000), pp 161–81.   93 *DED*, pp 345–6.   94 Ibid., p. 348.   95 Ibid., pp 348–9.   96 Ibid., p. 350.

proper to itself. It has the ability to know the natures of bodies, which would be impeded if the intellective soul was itself corporeal.[97] Moore's argument rested on this fundamental Thomist point. Fowler captures the argument quite neatly: 'the intellective soul, while truly the form of the human body, was not a material form like all other forms, but an immaterial and self-subsisting form, unique among substantial forms, not dependent on the body in its highest operations and therefore capable of existing apart from it'.[98] From this one can deduce that the 'mens' is immortal, and that this interpretation flows from an *Aristotelian* understanding of the soul, though this was precisely the argument used by Aquinas.[99] Moore provided a series of supporting passages from Aristotelian texts, in an attempt to illustrate that the natural deduction from his theories was that the soul was immortal.[1] Later in the text Moore argued that the intellective soul is incorruptible, self-subsisting form and cannot be destroyed. It is unconnected with the human body (or any matter) because it has operations proper to itself and therefore the death of the body does not necessitate the death of the intellective soul, which is 'without any controversy' immortal.[2] Moore believed he had demonstrated the immortality of the soul through rational philosophy, and just as importantly, as he put it, 'from Aristotle *alone*'.[3]

Debate about the immortality of the soul caused serious problems for both Cartesians and Aristotelians. While Moore argued that Descartes' theory of the soul ultimately led him to a fideist position, he also knew that some 'secular' or 'radical' Aristotelians made a similar case.[4] This meant that there could be no perceived advantage in Aristotle over Descartes; in fact the debate was pointless. To refute the secular Aristotelians, Moore turned, at the end of *De existentia Dei*, to one of the best known rejections of the possibility of rational demonstration of the soul's immortality, by the Italian Aristotelian, Pietro Pomponazzi.[5] In the pref-

---

97 *DED*, pp 350–1. Therefore the intellective soul is not 'mixed' with the body. For further analysis of Moore's discussion of the soul, see chapter six.   98 Fowler, *Descartes on the human soul*, p. 91.   99 *DED*, p. 351; Garber, 'Soul and mind: life and thought in the seventeenth century', p. 761.   1 *DED*, pp 352–9. Moore also noted that passages in the writings of Plutarch and Cicero asserted that Aristotle *positively* held the soul to be immortal and that Aquinas's opinion on the question was clearly based on the 'science of Aristotle' (ibid., p. 359).   2 *DED*, p. 376. The proof is detailed in syllogistic format on pages 377–8 and a full demonstration is provided on pages 396–403.   3 Ibid., pp 379–81.   4 Descartes, argues Fowler, was content that he had provided the conditions for immortality through his distinction of body and mind, since this was fully in line with scholastic thought. He had shown that the death of the body did not necessitate the death of the soul. However he maintained the line that 'only a revelation of God's will in this regard could transform knowledge of the immortal nature of the soul to knowledge of the fact of eternal life.' See: Fowler, *Descartes on the human soul*, pp 218, 228, 272. On difficulties for Aristotelianism, and the argument that Descartes did not occupy a fideism similar to Montaigne or Bayle, ibid., pp 71–113; on the demonstration in the second meditation and Mersenne's response, which forms the basis of Moore's discussion, ibid., pp 187–219. See also: Prendergast, 'Descartes: immortality, human bodies, and God's absolute freedom', pp 37, 46.   5 Pomponazzi's radical Aristotelian position fuelled debate well into the seventeenth-century. An edition of his work on the soul was published in Paris in 1634. See: Fowler, *Descartes on the human soul*, pp 83, note 34, 91–6, 192, 213–14.

ace, Moore commented that: 'we will try to answer the objections of Pomponazzi, whom we have heard praised frequently by certain parties because he thought that, *according to the doctrine of Aristotle*, it must be said that the soul of man is material and mortal'.[6] Pomponazzi argued this in his *De immortalitate animae* (1516). His position stood in stark contrast to the decision of the Fifth Lateran Council three years earlier that the immortality of the human soul was philosophically demonstrable.[7] As Fowler puts it: 'The "Christian philosopher" in his treatment of the human soul was expected to arrive at these doctrinal conclusions.'[8] Descartes was well aware of this, as he comments in the *Meditations*:

> As regards the soul, many people have considered that it is not easy to discover its nature, and some have even had the audacity to assert that as far as human reasoning goes, there are persuasive grounds for holding that the soul dies along with the body and that the opposite view is based on faith alone. But in its eighth session the Lateran council held under Leo X condemned those who take this position, and expressly enjoined Christian philosophers to refute their arguments and use all their powers to establish the truth; so I have no hesitated to attempt this task as well.[9]

Pomponazzi's 'double truth', that the immortality of the human soul could be 'true' in faith, but undemonstrable, or even 'false', in reason, led to claims that the author's Christianity was suspect.[10] Indeed, by explicitly linking Descartes and Pomponazzi, Moore was suggesting that Cartesianism could not provide an adequate 'Christian' philosophy. This rejected Cartesian claims that Descartes, by providing a demonstration of the distinction between mind and body, had avoided the Aristotelian problem created by the first principle that all knowledge is derived through the senses. This was the difficulty at the root of Pomponazzi's theories.

Moore argued that Pomponazzi was not a real Aristotelian. He pointed out that Pomponazzi accepted that the intellective or rational soul in man was theoretically separable from the body; its immortality depended on having operations proper to itself. Pomponazzi's point of departure was his argument that all operations of the rational soul were ultimately linked to the other parts of the soul, because all our knowledge is derived from sense experience.[11] Moore took the standard Aristotelian line that some of the operations of the rational soul are unconnected to the body and, in consequence, part of the rational soul in humans is immateri-

6 *DED*, preface (unpaginated), my italics, see also p. 411.   7 Pietro Pomponazzi, 'On the immortality of the soul', introduced by J.H. Randall Jr (1967); M.L. Pine, 'Pomponazzi, Pietro (1462–1525)' (1998).   8 Fowler, *Descartes on the human soul*, p. 3.   9 Descartes, *The philosophical writings*, ii, p. 4.   10 Pine, 'Pomponazzi, Pietro (1462–1525)', pp 529–30. See also: P.O. Kristeller, 'The myth of Renaissance atheism and the French tradition of free thought' (1968).   11 *DED*, pp 412–14; Pomponazzi, 'On the immortality of the soul', pp 272–4, 317–18. Pomponzzi concluded that the question was a 'neutral' one; it could not be affirmed or denied by reason alone.

al, unconnected with the body and therefore separable and immortal. Moore argued that Pomponazzi's distinction between the different parts of the soul was not rigid enough, a problem that had created similar difficulties for other followers of Aristotle.[12] Moore dealt with a series of claims from Pomponazzi's *De immortalitate animae*, some of which underlined the difficulties created by Christianising Aristotle. For example, Pomponazzi pointed out that for Aristotle the world was eternal, and if the human soul was immortal, then there would be an infinite number of souls in existence, which seemed illogical. Moore countered that such a multiplication is conceivable if souls are immaterial, but ultimately argued that Aristotle, as Aquinas pointed out, based his idea of the world's eternity on probable opinion only.[13]

Moore's discussion of Pomponazzi in a text explicitly concerned with Cartesianism is important because it underlines the tensions inherent within Aristotelianism.[14] As Roger Ariew has commented: 'What was taught in the schools during the seventeenth century was Aristotelian, but remains difficult to describe: probably not one of Aristotle's doctrines was held by all early modern scholastics.'[15] Moore's demonstrations of both God's existence and the immortality of the human soul are built on those propounded by Thomas Aquinas. But while Aquinas and others loom large throughout Moore's text, he specifically associates the demonstrations with Aristotle in the first instance. Moore, like many of his contemporaries at the University of Paris, was a Thomist Aristotelian.[16] The engagement with Pomponazzi indicates, not only the preparedness of scholars to challenge each other in the name of Aristotle, but also the search for the 'real' Aristotle. There was no monolithic understanding of Aristotle that could be appealed to simplistically, even though a contemporary Scholastic like Gabriel Daniel complained in 1690 that all Scholastics were indiscriminately labelled proponents of the 'old philosophy'.[17] The search was given an added sense of urgency in the first place by the humanism propounded by Pomponazzi, and by the emergence of a serious competing alternative in the shape of Cartesianism in the second half of the seventeenth-century.[18] Moore, too, recognised the deficiencies in Aristotle:

---

12 *DED*, pp 412–13, 414–18, 420.   **13** Ibid., pp 445–6. Moore deals with other problems raised by Pomponazzi on pp 422–45.   **14** The early seventeenth-century Paris Aristotelian Jean Cécile Frey had attacked Pomponazzi, and others, in his unpublished 1628 'Cribrum philosophorum'. See: A. Blair, 'The teaching of natural philosophy in early seventeenth century Paris: the case of Jean Cécile Frey' (1993), p. 118.   **15** R. Ariew, 'Aristotelianism in the 17th century' (1998), i, pp 386.   **16** Moore would have been very familiar with the most important competing Scholastic alternative, i.e., Scotism. His library contained the works of Scotus: 'Inventaire Aoust 1726' (AN, MC, ET/XVII/ 647). He may also have been aware of the work of the mid-century French Scotist, Claude Frassen, see: Rosenfield, 'Peripatetic adversaries of Cartesianism in 17th century France', p. 32. Ariew has argued recently that Scotism was much more influential in seventeenth century France than often assumed, in *Descartes and the last Scholastics*, pp 39–57.   **17** Cited in Rosenfield, 'Peripatetic adversaries of Cartesianism in 17th century France', p. 15.   **18** This is part of the explanation for Moore's stress on the importance of the Greek language as a fundamental tool of 'scientia' in his 1700 *Hortatio*, see

Although, however, some good faithful men, perhaps deservedly criticised Aristotle sometimes rejected him because of certain errors – *and I would not wish to defend Aristotle on these matters* – he was never totally despised by anyone except by someone who totally despised philosophy or at least, was quite ignorant of it.[19]

In the concluding section of *De existentia Dei* Moore directly compared the alternative, competing philosophies of Descartes and Aristotle. He suggested that the popularity of Cartesianism was a result of simplicity: 'The suggestion that this philosophy is very easy to learn is what appeals to most people today. It was such that one and a quarter hours was enough to learn the whole system.'[20] Moore believed that this popularity was transient: 'I have no doubt but that in due time posterity will be amazed that Descartes should have attained so much fame and have so many followers ...'[21] Ultimately, argued Moore, it was Aristotle who could provide the rational demonstrations discussed in his book. Moreover, Aristotle remained the most influential of philosophers because:

no other philosopher has ever treated more accurately, more fully or more fruitfully of moral law or civil law, of the natural discipline of a rational being, of metaphysics itself, or of rhetoric or of poetry. All these studies Aristotle either invented or perfected to the highest degree.[22]

The implication was that Aristotle was the foundation for all areas of rational enquiry. If one or more elements of Aristotelianism were discredited, an entire systematic body of knowledge or way of thinking was open to question. For an educator, the convenient pedagogical structure of Aristotelian thought, even allowing for its inherent eclecticism, was never fully supplanted in the seventeenth-century, and therefore remained at the core of university-taught philosophy.[23]

Charles Alan Kors has brilliantly characterised the 'great contest' between Aristotelians and Cartesians as follows:

If the debates did not turn on matters of such extraordinary substance as how the human mind ought to understand, structure and transmit its experience of the world in which it found itself, it might be tempting to see the great Aristotelian-Cartesian contest of early modern France simply as

---

chapter four.   **19** *DED*, p. 453. Translation by C. Connellan and A. Geraghty in Deane (ed.), *The Field Day anthology of Irish writing*, i, p. 965. My italics.   **20** Cited in Deane (ed.), *The field day anthology of Irish writing*, i, p. 966.   **21** Ibid.   **22** Ibid.   **23** M. Feingold, 'Aristotle and the English universities in the seventeenth century: a re-evaluation' (1998), pp 141–3. On the significance of early modern Aristotelianism, see also: C. Mercer, 'The vitality and importance of early modern Aristotelianism' (1993); R. Porter, 'The scientific revolution in the universities' (1996); Brockliss, 'Curricula'; Ariew, *Descartes and the last Scholastics*; É. Gilson, *Études sur le role de la pensée médiévale dans la formation du systéme Cartésien* (1930), pp 316–33.

a struggle for eminence, influence and institutional power among clerks and philosophers of competing schools. In its deepest terms, however, it was nothing less than a contest for status in which the highest ideal aspirations and the rawest ambitions touched and reinforced each other: the right to teach others in the name of Christendom ... Aristotelians and Cartesians in short, struggled for nothing less than the soul and mind of France, and for the satisfactions and rewards of winning that struggle.[24]

This was precisely the point Moore was making, that Aristotelianism alone could provide a metaphysics compatible with Christianity. The threat posed by Cartesianism went beyond metaphysical principles. The new philosophy presented early-modern society with an alternative to the prevailing Scholasticism in the universities; there were now two competing and opposed ways of understanding the world. This conflict was especially troublesome as the French ancien régime moved in an increasingly 'orthodox' direction against other strains of intellectual dissent, for example the Huguenots or Jansenists. The battle against Cartesianism was another aspect of the attempt to purify France internally. Thus Moore's project was part of an effort involving not only a group of philosophers at the Universtity of Paris, but the Catholic hierarchy, and the state itself. For example, the attempts to ban Cartesianism at the University of Paris in 1671, 1685 and 1691 all involved the monarchy, the archbishop of Paris and the university authorities. The intellectual disputes of the period were closely connected to the larger questions about how society was organised and regulated, indeed Cartesianism was ultimately portrayed as a threat to royal power.[25] François Babin, writing in 1679, commented on the dangers of Cartesianism:

> Their boldness is so criminal that it attacks God's power, enclosing him within the limits and the sphere of things he has made, as if creating from nothing would have exhausted his omnipotence. Their doctrine is yet more harmful to sovereigns and monarchs and tends towards the reversal of the political and civil state.[26]

Personal insecurity in 1691–2 also informed Moore's decision to underline his intellectual orthodoxy to the university and state authorities. It was in this way that Irish scholars, satirised as 'pedantic clerics and squabbling hibernians', adapted themselves and their skills to the intellectual world of the French state.[27]

There was an important Irish dimension to Moore's philosophy. It is no accident that *De existentia Dei* was published soon after his return to Paris from

---

24 Kors, *Atheism in France*, pp 265–6.   25 A. Tuilier, *Histoire de l'Université de Paris et de la Sorbonne* (1994), ii, p. 82; J. Israel, *Radical Enlightenment: philosophy and the making of modernity, 1650–1750* (2001), pp 38–42.   26 Cited in Ariew, 'Damned if you do: Cartesians and censorship, 1660–1706', p. 259. See also: M.C. Jacob, *The cultural meaning of the Scientific Revolution* (1988), pp 43–72.   27 Ó Ciosáin, 'Attitudes towards Ireland and the Irish in Enlightenment France', pp 141–6.

Dublin. However, Moore is not well understood by modern historians of ideas in Ireland. Andrew Cartpenter and Seamus Deane have commented:

> On the continent the Irish exiles in Louvain, Paris and other centres were still inclined to believe that it was possible to launch a kind of counter-ref-ormation against the onset of the modern world that had dispersed them so widely. Michael Moore, for example, tried to save the world from Carte-sianism. Like so many exiles, he wishes to re-establish what once was and to deny the basic assumptions which legitimised the world that had replaced it. Yet he and his compatriots were fighting an intellectual battle that had long been lost. They could no more heal the Cartesian split than they could restore either the power of Catholicism or the prestige of Gael-ic culture.[28]

An opposing opinion was ventured by Colm Connellan:

> This major work of Michael Moore deserves to be edited and studied in detail. His rejection of Descartes is still valid philosophically and it is fas-cinating, three hundred years later, to see what this Irish scholar said as he lived and worked at the very heart of the philosophical development of the time. The work illustrates how the writings of Aristotle were studied and used. It shows the manner in which philosophy was taught to a great many Irish students.[29]

Moore's interest as an Irish thinker lies somewhere between these opinions.[30] The intellectual battle had not 'long been lost' but was at its height in France in 1680s and 1690s. Aristotelianism remained fundamental to the stability of ancien régime France, which did not officially endorse full-blown Cartesianism until the very end of the seventeenth century.[31] Moore had witnessed the disintegration of Catholic aspirations in Ireland in 1690, and if Kors suggestion that Aristotelians and Cartesians struggled for the 'soul and mind of France' is largely correct, a similar struggle for the 'soul and mind of Ireland' was an important consideration for Moore.

He provides an important example of the difficulties faced, and methods employed by, Irish Catholics abroad in their maintenance of Irish Catholicism after 1690–1. His position at Trinity College, Dublin had been short-lived, and

---

28 A. Carpenter and S. Deane, 'The shifting perspective (1690–1830)' (1991). 29 Connellan, 'Michael Moore (1640–1726)', p. 268. Connellan was co-translator of the section from *DED* pub-lished in *The Field Day anthology of Irish writing*. 30 See also: T. Duddy, *A history of Irish thought* (2002), pp 78–81. 31 D. Clarke, 'Cartesian science in France, 1660–1700' (1985). From the 1690s, argues Brockliss, the Académie des Sciences increasingly replaced the Paris faculty of theology as the 'arbiter of philosophical orthodoxy'; see: 'Descartes, Gassendi and the mechanical philosophy in the French collèges de plein exercise, 1640–1730', p. 462.

the potential for the creation of an Irish Catholic ancien régime had quickly evaporated. The future of Irish Catholicism now rested on the Stuart monarch in exile at St Germain, a church under severe pressure, and the universities of Catholic Europe. In the early 1690s the social and religious fabric of Irish Catholicism was in a perilous position. Maintaining the intellectual orthodoxy of university curricula was part of the battle to preserve Irish Catholic identity. The open rivalry of Aristotelians and Cartesians must have deepened Moore's sense of insecurity. But, paradoxically, it also provided an opportunity for him to prove his intellectual capabilities in defence of the orthodox Aristotelianism. Personal and national insecurities combined to produce such a strident critique of Cartesianism in which there could be no room for compromise. As Charles Schmitt has suggested, Aristotelianism had ceased to provide an accepted 'comprehensive philosophy' but retained an important ideological role.[32]

Moore's prime focus was the debate *between* Catholics in France, but he was probably well aware from his recent sojourn in Ireland that the 'new' philosophy there was primarily associated with the emerging Protestant ascendancy. The new learning made a slow but steady progress in Ireland from the early efforts of Samuel Hartlib and others in the 1650s, through to the Dublin Philosophical Society founded in 1683.[33] There was a significant anti-Scholastic and Cartesian influence at the heart of the society, especially through one of its prime movers, William Molyneaux, who provided the first English translation of Descartes' *Meditations* in 1680, under the title: *Six metaphysical meditations wherein it is proved that there is a God.*[34] Indeed, Hoppen suggested that those attracted to the new learning were comprised of 'a small social caste made up of those who had settled or whose ancestors had settled in Ireland during the sixteenth and seventeenth centuries.'[35] While the Dublin Philosophical Society did not prohibit Catholic membership, only one Catholic, Mark Bagot, appears to have joined.[36] Moore's philosophical position stands in contrast to this strand within the Irish intellectual élite, but in others senses his writings fit a wider pattern. First, the course in philosophy taught in Trinity College at this point remained largely Aristotelian.[37] Second, the peculiar political circumstances of Ireland during the seventeenth and eighteenth centuries influenced its Protestant philosophers and theologians. The publication of John Toland's deist tract *Christianity not mysterious* in 1696 caused a huge storm because its rationalised Christianity appeared to undermine the Catholic-Protestant divisions on which the Irish administration was established. Subsequent pub-

32 C. Schmitt, *Aristotle and the Renaissance* (1983), p. 107. 33 T.C. Barnard, 'The Hartlib Circle and the origins of the Dublin Philosophical Society' (1974–5); K.T. Hoppen, *The common scientist in the seventeenth century: a study of the Dublin Philosophical Society, 1683–1708* (1970), pp 10–24, 73–83; idem, 'The papers of the Dublin Philosophical Society, 1683–1708: introductory material and index' (1982),. 34 Hoppen, 'The papers of the Dublin Philosophical Society, 1683–1708', pp 166–7. 35 Ibid., p. 161. 36 Hoppen, *The common scientist*, pp 25, 49, 235. The society was temporarily disbanded during the Jacobite period, ibid., pp 168–75. 37 Ibid., pp 53–72; idem, 'The papers of the Dublin Philosophical Society 1683–1708', pp 167–71.

lications during a 'golden age' of Irish philosophical writing, stretching from 1696 to 1757, had to deal with Toland's radical thought, producing a strong counter-enlightenment tendency within Irish philosophy.[38] Though Moore's continued support for Scholasticism was very different, he shared a heightened awareness concerning the religious implications of the new philosophy and its more radical manifestations. He was not alone in his concern with the political, social and religious implications of new philosophical trends.[39]

Most fundamentally, Moore reflects the philosophy which underpinned the intellectual world encountered by most Irish Catholics in Europe. Catholic centres of education succumbed slowly to Cartesianism, and then often only in natural philosophy. The work of Brockliss and others suggests that Louvain 'converted' around the 1670s, Paris and Padua by 1700, and Spanish universities as late as the mid-eighteenth century.[40] Indeed, Brockliss also points out, with reference to France, that 'Cartesian metaphysics, whatever the form, was never accepted by more than a handful of eighteenth century professors … In the teaching of metaphysics … Aristotelianism of a modified form remained a viable option until [1740].'[41] It can be inferred that the education experienced by most Irish Catholics reflected these patterns.[42]

Despite the publication of *De existentia Dei*, Moore failed to find employment in Paris. Walter Harris laid the blame firmly at the door of the exiled Stuart monarch:

> He [Moore] retired to Paris, and was there highly caressed on the score of his learning and integrity. King James, after his misfortunes at the Battle of the Boyne, was obliged to take refuge in the same place. The King's retirement pursued him here, and obliged him to forsake France, as he had done Ireland.[43]

38 David Berman's argument is outlined in: 'Enlightenment and counter-enlightenment in Irish philosophy' (1982); 'The culmination and causation of Irish philosophy' (1982); 'The Irish counter enlightenment' (1985). See also: *John Toland's Christianity not mysterious text, associated works and critical essays*, ed. P. McGuinness, A. Harrison and R. Kearney (1997).   39 For Moore and his Aristotelian colleagues in Paris, Descartes was the embodiment of the new philosophy. For Irish Protestant philosophers John Locke was the key figure. Berman argues that divergent interpretations of Locke lay at the heart of Irish philosophical discourse in the first half of the eighteenth-century. See: Berman, 'Enlightenment and counter-enlightenment in Irish philosophy', p. 149.   40 Brockliss, 'Curricula', pp 584, 586–7.   41 Brockliss, 'Philosophy teaching in France, 1600–1740', p. 141–2.   42 Irish Franciscans based in Rome and centred on Luke Wadding had spearheaded the revival of Scotism in the early seventeenth-century, culminating in the massive edition of Scotus's *Opera omnia* in 1639. See: B. Millet, 'Irish Scotists at St Isidore's College, Rome in the seventeenth century' (1968).   43 Ware, *The whole works*, ed. Harris, ii, p. 289. The fact that Moore returned to Paris only weeks after the death of James II in 1701 adds weight to this theory. French biographies provided no reason for Moore's departure for Italy, for example: Desmolets, *Continuation des mémoires*, iii, p. 202. On the Stuart court-in-exile see: E. Cruickshanks and E. Corp, *The Stuart court in exile and the Jacobites* (1995); E. Corp, 'The Irish at the Jacobite court of Saint Germain-en-Laye' (2001). The latter discusses the accusations of an Irish officer, printed in: Richard Hayes (ed.), 'Reflections of an Irish

Though he probably remained in Paris during 1691 and much of 1692, Moore was forced eventually to move again, this time to the Italian peninsula.[44]

brigade officer' (1950–1).   **44** The date of his departure is uncertain. He was certainly in Paris in 1691 and possessed papers related to the 'privilege du roi' granted for *DED* in 1692. Therefore it seems likely that he left Paris for Rome in late 1692. See: Boyle, 'Dr Michael Moore', p. 8; *DED*, 'Extrait du privilege du Roy', unpaginated; 'Inventaire, Aoust 1726' (AN, MC, ET/XVII/647, f. 18).

4

Double exile and rejuvenation:
Rome and Montefiascone, 1692–1701

While France, the Low Countries and the Iberian peninsula were the favoured destinations for the majority of Irish students and scholars, others made the longer journey to the Italian peninsula. The Irish Franciscans (1625), Augustinians (1656) and Dominicans (1677) all established colleges in Rome in the seventeenth century. The prominent Irish Franciscan, Luke Wadding, with the assistance of the cardinal protector of Ireland, Ludovico Ludovisi, established a Roman college for the Irish secular clergy, which opened to students on 1 January 1628. Ludovisi later placed the Jesuits in charge, much to Wadding's chagrin.[1] Though the colleges naturally attracted the majority of Irish students and priests, they were also to be found in seminaries and universities across the Italian states.[2] Michael Moore may well have had contacts among the Irish in Rome and he quickly found employment there as a censor of books. His life took an unexpected, but critically important, turn in 1696 when he took charge of a seminary in the small town of Montefiascone at the invitation of the local bishop, Marco Antonio Barbarigo. Although his decade-long stay in Italy amounted to a kind of double exile, from Ireland and France, he was able to rejuvenate his career in Rome and, especially, Montefiascone before his return to Paris in 1701, imbued with the reforming zeal of Italian Catholicism.[3]

The first part of Moore's career in Italy is the most difficult period of his life to document. Harris was aware that: 'He retired to Rome, [and] was made censor of books.'[4] This is conformed by the 'approbatio doctorum' Moore provided for Cornelius Nary's English translation of the New Testament:

> Ego infra scriptus Vicarius olim generalis illustrissimi et reverendissimi Patricii Russell Archiepiscopi Dubliniensis et Hiberniae primatis, sacrae theologiae lector et professor per annos septem cum in Gallia tum in Italia,

---

1 Ludovisi placed the Jesuits in charge in his will of 1629. After his death, in 1632, the will was hotly contested and the Jesuits only took charge after the dust had settled, in their favour, in 1635. See: P. Corish, 'The beginnings of the Irish college, Rome' (1957).   2 S. Creighton, 'The penal laws in Ireland, and the documents in the archives of Propaganda (1691–1731)' (1962). Creighton noted the presence of Irish students at Naples, Milan, Turin, Genoa, Bologna and Rome.   3 Previous historians have noted the presence of Irish students at Montefiascone: Bellesheim, *Geschichte der Katholischen Kirche in Irland*, iii, p. 35; Creighton, 'The penal laws in Ireland, and the documents in the archives of Propaganda (1691–1731)', p. 8.   4 Ware, *The whole works*, ii, p. 289.

librorum censor in Italia a Magistro Sacri Palatii Deputatus, antiquus Parisiensis Academiae rector, Professor Regius et in Regia Navarra primarius …'[5]

Moore was still in Rome in late 1695 when he provided information at the processus datariae of two candidates for vacant Irish bishoprics, Maurice Donnellan (Clonfert) and Edward Comerford (Cashel), on 15–16 September.[6] On 5 January 1696 Moore acted at witness at the processus of William Daton, candidate for the diocese of Ossory. A note was attached to the proceedings observing that Moore was 'about to leave Rome', requesting that the process would be speeded up to accommodate his evidence, both in Daton's case, and that of another episcopal candidate, Patrick O'Donnelly.[7] Moore probably left Rome for Montefiascone shortly after 5 January 1696 and certainly arrived there before May 1696.[8]

Moore met Marco Antonio Barbarigo in Rome in 1695 and later wrote that he was 'called' to Montefiascone to take charge of the local seminary. Barbarigo's biographer, Pietro Bergamaschi, simply noted that Moore admired Barbarigo's work in Rome, in turn Barbarigo offered him the chance of employment at Montefiascone.[9] But the connection may have run deeper than the requirements of Barbarigo's seminary. Both men had been forced into unofficial exile as a result of competition between civil and religious authorities.[10] Moore and Barbarigo were roughly the same age; the latter was born into a Venetian noble family in 1640. With the encouragement of his relative, the reforming Cardinal Gregorio Barbarigo, archbishop of Padua, Marco Antonio Barbarigo was ordained a priest in 1671.[11] In 1676 he accompanied Gregorio to the papal conclave which elected Innocent

5 'I the undersigned, formerly vicar general of the most illustrious and reverend Patrick Russell, Archbishop of Dublin, primate of Ireland, for seven years reader and professor of sacred theology both in France and Italy, censor of books in Italy with the Masters of the Sacred Palace of Deputies, former rector of the University of Paris, royal professor and principal at the Collège de Navarre …' It was dated February, 1715. [C. Nary] (trans.), *The New Testament of Our Lord and Saviour Jesus Christ …* (1718), unpaginated. Despite Moore's approbation Nary's text was later criticised and even censored.   6 Giblin, 'The *processus datariae* and the appointment of Irish bishops in the seventeenth century', pp 606–10.   7 Ibid., pp 610–12. Donnelly's case was postponed until 16 June 1697. Moore was not a witness (ibid., pp 614–16).   8 *Secundus synodus dioepcesana Montefalisci et Corneti …*(1700), p. 122.   9 Moore, *Hortatio*, pp 3–4; P. Bergamaschi, *Vita del servo di Dio Card. Marc'Antonio Barbarigo Vescovo di Montefiascone e Corneto* (1919), ii, p. 430. A Cardinal Barbarigo (it is not clear if this was Marco Antonio or Gregorio) visited the Irish Franciscans in Rome in 1693: Bellesheim, *Geschichte der Katholischen Kirche in Irland*, iii, p. 227.   10 An English language life of Barbarigo is available, though it is highly hagiographic in tone and has not supplanted Bergamaschi in terms of detail: M. Rocca, *Cardinal Mark Anthony Barbarigo*, ed. and trans. M. Marchione (1992). The following are also useful: *Dictionario biografico degli Italiano*, vi (1964), pp 73–5; A. Volpini, *De vita et moribus M. Antonii Barbadici Card. Pontificis Faliscodunensium et Cornetanorum* (1877); G. Marangoni, *Vita del servo di Dio Card. Marco Antonio Barbarigo vescovo di Montefiascone e Corneto* (1930). Marangoni's manuscript life was written in 1716, ten years after his subject's death.   11 The following account of Barbarigo's early career is based on: Bergamaschi, *Vita del servo di Dio Card. Marc'Antonio Barbarigo*, i, pp 31–235; Rocca, *Cardinal Mark Anthony Barbarigo*, pp 23–79; *Dictionario biografico degli Italiano*, vi (1964), pp 73–5.

XI. The two men remained in Rome at the pope's request continuing the reforming work that characterised Gregorio Barbarigo's Paduan episcopate. In 1678 Marco Antonio was appointed archbishop of Corfu, a Venetian possession in the Adriatic Sea, and a centre of political and religious tensions. The island was strategically crucial in the long-running Venetian conflict with the Ottoman Empire.[12]

While Barbarigo was in Corfu, he became embroiled in a dispute with the Venetian governor, Girolamo Corner, ostensibly concerning precedence at ecclesiastical functions. This squabble about the superiority of temporal or religious authority was complicated by an underlying tension between two branches of the Venetian nobility. An attempted reconciliation in 1685, when Barbarigo sailed from Venice to Corfu with a fleet under Francesco Morosini, prepared to engage with the Turks, backfired when a similar dispute broke out between Morosini and Barbarigo. Barbarigo refused to perform a ceremony at the island's cathedral, at which Morosini expected to assume the position of celebrant. Barbarigo was ordered to Venice by the city's senate, but Rome commanded him to remain. In 1686, under extreme pressure, he travelled to Venice, where he was severely rebuked before proceeding to Rome. Attempts to reinstate him in Corfu proved futile, but Barbarigo was raised to the cardinalate later in the same year. In 1687 he was appointed archbishop of the small, impoverished dioceses of Montefiascone and Corneto. This distanced him from the Venetian problems, but was effectively intended as a kind of exile. From 1687 until his death in 1706, Barbarigo endeavoured to reform the dioceses using the experience he had built up in Venice, Padua, Rome and Corfu since the early 1670s. Like Moore, Barbarigo had fallen victim to a struggle between clerical and secular authorities played out against the backdrop of significant international events. In both cases the result was unofficial exile.

Marco Antonio Barbarigo and Michael Moore had an opportunity to renew their careers in the dioceses of Montefiascone and Corneto. This involved the implementation of Tridentine reforms, including the expansion of lay and clerical education, the development of church infrastructure and the establishment of a disciplined and well-educated clergy. Indeed, the lack of earlier reform in the region provided Barbarigo with a clean slate on which to arrange the church according to his own well-developed ideas. The improvement of lay and clerical education was central to his plans, and he quickly established Schools of Christian Doctrine, a sixteenth-century innovation designed to impart basic religious education to children and adults.[13] Rosa Venerini and Lucia Filippini, both involved in female education, carried out the most influential educational reforms in the dioceses. Venerini was invited by Barbarigo to come to Montefiascone from Viterbo to open a school, while Filippini, a local girl from Corneto, was placed in charge of the new Institute of Religious Teachers (L'Instituto delle Maestre Pie) formed to oversee the task. The pair established schools around the diocese in the

12 There were three periods of intense conflict between 1645 and 1718. For a basic account: D. Sella, *Italy in the seventeenth century* (1997), pp 11–13.   13 Sella, *Italy in the seventeenth century*, pp 83–99.

1690s, though tensions arose during the early 1700s between those drawn towards the contemplative and teaching strands of the order. A school was opened in Rome in 1707, at the request of Clement XI, but Filippini was dogged by accusations of Quietism, while her relationship with Venerini deteriorated due to disagreements concerning teaching methods. Despite the problems, the work of Venerini and Filippini highlighted the dramatic reforms under way at Montefiascone and Corneto to a wider Italian audience.[14] An important tool in any Tridentine reform was the diocesan synod. Barbarigo gathered the local clergy together for the first time in seven decades in 1692. He repeated the exercise four years later in an attempt to monitor the rate of change. By this stage Michael Moore had arrived in the diocese to take charge of one of the cornerstones of diocesan reform, the local seminary.[15]

When Moore arrived in Montefiascone he must have been overwhelmed by the picturesque beauty of the medieval town, built on top of the highest point in the Volsini hills, overlooking Lake Bolsena. From the ruined medieval papal fortress, the Rocca dei Papi, at the summit of the town there would have been (as there are today) commanding views of the surrounding countryside. The development of the cathedral and seminary under Barbarigo's episcopacy enhanced the walled medieval city's reputation as a local administrative and spiritual centre. Moore arrived at a particularly difficult time for the region, which experienced a major earthquake on 11 July 1695. Montefiascone did not suffer to the same extent as other towns in the dioceses, particularly Bagnorea and Celleno.[16] To judge by Barbarigo's diocesan reports (relatio status) for the years 1694 and 1699 there was no noticeable decrease in population, though these figures probably do not provide reliable indicators of short term population change.[17] In the mid-1690s 3,607 'souls' (animae) lived in Montefiascone. It was easily the largest urban centre in dioceses, which had a population of around 17,000 people.[18]

The Montefiascone seminary, of which Moore took charge, was the cornerstone of Barbarigo's reforming programme.[19] Seminaries were only gradually established in Italy and often as rudimentary establishments that did not meet the lofty expectations of Trent.[20] In 1666 Barbarigo's predecessor, Cardinal Paluzzi-

14 For a useful introduction see: M. Marchione (trans. and adaption), *From the land of the Etruscans: the life of Lucy Filippini by Pietro Bergamaschi* (1986), based on Bergamaschi's *Vita di Lucia Filippini* (1916).   15 *Synodus dioecesana I, Montis Falisci et Corneti* … (1693); *Secundus synodus dioecesana Montefalisci et Corneti*, p. 122.   16 Rocca, *Cardinal Mark Anthony Barbarigo*, pp 137–9. Montefiascone experienced another earthquake in 1700 and the entire region was severely damaged in 1703. 17 Diocesan reports of Cardinal Marco Antonio Barbarigo for the years 1689, 1694, 1696, 1699, 1702, 1706 (ASV, Congregazione del Concilio, Relationes Dioecesium, 541A, ff 306–58).   18 Based on the reports dated 3 April 1694 (ASV, Congreg. Concilio, Relat. Dioec., 541A ff 334v-335) and 21 October 1699 (ibid., ff 345v-346).   19 A useful history of the seminary was published in 1990 to commemorate the tercentenary of the institution 'founded' by Barbarigo: A. Patrizi, *Storia del Seminario di Montefiascone* (1990). He provides a brief historiography (ibid., pp 17–21).   20 For a brief overview of Italian clergy in the seventeenth-century see: Sella, *Italy in the seventeenth century*, pp 106–21. The majority of Italy's 315 dioceses did not have a seminary by the end of the century (ibid., pp 108, 113–14).

Altieri, had founded a 'piccolo seminario' with five students and a prefect of studies.[21] The institution had not expanded over the subsequent two decades. Barbarigo reported in his first relatio status in 1689 that the seminary comprised six students who were instructed in piety and the humanities.[22] Until his death in 1706 Barbarigo undertook the large-scale re-development of the seminary, involving the expansion of seminary buildings, the drawing up of regulations, the augmentation of available courses, an increase in the number of students and the attraction of capable staff.[23] Barbarigo invested heavily in the building work for the seminary in the hope of ensuring the construction of a significant centre of learning and piety.[24] Marangoni, for instance, noted that he spent 30,000 scudi on the project and maintained twenty students free of charge.[25] In 1693 he united a seminary he had established at Corneto with the institution at Montefiascone to form the 'Seminary of Montefiascone and Corneto'.[26] In his first diocesan synod Barbarigo outlined the type of regime suitable to seminary training. This involved a tightly knit structure focusing not only on academic activity, but also on the spiritual growth of the students and the daily minutiae of seminary life.[27] There were two key sources of inspiration for the regulation of the seminary. One was the Paduan seminary founded by Gregorio Barbarigo, with which Marco Antonio Barbarigo was very familiar. Common to both systems was the influence of the counter-reformation prelate, Carlo Borromeo, the sixteenth-century archbishop of Milan.[28]

The purpose of the newly regulated seminary, noted Barbarigo in 1693, was the 'santa riforma della disciplini ecclesiastica' in the church of Montefiascone.[29] In practice this meant a stress on the maintenance of discipline at the diocesan seminary. As well as dealing with academic study, the rules outlined pious exercises and daily routines which had to be followed by the seminarians. For example, much stress was placed on sacramental observance, meditation and examination of conscience. Every academic year spiritual exercises were to be undertaken between 24 October and 4 November, and devotion to Mary was particularly promoted.[30] Above all, the 'regole' stressed obedience. The system was designed to encourage what amounted to character building by promoting honesty, equality and an atmosphere of community.[31]

21 Bergamaschi, *Vita del servo di Dio Card. Marc'Antonio Barbarigo*, i, pp 329–37; Patrizi, *Storia del Seminario*, pp 139–40.   22 Diocesan report by Barbarigo, 9 November 1689 (ASV, Congreg. Concilio, Relat. Dioec., 541A ff 309–309v).   23 For a sketchy overview see: Patrizi, *Storia del Seminario*, pp 135–49, 159–67.   24 See Bergamaschi's description of the seminary: *Vita del servo di Dio Card. Marc'Antonio Barbarigo*, i, pp 337–55.   25 Marangoni, *Vita del servo di Dio Card. Marco Antonio Barbarigo*, pp 151–3.   26 Diocesan report by Barbarigo, 3 April 1694 (ASV, Congreg. Concilio, Relat. Dioec., 541A, f. 331v).   27 *Synodus dioecesana I, Montis Falisci et Corneti*, appendix synodi: 'Dioecesanae continens regulas seminarii, aliaque ad parochorum commoditatem', pp 33–64.   28 Bergamaschi, *Vita del servo di Dio Card. Marc'Antonio Barbarigo*, i, pp 372–4. The 'Regole' were printed in 1693, followed by a second edition in 1742, acknowledging the influence of Borromeo: *Regole per il Seminario di Montefiascone ...* (1742), pp 3–5.   29 *Regole*, p. 3.   30 Based on *Regole*, pp 7–34; *Synodus dioecesana I, Montis Falisci et Corneti*, appendix synodi: 'Dioecesanae continens regulas seminarii, aliaque ad parochorum commoditatem', pp 33–64. For an overview see: Bergamaschi, *Vita del servo di Dio Card. Marc'Antonio Barbarigo*, i, pp 372–80.   31 Bergamaschi, *Vita del servo di*

On Barbarigo's arrival in Montefiascone, the tiny seminary provided a basic education in the humanities. Over the following decade, the seminary evolved into a self-contained educational institution that provided instruction in all areas of study pertinent to the clerical life. In 1696, the year of Michael Moore's arrival, Barbarigo was able to report the existence of a seminary in Montefiascone of which he was evidently proud:

> Seminarii domus meis sumptibus edificata, quae alterius relationis sempore imperfecta erat, nunc Diuini Huminis ope perfecta conspicutur, in qua plures quam sex[a]ginta adolescentes ad scientias ne dum Latinarum, et Grecarum Literarum, sed etiam Philosophia, et Theologiae comporandus, moresque formandas optimis unde quoque collectis praeceptoribus in presens aluntur. Ecclesia euisdem seminarii ad huc imperfecta remanet, sed breui perficienda spero.[32]

During the synod of the same year a number of students publicly defended theses in philosophy and theology.[33]

The expansion in the educational capacity of the seminary was based on the Paduan version of the 'ratio studiorum' and included the addition of an impressive library and a printing facility.[34] Additional subjects were added to the curriculum, which provided courses in theology (two lecturers), philosophy (three lecturers), sacred scripture, law, languages, mathematics, history, geography and chronology in the 'upper' half of the institution. The 'lower' provided instruction in the humanities, grammar and rhetoric.[35] The courses were largely rooted in traditional sources, for instance the writings of Aristotle and the commentators of Coimbra for philosophy and Thomas Aquinas and Laymann in theology.

The rector was responsible for discipline and normally taught either philosophy or theology. Domenico Duranti held the position from the inception of Barbarigo's reforms at the seminary in 1690 until December 1695 when the responsibility passed to Antonio Ruggero. Ruggero's tenure was short-lived, probably in a caretaker capacity, until Moore's arrival in early 1696.[36] At the second diocesan synod, held in 1696, Moore was described as: 'sacrae theologiae professor sacerdos et seminarii rector'.[37] Bergamaschi noted that he was rector, prefect of studies and lecturer in dogamatic theology, sacred scripture and Greek and Hebrew.[38] This evidently encompassed every post he held, since in 1700 he described him-

Dio Card. Marc'Antonio Barbarigo, i, p. 381.   **32** 'The seminary building has been constructed at my expense, which was always incomplete in other reports, now, by the work of God and man has been completed, in which as many as sixty young men are prepared in knowledge not only of Latin and Greek letters, but also philosophy and theology, and formed in the highest morals, from which the teachers gathered here are also increased. The church of the seminary remains incomplete, but I hope it will soon be finished.' Diocesan report by Barbarigo, 16 June 1696 (ASV, Congreg. Concilio, Relat. Dioec., 541A ff 340–340v).   **33** Ibid.   **34** Bergamaschi, *Vita del servo di Dio Card. Marc'Antonio Barbarigo,* i, p. 419.   **35** Ibid., i, p. 420.   **36** Ibid., i, pp 385–7.   **37** *Secundus synodus dioecesana Montefalisci et Corneti,* p. 122.   **38** For brief biographies see: Bergamaschi, *Vita del servo di Dio Card. Marc'Antonio Barbarigo,* i, pp 429–31; *Laudatio funebris Benedicti Bonelli nobilis Tyrolensis in seminario*

self as: 'Dicti seminarii rectore, et in eodem Sacrae Scripturae, et linguarum Graecae, et Hebraicae Professore.'[39]

Moore's rectorship was part of an attempt to create a profile for the nascent institution and boost its academic prestige. Barbarigo was also attracted by the idea that his seminary could prepare students for a role outside Italy. Indeed, the seminary quickly attracted students from all over Europe. Most revealingly, Barbarigo reported in 1699 that the flourishing seminary included a number of Irish students who were being trained, at the archbishop's expense, in 'piety and science' before returning to Ireland to combat 'heresy'.[40] Though Barbarigo did not cite Moore by name, it is clear that the concentration of Irish students at Montefiascone was the result of his indirect patronage. Barbarigo had made no mention of the presence of any Irish students in his previous report, compiled a few months after Moore's arrival in 1696. They were successfully integrated at the seminary. For example, Nicolas Nevil (Neville, or possibly Newel) entered the seminary on 12 July 1696 and later became professor of philosophy.[41] Other Irish students included Niccolo Dempsy and Dominicus de Burgo.[42]

By the early eighteenth century the seminary had grown into a community of roughly two hundred students. Barbarigo encouraged the recruitment of staff and students from all over Europe. Bergamaschi notes the presence of students from Italy, France, the Low Countries, Spain, England, and the Ionian islands (Barbarigo's former home), as well as Ireland.[43] The most interesting English-speaking student was Richard Howard, who entered the seminary in 1699.[44] He was a member of a prominent English Catholic gentry family, the Howards of Norfolk, whose sons and daughters were largely educated on continental Europe during the seventeenth and eighteenth centuries. His grand uncle, the English Dominican cardinal, Philip Howard of Norfolk, had died in Rome in 1694. His uncle, Henry, was the seventh duke of Norfolk, while his elder brothers, Thomas and Edward, were the eighth and ninth dukes respectively.[45] Richard Howard was born in 1683 and may have encountered Michael Moore in Paris, where he and his siblings stayed for safety from 1689 to 1693 before returning to England. He was later ordained and became a canon of St Peter's in Rome with the title Monsignor Howard de Norfolk.[46]

et collegio Falisco theologiae dogmaticae lect. (1787), pp xxi–xxii; Patrizi, *Storia del Seminario,* pp 161–2. All three add little to our stock of knowledge but they view Moore as the first 'famous' official at the seminary. **39** *Hortatio,* title page. **40** Diocesan report by Barbarigo, 21 October 1699 (ASV, Congreg. Concilio, Relat. Dioec., 541A, f. 344). **41** Archivio della Sacra Congregazione di Propaganda Fide, Acta, volume 67 (1697), ff 47v–48v; volume 68 (1698), ff 329–29v (examined on microfilm, NLI, p. 5156); Patrizi, *Storia del Seminario,* p. 165; Bergamaschi, *Vita del servo di Dio Card. Marc' Antonio Barbarigo,* i, p. 448. **42** Archivio della Sacra Congregazione di Propaganda Fide, Acta, volume 67 (1697), ff 47v–48v; Alunni e convitti del Ven. Seminario o di Montefiascone 1700–1701 (Seminario Barbarigo, Archivio, MS 140, ff 1–2v), provides a list of students; Bergamaschi, *Vita del servo di Dio Card. Marc'Antonio Barbarigo,* i, p. 455. **43** Bergamaschi, *Vita del servo di Dio Card. Marc'Antonio Barbarigo,* i, p. 435. **44** Patrizi, *Storia del Seminario,* p. 166. **45** J.M. Robinson, *The dukes of Norfolk,* 2nd edn (1995), pp 117–65. **46** Ibid., p. 148; J. Ingamelis, *A dictionary of British*

As part of the expansion of the college curriculum Moore published a study of Greek and Hebrew in 1700 entitled: *Hortatio ad studium linguae Graecae et Hebraicae, recitata coram eminentissimo D.D. Marco Antonio Barbadico*.[47] This was the shortest of Moore's publications and the only one that did not deal specifically with a philosophical subject. Indeed the audience to which Moore was addressing his oration, the students of the seminary at Montefiascone, and the freedom of argument which the subject accorded, meant that the *Hortatio* was probably the frankest of Moore's works. Greek was already an integral part of the seminary curriculum by 1700. According to Moore, students were able to understand and interpret Greek authors, and sustain theses on philosophy in Greek 'with ease'. Moore's oration provided an opportunity to expand the curriculum further by introducing the study of Hebrew.[48] Moore delivered his oration shortly after the feast of Pentecost, therefore he used the Pentecost story to highlight the religious importance of languages. Above all, he argued that Greek and Hebrew deserved special attention as languages of 'scientia'.[49]

Moore's central argument, that Greek and Hebrew were necessary to the study of scripture, presented the author with a problem. As Moore himself noted, the Council of Trent had confirmed the centrality of the Vulgate (Latin) Bible as the authentic translation, accepted by the entire church as a sufficient basis for resolving controversy. Moore was therefore quick to adhere to the judgement: 'Ego quoque huic Ecclesiae judicio lubentissime subscribo, et vulgatam nostram versionem reverenter agnosco, nec quidquam unquam ejus authoritati mea oratione detractum esse velim.'[50] This, he argued, did not preclude biblical inquiry based on other versions or languages, in his defence citing the opinion of Roberto Bellarmino, Melchior Canus and Augustine. Indeed, while the Vulgate of Jerome provided the critical starting point for the student, Moore suggested that not even the saint himself was entirely satisfied by his translation.[51]

Moore proceeded to the problem of the Greek language and its study, in which he underlined the vital importance of the language and drew a connection between ignorance of Greek and the collapse of traditional 'scientia'. At a simple level the language was necessary to understand the ancient Greek authors such as Homer, Pinardo, Menandro, Sophocles, Euripides, Herodotus, Thucydides, Isocrates and Demosthenes. Despite this, Moore argued that Greek had been abandoned in the 'schools', leading to a general ignorance of the language and its philosophical significance.[52] Above all, there was a connection between the rise of Cartesianism and the neglect of Greek, even among the learned in society.

and Irish travellers in Italy 1701–1800 (1997), p. 530. **47** 'Oration on the study of the Greek and Hebrew languages, recited in the presence of the most eminent Marco Antonio Barbarigo.' Published by the seminary press at Montefiascone in 1700. To date only two copies of this work have been located, both held at the Biblioteca Apostolica Vaticana (Barberini.Y.III.77, 78). **48** *Hortatio,* pp 4–6. **49** Ibid., pp 7–9. **50** Ibid., p. 9. 'I also subscribe to this most joyful judgement of the church and I reverently recognise our Vulgate version, nor would I ever want its authority to be detracted by my oration.' **51** *Hortatio,* pp 9–11. **52** Ibid., pp 12–13.

Moore had already presented his opinions on the destructiveness of Cartesian philosophy in his *De existentia Dei*. In his *Hortatio* Moore was not constrained by the academic audience to which he was appealing in the University of Paris and therefore presented a more wide-ranging and, in fact, revealing argument concerning the implications of Cartesianism for society and religion.[53] Moore argued that while Descartes was steeped in mathematics, he was completely ignorant of reason and natural science or peripatetic doctrine; he was 'taken' by Epicurean philosophy and 'deserved to be cursed' (*execrandum*) by all 'good and pious men'.[54] Moore's central concern was the dangers of the self-contained materialist universe of the Cartesians. Moore argued that this system allowed no place for providence, for 'rational purpose' (*finis ratio*), in fact it left no room for the divine. Descartes' world was therefore predicated on the necessary advancement of everything from 'a single natural matter' (*ex sola materie natura*). The author provided a cynical journey through this astonishing Cartesian world in which the movement of particular matter appears inexplicable. The entire world, the stars, the planets and the natural features of the earth, as well as plants, animals and men, are all composed of this same natural matter or body. The whole system, argued Moore, was unnatural. Not only was it unable to explain such critical notions as the immortality of the human soul, but it was contrary to the judgment of scripture and the fathers of the church. Indeed it contradicted the judgement of all people of faith.[55]

Moore was quite willing, before his audience at Montefiascone, to deploy the full range of philosophical *and* religious ammunition against what he saw as a major threat to established religious orthodoxy. For, despite the obvious (to Moore) objections to Cartesianism, 'haec monstra, haec portenta creduntur; et ab haereticis omnibus, et impiis avidissime corripiuntur imprimis'.[56] Moore argued that these doctrines were contrary to the Catholic faith, especially in relation to the explanation of transubstantiation, and had been condemned deservedly by the papacy.[57] This brought the author to one of his central points, for Moore a significant cause of the collapse of the 'old philosophy' was the neglect of the Greek language in the schools.[58] Moore took the example of the church fathers and argued that the Greek of Basil, Gregory, John Chrysostom, Cyrillian or Theodoretos was a match for the ancient classics. This meant that no Latin translation could possibly do them justice and 'plane negliguntur, quia non intelliguntur'.[59] A

---

53 The hard-line position of Italian Catholicism in the seventeenth-century had significant implications for Irish politics, as the case of Rinuccini suggests. See: T. Ó hAnnracháin, '"Though hereticks and politicians should misinterpret their good zeal": political ideology and Catholicism in early modern Ireland' (2000), p. 169. On the spread of Cartesianism in Italy see: Israel, *Radical Enlightenment*, pp 43–58.   54 *Hortatio*, p. 13.   55 Ibid., pp 13–15.   56 Ibid., p. 15: 'these monstrosities, these fictions are believed, and they are seized on most eagerly by all the heretics and the impious'.   57 *Hortatio*, pp 15–16. It was precisely this problem that had caused the 1671 debate on Cartesianism in Paris, in which Moore was probably involved. For a recent discussion see: Nadler, 'Arnauld, Descartes and transubstantiation: reconciling Cartesian metaphysics and the real presence', pp 229–46.   58 Hortatio, p. 16.   59 Ibid.: 'clearly they are neglected because they are not understood'.

return to the sources was urgently required and a rethink about how these could be presented to students.[60] The implication was that an entire way of thinking, within the Catholic church, was under threat if scholars continued to ignore the importance of Greek.

By urging a similar rejuvenation in the study of Hebrew, Moore dealt with a different, though in his mind related, set of enemies. Hebrew was a 'sacred language', 'divinely instituted', not the result of human transgression at Tower of Babel like other languages, but owed its origin directly to the divine creator, free from the disgrace of sin. Through Hebrew, Adam had imposed names on all created things and, as Augustine pointed out, Hebrew was the language used by God to communicate the Mosaic law: 'Quod ea divina lex, non atramento, non calamo, non penicillo, sed Dei ipsius, ut ita dicam manu, ac digito conscripta fuerit in tabulis quidem Lapideis ...'[61] Moore wanted to make a case for the study of Hebrew as an integral part of the seminary curriculum.[62] He pointed out that some of the parables most familiar to Christians were written in Hebrew, particularly those of Solomon, and that without knowledge of Hebrew their deepest meaning would remain mysterious. The argument holds, Moore stated, not just for the writings of Solomon, but also for the entire Bible. Obviously the Old Testament provided a direct point of usage, but the New Testament, while written in Greek, could only be contextualised by the Old, written in Hebrew. A deeper knowledge of scripture was therefore dependent on an understanding of Hebrew.[63] Moore provided some concrete instances of this point using examples of the complexity of Hebrew grammatical structures to illustrate how only a reader with a knowledge of Hebrew could hope to penetrate the deeper meanings of biblical writers.[64]

Having made a substantial case for the study of Hebrew on its own merits, Moore's argument shifted to the practical benefits and necessity of the language. The ignorance of Hebrew and the difficulty of attempting to penetrate the mysteries of the sacred text resulted in neglect of the bible. The bible, urged Moore, should be read constantly, despite the difficulties it presented.[65] Moore argued that neglect of biblical study based on Greek and Hebrew was gravely dangerous:

> Judaei enim solum Hebraicum textum agnoscunt, Haeretici semper ad Graecos, et Hebraicos fontes provocant, vulgatam nostram non reverenter, non probant, his linguis gnaviter incumbunt; in iis addiscendis diu noctuque desudant; earum tanta est apud ipsos existimatio, ut non dubitaverit asserere Lutherus.[66]

---

60 *Hortatio*, pp 16–17.   61 Ibid., p. 18: 'The divine law was not written by ink, pen or pencil, but by God himself, by his hand and finger ... in tablets of stone ...' The lengthy introduction to Hebrew as a divine language occupies pages 17–20.   62 Ibid., pp 20–1.   63 Ibid., pp 21–2.   64 Ibid., pp 22–4.   65 *Hortatio*, pp 25–6.   66 Ibid., p. 27: 'For the Jews alone recognise the Hebrew text, the heretics always challenge the sources in Greek and Hebrew, they do not respect our Vulgate, they do not approve it, they diligently choose these languages; they make great exertion in them by day and

Moore highlighted the danger presented by well-educated Protestants, armed with knowledge of Greek and Hebrew, pointing to the spread of the Reformation throughout Europe, in Germany, Holland, Britain, Poland and Transylvania. Greek and Hebrew were more than classical languages; they were tools in the theological battle for the future of Catholicism.[67]

Moore used two scriptural passages to show how knowledge of Greek and Hebrew were essential tools in the battle for Christianity in Europe. First, using a passage form Paul's First Letter to Timothy, he demonstrated how the Italian-born reformer Laelius Socinus was able to exploit the differences between Latin and Greek texts to attack Catholic doctrine.[68] Second, Moore raised an important test case from the work of Calvin and Zwingli, concerning the Eucharist. Moore's discussion was based on the passage in Luke's gospel in which the sacrament was instituted, in the Vulgate version: 'Hic est calix, novum testamentum in sanguine meo, qui pro vobis fundetur.'[69] Moore undertook a lengthy grammatical discussion which illustrated how Calvin and others exploited Greek and Hebrew sources to raise doubts about, and ultimately reject, the Catholic interpretation of the Eucharist.[70] The point of these grammatical discussions was clear: the Greek and Hebrew languages were not simply useful; they were necessary weapons in the fight against 'heretics and Jews'.[71]

Moore acknowledged that Italy had been spared the spread of Protestantism, but noted that there were many Jews in the states of the Italian peninsula, not to mention the fact that it was the birth place of Socinus. Moreover, England provided a striking lesson to the complacent. At the start of the sixteenth century it appeared immune from heresy and was a staunchly Catholic country, but in a very short space of time the situation changed. A similar situation pertained in Holland, France, Germany and Poland, which were all partly affected, while Denmark, Sweden and Norway had been 'completely corrupted'.[72] Clearly the need for preparation and defence against the attacks of Protestants was an important subject for Moore. Strangely, though, he never mentioned Ireland.

At the heart of Moore's argument was the centrality of education in the defence of Catholicism. At the Council of Vienne (1311–12), Clement V had ordered the establishment of chairs of Hebrew, Arabic and Chaldean at the Universities of Bologna, Oxford, Paris and Salamanca. The renaissance papacies of Nicholas V and Leo X had re-invigorated the study of classical languages in Italy. Moore also drew attention to three model educational centres: his future employer in Paris, the Collège de France, the seminary of Gregorio Barbarigo at Padua

---

night; it is so much the opinion among themselves, that Luther did not hesitate to agree.' **67** *Hortatio*, pp 27–8. **68** Ibid., p. 29–33. Laelius Socinus (or Lelio Sozini) (1525–62) was born in Sienna but later settled in Zurich. His ideas were developed by his nephew Faustus Socinus (1539–1604) into the doctrine known as Socinianism. **69** Ibid., p. 34. Taken from Luke 22:22. **70** Ibid., pp 33–9. **71** Ibid., pp 39–42. Moore also rejected the idea that the Hebrew sources were corrupted, by suggesting, for example, that if this had been the case Christ himself and the Jewish apostles would have raised objections to them (p. 42). **72** *Hortatio*, pp 42–3.

and the University of Alcalá de Henares in Spain which was responsible for the multi-lingual *Biblia Poliglota Complutense* (1622).[73] But the study of Greek and Hebrew had once again diminished to the point of extinction. Indeed, Moore's institutional promotion of Hebrew was particularly remarkable. Hebrew was not on the curriculum at the University of Paris during this period, though it was taught by a number of pioneers such as Pierre Billet, Étienne Fourmont and the early university Cartesian, Edmund Pourchot.[74] Moore's *Hortatio* can be read as an argument for the creation of a model centre of education at Montefiascone, rooted in the traditions of Italian humanism and the ideas of Tridentine education. Behind this lay the danger posed by the 'enemies' of Catholicism: internally the philosophical theories of Cartesianism and externally the heterodoxy of Protestantism.[75] He envisaged that Greek and Hebrew scholarship would be deployed in the dogmatic struggle for the spiritual control of Italy and Europe.[76]

The curriculum of the seminary at Montefiascone expanded as the seminary grew in physical size, students and staff. Clement XI even announced to the college of cardinals in 1700 that he planned to place his nephew in the care of the seminary, a clear indication of Rome's approval.[77] The college managed to attract impressive academic staff. Moore's successor, Alessandro Mazzinelli, was groomed for the role he undertook in 1701, for the bulk of correspondence Barbarigo sent to the college was directed to him.[78] Barbarigo's successor, Sebastiano Pompilio Bonaventura, noted the existence of a flourishing seminary in his first diocesan report of 1710. Moore's promotion of the study of Hebrew, as well as Greek, was successful, and the subject was taught from at least 1700. On Moore's departure a French professor, Giovanni Bouget, was appointed lecturer of Greek and Hebrew and later published a *Grammatica Ebraica* at Montefiascone in 1717.[79] The eighteenth-century standing of the town and diocese is attested to by the marriage there. on 1 September 1719, of the Stuart pretender James III and his Polish princess, Clementina Sobiescki.[80]

Moore was influenced by the 'Tridentine revival' of the late seventeenth-century.[81] While he was keen to impress on his audience the need for vigilance in the struggle against Protestantism, he also stressed the need for academic formation and rejuvenation. Moore combined the humanist 'return to the sources', in this

73 *Hortatio*, p. 43. There was an Irish College in Alcalá de Henares in the seventeenth and eighteenth centuries: Patricia O Connell, *The Irish College at Alcalá de Henares, 1649–1785* (1997), pp 12–16. 74 Jourdain, *Histoire de l'Université de Paris*, p. 320. Hebrew was allegedly taught at some underground Catholic schools in Ireland: W.B. Stanford, *Ireland and the classical tradition*, 2nd edn (1984), pp 36–7. 75 *Hortatio*, pp 43–5. 76 See: A. Hamilton, 'Humanists and the Bible' (1996). 77 Patrizi, *Storia del seminario*, p. 162; *Laudatio funebris Benedicti Bonelli*, pp xxi–xxii. 78 Bergamaschi, *Vita del servo di Dio Card. Marc'Antonio Barbarigo*, i, pp 437–8. On the early staff see: Patrizi, *Storia del seminario*, pp 161–6. 79 Bonaventura's first report, dated 20 November 1710 (ASV, Congreg. Concilio, Relat. Dioec., 541A ff 367–369v); Patrizi, *Storia del seminario*, pp 163–4. 80 Bergamaschi, *Vita del servo di Dio Card. Marc'Antonio Barbarigo*, ii, p. 463. Sobieski was rescued from imprisonment at Innsbruck by a group of Jacobites led by Moore's kinsman, Charles Wogan, originally from north Kildare. 81 Sella, *Italy in the seventeenth century*, p. 107.

96 *Michael Moore, c.1639–1726*

case biblical, with Aristotelian Scholasticism. He championed the progressive educational ideas embodied in these scholarly traditions, invigorated by the counter-reformation. While the protagonists of the new science castigated humanists as much as scholastics, Moore's reforms at Montefiascone show that they were capable of enhancing educational standards. Moore's seminary, following the example of Borromeo in the sixteenth century, 'aimed at turning out priests who, in terms of education, piety, moral conduct and outward decorum would stand as models of Christian living and exude the high dignity and the distinct nature of the clerical status.'[82] His *Hortatio* stressed not simply the importance of the study of Greek and Hebrew for purely academic reasons, but pointed out the moral and spiritual benefits that they accorded.[83]

The decade Moore spent in the Papal States illustrates the apparent ease with which an Irish exile was able to move across Catholic Europe. Though he left Montefiascone in late September or early October 1701 and returned to Paris, the seminary at Montefiascone would provide a blueprint for Moore's activities at the University of Paris in the early eighteenth century. Moore instituted a major reform of the Collège de Navarre, based on ideas with which he had become familiar at the seminary of Marco Antonio Barbarigo. Moore returned to Paris imbued with two central features of the counter-reformation: the stress on individual piety encouraged by educational achievement and need for order and discipline.[84] As a professor at the Collège de France from 1703, he continued to wage a battle against Cartesianism. However, Moore was missing from the University of Paris during the crucial 1690s, when Cartesian ideas were increasingly incorporated in the philosophical curriculum. Moore's reforms at the Collège de Navarre would be accompanied by an increasingly minority argument for the retention of Aristotelian natural philosophy.

82 Sella, *Italy in the seventeenth century*, p. 116.   83 A. Grafton, 'The new science and the traditions of humanism' (1996). On the humanist challenge see: Brockliss, 'The University of Paris in the sixteenth and seventeenth centuries', pp 115–38. At Paris, Greek had been added to the curriculum in the sixteenth century.   84 R. Bireley, *The refashioning of Catholicism, 1450–1700: a reassessment of the counter-reformation* (1999), pp 201–2.

5

'As in a little seminary': the University of Paris, 1701–20

During the first two decades of the eighteenth century Moore held three influential academic posts in Paris. As well as serving a term as rector in 1701–2, he became principal of philosophy students at the Collège de Navarre in 1702 and professor of Greek and Latin philosophy at the Collège de France the following year. The only Irish rector of the University of Paris in the seventeenth and eighteenth centuries, Moore's prominence marked a turning point for the Irish community generally as they became a more visible presence in the university. During the eighteenth century Irish clerics even captured prestigious chairs of theology, which had been out of their compatriots' reach a century earlier. Moore's successful return to Paris was predicated on a dual strategy for the future of the university, emphasising the need for reform along the model he had become familiar with in Montefiascone, while at the same time opposing the encroachment of Cartesianism. Educational reform and intellectual orthodoxy became the twin pillars of his career in early eighteenth-century Paris.[1]

James II died at his court in Saint Germain-en-Laye on 5 September 1701.[2] A month later Moore was back in the French capital, and on 10 October 1701 he was elected rector of the University of Paris. A description of the election was proudly entered in the register of the Nation d'Allemagne:

> The four procurators … entering the conclave under good and happy omens with rare unanimity proclaimed Rector a man long desired by all, who had just returned from the arms of the sovereign pontiff, Clement XI, and those of the most eminent Cardinal Barbarigo, namely, Master Michael Morus, alias O'Morigh (Morra), an Irishman, sometime professor emeritus of eloquence [rhetoric] and philosophy at the Collège des Grassins, and though he objected to accept the proffered honour and wished to decline (as on a former occasion) the office of Rector, they invested him with the purple. He returned thanks with a grateful and polished speech, and even drew tears from some of the heads of the university by his references to the past.[3]

1 Some of the ideas presented in chapters five and six have been discussed in L. Chambers, 'Knowledge and piety: Michael Moore's career at the University of Paris and *Collège de France*, 1701–20' (2002). 2 J. Miller, *James II*, 3rd edn (2000), p. 240. 3 Livre des conclusions. Nation d'Allemagne

Though shorn of much of his real power by the end of the seventeenth century, the rector was, as Maxime Targe has noted, the 'chef suprême' of the university.[4] The rector was elected by the representatives of the four nations and was always a member of the faculty of arts.[5] The masters of the faculty of arts closely guarded their authority to elect the rector. Du Boulay claimed, in an important pamphlet on the office published in 1668, that the other faculties merely confirmed what the arts faculty had already decided, which ensured equilibrium between the faculties.[6] Although the position entailed little actual power, the debate about the source of the rector's authority and the election process remained controversial. Du Boulay's pamphlet was a reaction to an attempted encroachment by the faculty of theology.[7] The rector convoked assemblies, was responsible for academic discipline and the visitation of colleges and had the power to cancel classes if necessary.[8] Despite the limitations, for Du Boulay: 'Neanmoins il est tres evident par les actes que nous avons rapportes qu'il a une veritable Jurisdiction et qu'il la peut exercer par information et audition de tesmoins et infliction de peines.'[9] Targe's assessment was more accurate: 'Au XVIIe et au XVIIIe siècles, les recteurs, dépouillés de toute influence religieuse ou politique, s'étaient maintenus en possession de quelques droits honorifiques et ils y tenaient d'autant plus qu'ils avaient perdu tous les autres.'[10]

Traditionally the rector served for one academic year, during which Moore was re-integrated within the exile Jacobite community in Paris.[11] In his new capacity, Moore led the university in their commemoration of James II in December 1701:

> On the 14th of December [1701], Doctor Moor, (Irish by nation) being chosen Rector of the University of Paris, brought the whole University of Paris in procession &c, to St Edmund's [the English Benedictine Priory] to do the King honour. And a noble ceremony it was.[12]

de l'an 1698 à l'an 1730 (AUP, registre 38, f. 38v). The translation was made by Boyle in 'Dr Michael Moore', p. 9. The election was also recorded in Conclusions de l'Université (1693–1708) (AUP, registre 37, f. 103v).   **4** Targe, *Professeurs et régents*, p. 4. Brockliss notes two basic functions: the rector was the chief dignitary and executive official of the university: 'The University of Paris in the sixteenth and seventeenth centuries', pp 45–8.   **5** M. Cesar Egasse du Boulay, *Remarques sur la dignité, rang, préséance, autorité et jurisdiction du Recteur de l'Université de Paris* (1668), pp 10–13.   **6** Du Boulay, *Remarques*, pp 9, 14.   **7** Anon., *Vetera acta et instrumenta sacrae facultatis theologiae Parisiensis adversus Rectorem et facultatem artium* (1668); Du Boulay, *Remarques*, pp 137–48.   **8** Du Boulay, *Remarques*, pp 78–94.   **9** Ibid., p. 126: 'Nevertheless, it is very evident from that acts that we have cited that he has a real jurisdiction, and that he can exercise it by information and examination of witnesses and the infliction of penalties.'   **10** Targe, *Professeurs et régents*, p. 12: 'In the seventeenth and eighteenth centuries, the rectors, deprived of all political or religious influence, had held steady in possession of some honorific rights and held them even more as they had lost all the others.'   **11** Arrest de continuation en faveur de Mr Morus, 17 Mars 1702 (AUP, Carton 13, E21); Conclusions de l'Université (1693–1708) (AUP, registre 37, ff 103v–108v).   **12** B. Weldon, *Chronological notes, containing the rise, growth, and present state of the English Congregation of the Order of St Benedict*, ed. G. Nolan (1881), p. 250. My thanks to Niall MacKenzie for bring this reference to my attention. Parts of James II's corpse were buried in five different locations: the parish church at St Germain, the English Jesuit college at

A few months later Moore delivered the annual panegyric on Louis XIV. This was founded by the city of Paris in 1684 to commemorate the accession of the king to the throne on 15 May, a practice which continued until Louis' death in 1715.[13] Moore's speech was described by a contemporary:

> ... the most illustrious Rector, surrounded by a large attendance of all the faculties, delivered the panegyric oration in honour of Louis the Great in the halls of the College of Navarre, at which were present many of the most distinguished of the nobility of Paris, the prefect of the city, together with the first president and the municipal officers. There were also present the principal ministers and officers of the most august King of Great Britain [James III]. The most illustrious Lord Rector won the attention and admiration of all by his admirable eloquence. With such consistent and admirable harmony did he present everything that related to the glory of the most Christian King that he had as many witnesses as he had hearers, of his sound learning and not that empty and profane science which puffeth up.[14]

The reference to 'his sound learning' suggests that Moore's opposition to Cartesianism was an important factor in his appointment.

From October 1701 until March 1702, Moore resided at the Collège d'Hubant, one of the residential colleges attached to the university.[15] On 1 February 1702 Moore welcomed Jacques Benigne Bossuet, bishop of Meaux to the university. Bossuet was clearly impressed, for he was responsible for Moore's appointment later in the same month as principal of 'artiers', essentially philosophy students, at the Collège Royal de Navarre.[16] The college was one of the oldest and most prestigious teaching institutions in France, founded by Jeanne de Champagne, the queen of Navarre, on the site of the present École Polytechnique, in 1304. Uniquely among the Parisian collèges de plein exercise, the Collège de Navarre provided instruction in theology, as well as humanities and philosophy.[17] The col-

St Omers, the Scots College in Paris, Chaillot and the English Benedictine College in Paris. See: Miller, *James II*, p. 240. **13** *Contrat de la ville de Paris avec l'Université pour faire un eloge du Roy le 15 May de chaque année, jour de l'avenement de sa majesté de la couronne* (1685) (AN, MM 242, pièce 23); Jourdain, *Histoire*, pp 261–2. **14** Livre des conclusions. Nation d'Allemagne de l'an 1698 à l'an 1730 (AUP, registre 38, f. 50). The translation was made by Boyle in 'Dr Michael Moore', p. 11. **15** Conclusions de l'Université (1693–1708) (AUP, registre 37, ff 103v–108v). He received a second letter of naturalisation in April 1702. ('Naturalité en faveur de Michel Morus, natif de Dublin, Recteur en l'Université de Paris au mois d'Avril 1702 ...' (AN, Le secretariat d'état de la Maison du Roi, O1 46, f. 236v).) **16** François Lediëu. *Les devarères années de Bossuet: Journal de Lediëu*, ed. C. Urbain and E. Levesque (Paris, 2 vols, 1928), i, 278–83. Prise de possession, 27 Fevrier 1702 (AN, M.C., ET/XI/357). The document is in the files of the notary Andre Valet, not Jean Fromont. Moore took up the post on 27 February. According to this document Moore was 'doyen de la nation d'Allemagne' and resided at the Collège d'Ave Maria on the Montagne Sainte-Geneviève. **17** For some historical background see: Notes et documents sur l'histoire du Collège de Navarre, n.d. [seventeenth- and eighteenth-centuries] (BN, MS Latin 9962); Rene Taton (ed.), *Enseignement et diffusion des sciences en France du dix huitième siècle,* 2nd edn (1986), p. 153.

lege was an impressive institution, eliciting a positive reaction from visitors like Charles Bertie in the early 1660s:

> Here is within an ancient cloister which I saw in no other college. Here I saw an act of the scholars or masque, which they performed in Latin, being very well dressed, and at the end of every part there were dancing that acted the furies and many other antique postures. The music played till they had ended their act. All this time the Masters and Presidents of the college were present to see who performed his part best, and to them that did well not only then but in the school they presented books, which custom they have not only in one particular college but throughout the whole university, as a reward for their industry in their studies all the year before.[18]

Bassuet (d.1704) hoped that Moore's appointment would encourage 'la réforme du collège de Navarre.' During his first years in charge, Moore, with the co-operation of the principal of grammar or humanities students, Arthur Artus, did indeed undertake a radical reform of the educational system at the college, which provides an important insight into the educational practice of a prominent Irish exile.[19] As early as 1703, one commentator recorded how Moore had reintroduced the practice 'de faire tous les dimanches une instruction aux ecoliers en forme de petit sermon', and also of a catechism in which he questioned the philosophy students.[20] The source added that: 'La pension de Mr Morus s'augmente tous les jours, aussi elle est forte reglée; les pennsionnaires vivent chez luy aussi bien que les boursiers comme dans un petit seminaire.'[21] Moore was concerned with the moral and spiritual education of his students as well as discipline and the efficient administration of the institution. By early August 1704, the university had 'publiquement approuve' major reforms drawn up by Moore and Artus, who sought the final approval of the college superior, the archbishop of Paris, Cardinal Louis-Antoine de Noailles. Moore and Artus presented a 'Memoire' on discipline, including proposed new rules drawn up by the principals accompanied by citations from supporting university statutes with explanatory notes.[22] The covering letter reveals much about what Moore and Artus felt they were trying to do at the college. Essentially the principals wanted to establish 'bon ordre' and discipline and believed that their positions were compromised by the power of the 'maitres de pension' who were in turn supported by the 'grands maitres'. The suppliants argued that this situation

---

18 Cited in Lough, *France observed*, p. 270.   19 Recueil des pièces concernant l'université, XVIIᵉ à XVIIIᵉ siècles (AN, MM 242 à 246). Ledèu, *Les dernières années*, p. 283.   20 Untitled, Avril [?] 1703 (AN, MM 243, no reference number, inserted between pièces 49 and 50). Moore may have written the document himself. 'of making every Sunday an instruction to the students in the form of a small sermon.'   21 Untitled, Avril [?] 1703 (AN, MM 243, no reference number, inserted between pièces 49 et 50): 'The pension of Mr Moore grows every day; also it is very well regulated; the pensionnaires and boursiers live with him, as in a small seminary.'   22 'Memoire concernant la discipline du Collège de Navarre presenté par les principaux du dit collège ... à Mr le Card[in]al de Noailles ... sup[erieu]r du Navarre au comencement d'Aoust 1704.' (AN, MM 243, pièce 51). Moore and Artus signed the covering letter.

was 'au prejudice des regles et du bon ordre que les principaux ont voulu faire observer aux escoliers qui demeurent dans leur pension dont ils ont eté souvent insultes sans en avoir pu avoir de justice'.[23] The petitioners were careful to argue that they wished to reinstate 'l'ancienne discipline', not radically alter the government of the college. The 'Reglements' drawn up by the principals were accompanied by carefully selected extracts from the university statutes designed to support their changes and appeal to precedent and the duty of principals.[24]

The 'sousprincipaux' at the Collège de Navarre deeply opposed any changes and presented their counter-arguments to Cardinal de Noailles in September 1704.[25] The under-principals argued that the articles of reform proposed by Moore and Artus would adversely affect the smooth running of the college and diminish their own power. They argued that the plans had been drawn up without consulting either them, or more importantly, the 'grand maitre', the principal of theology students, and effective head of the college. They also asserted that the reforming statutes would threaten the authority of the 'grand maitre', not to mention the external power of the king and de Noailles. Perhaps, it was suggested, Moore and Artus wanted to replace one 'grand maitre' with three. More practically, the under-principals argued that discipline already existed and a new system, far from encouraging good behaviour, would actually ruin the college. They argued that 'la pluralité des maitres de pension' created no difficulties in the maintenance of discipline. As the under-principals commented: 'Il est impossible de voir la discipline observer avec la meme exactitude qu'elle etoit autrefois.'[26] The reform would also, it was argued, infringe on the rights of the boursiers in the community. The petition concluded by suggesting that reform would benefit Artus financially, implying that the plans were little more than self-aggrandisement. The petition illustrates that Moore and Artus were undertaking their reform in the face of entrenched interests from within the existing system. Their plan envisaged the centralisation of authority, over humanities and philosophy students, in their own hands, which would have subverted the existing system whereby students were accorded quite a large degree of autonomy.

In July 1705 Moore presented his vision of the daily life of the college in yet another petition to de Noailles. This system was apparently intended for boursiers only, an indication that the more powerful pensionnaires retained more freedom than their non-fee paying fellow students. Moore's case was prefaced by an interesting maxim: 'La science etant un vain ornement, si elle n'est [pas] accompagnée

---

23 Ibid., covering letter: 'to the prejudice of the rules and of good order that the principals want to point out to the students who live in their *pension*, in which they have often been insulted without having been able to have justice.' 24 'Reglements faits par Mrs les ppaux', 'Articles des statuts de l'Université qui font voir le droit des ppaux sur la discipline des colleges' in 'Memoire concernant la discipline du Collège de Navarre' (AN, MM 243, pièce 51). 25 'Request des sousprincipaux du Collège de Navarre contre [Moore and Artus]', 6 Septembre 1704 (AN, MM 243, pièce 52). 26 'Request des sousprincipaux du Collège de Navarre contre [Moore and Artus]', 6 Septembre 1704 (AN, MM 243, pièce 52, f. 3): 'It is impossible to see discipline observed with the same exactitude that existed in

d'une solide pieté.'[27] The daily routine lasted from 5.30 a.m. until 9.30 p.m. The students were expected to participate in public prayers at 6.00 a.m. and then retire in silence until mass. The time at which mass was celebrated was not stipulated in the plan, but it was presumably around 7.00 a.m. The 'escoliers' were expected to assist at divine office on Sundays, feast days and at 'grande messe'. The students were required to go to confession and receive communion once a month in the chapel. On exiting from divine office, the students retired 'modestly' to their rooms to study. At 8.00 a.m. they prepared for class and breakfast and were not allowed to return to their rooms until after class. At 11.00 a.m. a meal was served in the refectory, where the students washed their hands and took their places. The blessing and a spiritual reading followed. No one was permitted to leave until the final grace was said. The same pattern was repeated at the evening meal. After dinner and supper, students were permitted to take 'une honneste recreation' for half an hour, before retiring to their rooms for study. Each boursier was to take a turn at serving in the refectory. One boursier was chosen as an 'econome ou procureur', and would present an exact account of finances when required. Each student was required to make his own bed in the morning, and place the 'ordures' in the corner of the room. A valet was engaged to remove them. The daily system attempted to instil internal values through external regulation. For instance, one point in the plan stated: 'Ils garderont entre'eux une grande honnesteté de paroles sans aucun ose traitter injurieusement ou battre son compagnon sous peine d'en etre chastié severement.'[28] Chastisement was to be expected for other offences, including absence from class, leaving the college without permission, returning after 6.30 in the evening, failing to study, failing to observe the rule exactly or if a student 'ne profite pas dans ses etudes'. A particularly dim view would be taken of students who were deemed insolent towards the principal.

The principal possessed the authority to visit rooms, to check books and to undertake 'repetitions' or 'conferences' in philosophy or theology each day, in which the boursiers were expected to participate. Moore stressed the importance of both 'piety' and 'science'. For instance, upon entering the college each student would undertake an examination of capability under the principal. As Moore commented: 'et on aura egard non seulement leur capacité mais aussi a leurs meurs ou bonne conduite puisque selon la fondations ils sont tous destiner a l'etat ecclesiastique'.[29] Assemblies would be held weekly, at which students would publicly 'avertir' faults against the rule, after three public reprimands they might be required to retire from the 'community'. Moore even made the point that the-

---

the past.'   **27** Untitled petition, Michael Moore to Cardinal de Noailles, July 1705 (AN, MM 243, pièce 54): 'Science is a vain ornament if it is not accompanied by a solid piety.' The following comments are based on this document. For comparison see R.A. Muller, 'Student education, student life' (1996), pp 339–43.   **28** Untitled petition, Michael Moore to Cardinal de Noailles, July 1705 (AN, MM 243, pièce 54): 'They will maintain a great honesty of talk between them without daring to treat abusively or to strike their companion, under pain of being severely chastised.'   **29** Ibid.: 'And he will have regard not only for their capacity but also for their morals and good conduct since according to

ologians and 'maitres-es-arts' were not exempt and, indeed, were expected to provide a good example to the other students. Finally, if the under-principal was not carrying out his responsibilities, the principal could name a temporary replacement, until a permanent under-principal was appointed. This effectively placed the principal in a position of autonomous authority, answerable only to the 'grand maitre' who had charge of theology students.[30]

In a separate document Moore and Artus addressed the underlying problem of authority at the college.[31] The document argued that all students other than theologians (both boursiers and pennssionnaires) should be united in the same 'cour' under the supervision of the principal. This being the case, the number of positions could be reduced to two key posts, the 'Grand Maitre' and 'Principal ou Maitre des Artiers'. The grand maître's authority over theologians was clear and consequently his position as the 'le premier homme de tout le College' was assured. However, the document stressed that to accord the 'grand maitre' an absolute superiority over the arts principal was dangerous. Students could then circumvent the principal's authority, something particularly true of the maitres-de-pension, leading to breakdown in discipline. The role of the principal of artiers was described as follows: 'Il doit étre attentif à les former à la science et à la piete.'[32] He was to supervise morning and evening prayers and give 'instructions' on Sundays and feast days. He was to monitor their behaviour and provide encouragement, but 'Les escolires ne doivent jamais étre sans surveillans.'[33] Indeed a claim was made for the right of the principal to choose the professors, which probably related to a fear on Moore's behalf that Cartesian thinkers would gain chairs of philosophy.

Central to Moore's vision for education at the Collège de Navarre was the linkage of science and piety, of erudition and Christian morality. The collegiate system of education which dominated third-level institutions in England and Spain, as well as France, was open to the option of a strictly controlled daily routine, both of the boursiers (usually poorer students who had received a bourse or scholarship to attend a particular university) and the pensionnaires (fee paying students who lived within the college buildings).[34] In reality this centralised and controlled ideal of discipline was not enforced during the early seventeenth century, largely

the [college] foundations they are all destined for the clerical state.' This was obviously a hangover from the past that Moore was prepared to use to his full advantage. **30** A separate undated and anonymous document, now housed at the Archives Nationales, outlines very similar reforms and may have been the equivalent rules drawn up by Artus for humanities students. 'Regles concernantes la discipline du College Royal de Navarre', undated (AN, S. 6181/8 Vitus, memoires, réglements concernant le Collège de Navarre 1567–1767, liasse 7e). **31** 'Plan de reformation pour le College de Navarre' (AN, S. 6181/8, liasse 7e). The document is undated, but it mentions the authority of de Noailles who was created cardinal in 1700 and died in 1729. Internal evidence suggests that Moore was the author. The following comments are based on this text. **32** Ibid.: 'He must be attentive to form them in science and piety.' **33** Ibid.: 'The students must never be without supervision.' **34** For a general comment see: Muller, 'Student education, student life', especially pp 333–9. He cites the Collège de Navarre, among others, as an example of the hierarchic nature of student life in early-modern France.

because only a minority of students actually resided, full-time, within the college's sphere of regulation.[35] Moore was attempting to create a novel, at least in the case of the Collège de Navarre, system of boarding establishment through which *all* the students' daily activities would be closely monitored by the principal in the pennsionnat.

Moore's reforms drew directly on his experiences at Montefiascone. But they also reflected trends in seventeenth-century France where, in the second half of the century, seminary training for the clergy became widespread. The Jesuits and other orders had also adopted the disciplined model used by Moore.[36] This model of centralised authority had further resonance for, as Brockliss has noted, placing authority in the hands of one man (a principal, superior or rector) reflected the institutions of the absolute state.[37] At Montefiascone, Moore had an effective carte blanche on which to impress his educational vision. The Collège de Navarre, however, had a relatively powerful student body, which jealously guarded their existing privileges and rights. Moore effectively usurped the traditional power of the boursiers, and therefore had to fight to push through his programme of reform.

Moore's reforms were strikingly similar to the Jesuit emphasis on the need for a carefully controlled timetable, itself quite innovative, and constant monitoring of students. While the majority of the French colleges gradually adopted this model during the mid-seventeenth century, the Collège de Navarre had not reformed by 1670, and had clearly not undertaken any systematic changes by the time Moore arrived in early 1702.[38] The counter-reformation emphasis on seminary education was a major inspiration for Moore's reforms. Therefore, it is possible that Bossuet, in choosing Moore, hoped to encourage reform based on the new incumbent's experience of the tightly organised regime at Montefiascone, a successful experiment in counter-reformation educational ideals.

Moore's aims as principal of artiers at the Collège de Navarre during the early eighteenth century conformed to the general pattern of change occurring around him. He viewed education as a means of producing 'rounded' citizens. The role of the teacher was not simply to impart knowledge; the profane and religious were both stressed. He was certainly creating a seminary atmosphere within the college, hence the comments that his pension was 'comme un petit seminaire' and his own argument that strictly speaking the collegiate system was designed for prospective clerics.[39] Brockliss has noted three important functions

35 Brockliss, *French higher education*, p. 82. The section entitled 'The internes' (pp 82–95) provides a useful summary of his thinking on the subject under discussion. See also: M.M. Compère, *Du collège au lycée (1500–1800)* (1985), pp 63–132; D. Julia, 'Les institutions et les hommes' (1986).   36 Brockliss, *French higher education*, pp 30, 62–71, 83–7; R. Briggs, *Communities of belief: cultural and social tensions in early modern France* (1989), pp 190, 198; J. McManners, *Church and society in eighteenth century France*, (1999), i, pp 198–207.   37 Brockliss, *French higher education*, pp 38–9. On the rights of boursiers at the colleges of the University of Paris, see footnote 71.   38 Ibid., pp 83–6, footnote 94.
39 Compère, *Du collège au lycée*, p. 103.

of the Jesuit system, which apply neatly to Moore's reform project. The principal hoped to create 'polite and civilized citizens', to encourage 'religious devotion' and finally, to act as a 'personal tutor'.[40] As Brockliss has noted: 'Everything was done to ensure that the student would emerge as a redoubtable Catholic and model citizen.'[41]

The success or otherwise of Moore's reforms is not clear, though he continued in his position as principal for the first two decades of the eighteenth century.[42] Shortly after becoming principal at the Collège de Navarre, Moore gained a teaching position at the other royal college in Paris, the Collège de France. This was a controversial appointment, for it linked Moore with the resurgent Jansenism of early eighteenth-century Paris. Indeed, Moore was accused of having Janesenist leanings, which can be explored through four key incidents: the 1702 claims of Thomas Sheridan (noted in chapter two); his appointment to the Collège de France in 1703; his alleged authorship of an early eighteenth-century, Jansenist tinged, *Theologie morale*; and his extraordinarily close links with the Irish Jansenist, and later convulsionnaire, Matthew Barnewall.

From the mid-seventeenth century, Jansenism and other associated politico-religious divisions in French society, in particular the debate about Gallicanism, threatened to tear the French church apart. The movement took its name from the bishop of Ypres, Cornelius Jansen, whose posthumous *Augustinius* became the pivotal text of the early debate. Theologically, the debate concerned the workings of divine grace in the context of human salvation. The standard Catholic position recognised two types of grace. Sufficient grace was a general assistance provided by God to all people and worked in conjunction with free will. Efficient grace was provided in conjunction with a specific action and was irresistible. Jansen, influenced by a certain reading of Augustine, argued that sufficient grace did not exist

---

40 Brockliss, *French higher education*, pp 88–90. He comments that: 'Evidently, the Jesuits and their imitators saw the pensionnat as something other than a prison in which students were incarcerated outside the classroom. On the contrary, it was a vehicle for the promotion of the social, spiritual, and intellectual development of the pensionnaire' (ibid., p. 90). On the importance of the concept of 'civility' see: H. Robinson-Hammerstein, 'Preface' in idem (ed.), *European universities in the age of reformation and counter-reformation* (1998), pp vii–x.   41 Brockliss, 'The University of Paris in the sixteenth and seventeenth centuries', p. 97 (in general see: pp 86–110).   42 Later plans for reform at the Collège de Navarre, largely concerning the financial administration of the college, can be found in the following collections: AN, S.6181 7e liasse; S.6546 (Collège de Navarre où de Champagne, 1304–An. X). There are sources for some of Moore's day-to-day activities. For example, in September 1717 he supported the renewal of a bourse for a student, Nicholas Aumont. Michael Moore to —— , 8 September 1717, Collège de Navarre, Bourses du Sr Jacobini (BN, MS Joly de Fleury, tome 268, f. 204). There is a sizeable amount of documentation on Aumont's case (ibid., ff 191–208) and other boursiers at the Collège de Navarre (ibid., ff 178–258). He regularly attended the meetings of the college assembly until 15 May 1719 when he seems to have retired: Conclusions des Assemblés de Messieurs les Deputés de Collège Royal de Navarre, 1709–1774 (AN, MM 469). Notable absences occur in April–May 1716, April–June 1717 and periodically throughout 1718, though the meetings themselves were rather sporadic in the latter year. The previous register has not been located, but there was no mention of the disputes concerning the reform of the college after 1709.

and thus, technically at least, Jansenism developed as a rigorist theology which seemed dangerously close to predestinarian Calvinism and appeared to reject human free will in favour of a strict determinism.

Thereafter the French Jansenists were the subjects of intermittent attempts to stifle their theological opinions. In particular, the battle was waged between the Jansenists and the Jesuits. Five propositions from the writings of Jansen were condemned by the papal bull *De occasione* in 1653. The Jansenists, most famously through Antoine Arnauld and Blaise Pascal, continued to promote their ideas, though by the 1660s they had settled into a 'silence respectueux' on the question of the five propositions. In the early eighteenth century the question was 'reopened' under the pressure of a number of influential cases such as the arrest of Quesnel, the debate about the Jesuit Chinese mission and the 'cas-de-con-science', which directly challenged the validity of the respectful silence. The result was two papal condemnations of Jansenism in *Vineam Domini* (1705) and, more famously, *Unigenitus* (1713).[43]

The perceived 'cyrpto-Calvinism' of Jansenism did not attract many Irish, though there were prominent exceptions, such as John Barnewall, Florence Conry, John Sinnich, John Callaghan, Matthew Barnewall and Matthew Kelly. Moreover, the nascent and homeless Irish community were susceptible to involvement in Jansenist disputes during the mid-seventeenth century, most notably during the 'Affaire des Hibernois' in 1651. This split the Irish students between those who were prepared to condemn pre-emptorily the five propositions and a more reticent, and possibly Jansenist-leaning, group. In any case the anti-Jansenist petitioners drew the wrath of the University of Paris authorities.[44]

The contention that Moore was a Jansenist sympathiser is largely based on Thomas Sheridan's 1702 accusation that Moore was 'a person suspected for Jansenism, and twice forced to abjure that heresy'.[45] Evidence of these alleged abjurations has not been found. Moore was not a signatory to the 1676 rejection of

---

43 Literature on the history of French Jansenism is vast. For an overview see: L. Cognet, *Le Jansenisme* (1961); W. Doyle, *Jansenism: Catholic resistance to authority from the reformation to the French revolution* (2000); A. Sedgwick, *Jansenism in seventeenth century France: voices in the wilderness* (1977); Briggs, *Communities of belief*, pp 336–63. For an introduction to the conflict in the context of French education see: Brockliss, *French higher education*, pp 247–58. **44** J. O'Leary, 'The Irish and Jansenism in the seventeenth century' (1978); Ruth Clark, *Strangers and sojourners at Port Royal* (1932), pp 187–203; P.J. Corish, 'John Callaghan and the controversies among the Irish in Paris 1648–54' (1954); T. Wall, 'Irish entreprise in the University of Paris (1651–1653)' (1944); Jourdain, *Histoire*, p. 182; for a recent overview of the 1651 incident in the immediate context see: J.M. Gres-Gayer, *Jansénisme en Sorbonne, 1643–1656* (1996), pp 91–5. The 'Affaire des Hibernois' can be followed through: *Conclusion de la faculté de théologie de Paris pour les Hybernois. Contre le décret de Monsieur le Recteur de l'Université du 4 Mars 1651 et contre les Jansenistes* (Paris, 1651); *Memoires apologetiques pour les Recteur, Doyens, Procureurs et Supposts de l'Université de Paris. Contre l'entreprise de quelques Hibernois, la plupart estudians en l'Université* (Paris, s.d. [1651]). **45** HMC, *Stuart papers*, vi, p. 26. For the context see chapter two. For recent suggestions that Moore was a Jansenist see: R. Amadou, 'Saint-Ephrem-Des-Syriens du Collège des Lombards à nos jours', p. 125, note 130; E. Preclin et E. Jarry, *Les luttes politiques et doctrinales aux XVIIᵉ et XVIIIᵉ siècles* (1955–6), i, p. 329.

Jansenism, signed by Irish theologians in Paris, simply because he was not a theology student at that point.[46] Neither did he sign the University of Paris formularies against Cartesian and Jansenist principles in 1691, 1704 or 1705, since he was not a professor of philosophy at a collège de plein exercise.[47] It would therefore appear reasonable to assume that Sheridan's comments were simply intended to cast a slur, a particularly difficult one to disprove, on Moore's reputation.[48] This is all the more plausible given Sheridan's acrimonious disagreement with Richard Talbot in Ireland. Sheridan had been Talbot's chief secretary until 1688, when he was sacked. He later attacked Talbot's Irish administration, claiming among other things, that Talbot had been unable to install Moore in Trinity College.[49]

Michael Moore's appointment to a position at the Collège Royal de France in 1703 suggests that contemporaries did not consider him a Jansenist. The college was completely independent of the University of Paris and appointments were tightly centralised in the hands of the crown, or in reality the 'haute directeur', Cardinal de Noailles. On 4 June 1703 Michael Moore was appointed professor of Greek and Latin philosophy (or professor of physics) at the college.[50] The context to his appointment was the gradual collapse of the Jansenist 'silence respecteaux' in the late seventeenth century. In 1701 the Abbé Eustace, a confessor to the Jansenist religious at Port Royal, formulated a 'cas-de-conscience' to define clearly the orthodox position with regard to the silence. The case revolved around a penitent priest who willingly condemned the five propositions in the manner demanded by the church authorities but who maintained only an attitude of 'respectful silence' as to whether these propositions were in Jansen's writings, with the meaning described by the condemnations. The problem was then posed: 'Le confesseur peut-il continuer de donner l'absolution à cet ecclesiastique aussi longtemps que celui-ci persévérera dans les memes sentiments?'[51] The case was submitted to the faculty of theology at the University of Paris for consideration and, after six months consultation, nineteen senior theologians concluded that there was no impediment to continued absolution. Having gained the approval of de Noailles, the printed version of the decision appeared with forty signatures. However, during February and March 1703 the decision was condemned by Clement XI and, shortly after, by the archbishop of Paris, de Noailles. In 1705 the

---

46 'Protestation of Irish priests in Paris against Jansenism, 26 August 1676' in Moran, *Spicilegium Ossoriense*, ii, pp 218–20 The document had twenty signatures. For its context see: O'Leary, 'The Irish and Jansenism in the seventeenth century', pp 39–40.   47 Jourdain, *Histoire de l'Université de Paris*, pp 269–70, 286.   48 Moore's contemporary, the Dublin priest, Cornelius Nary, who had studied in Paris, was dogged by accusations of Jansenism which appear to have been unfounded, see: Fagan, *Dublin's turbulent priest*, pp 14, 97–8.   49 Millar, 'Thomas Sheridan and his "Narrative"', (1976.).
50 'Provision de professeur en physique au College Royal pour le Sr Morus, a Versailles le 4 Juin 1703' (AN, Le secretariat d'état de la Maison du Roi, O1 47, ff 89–90). He took up the post on 5 July, see: Registre des délibérations du conseil des lecteurs royaux, Collège de France, 1674–1731 (ACF, f. 74v).
51 Jourdain, *Histoire de l'Université de Paris*, pp 284–5. 'Can the confessor continue to give absolution to this ecclesiastic as long as he perseveres in the same feelings?'

papal bull *Vineam Domini* reiterated the papal condemnation in even stronger terms. The importance of the controversy lay, as Gres-Gayer has pointed out, in creating the conditions for the 'rebirth' of Jansenism in France.[52]

A recantation was ordered from those who had signed, and three signatories were exiled internally within France.[53] Ellies Louis Dupin was an incumbent professor of Greek and Latin philosophy at the Collège de France and had been the initial recipient of the unresolved case. He signed the original document in favour of the traditional respectful silence and, despite the fact that he was not a fervent Jansenist, he was exiled internally to Chatelleraut.[54] He later made an apology, and attempted to draw a distinction between his role in this theological controversy and his position as a philosophy lecturer, but to no avail. Jansenist commentators claimed that Dupin was victimised for his role in the affair.[55] Michael Moore received the professorship which Dupin had lost. The fact that de Noailles initially supported the signatories suggests that Moore's appointment to the position Dupin had lost was an attempt to placate Dupin's supporters. It is even possible that Alexis de Barjot, one of only five doctors who refused to condemn the recalcitrant signatories at a meeting of the faculty of theology in September 1704, was important in securing Moore's appointment.[56] Another reading of events is possible. In the 1730s a group of high profile Irish clerics were appointed to positions in the faculty of theology after the incumbents were ejected for their continued opposition to the anti-Jansenist papal bull *Unigenitus*. As foreigners, the Irish were unconcerned with the Gallicanism which influenced so many of their French contemporaries against the acceptance of papal edicts.[57] It could be argued that Moore's career foreshadowed this development and greater Irish involvement in the University of Paris in the eighteenth century. Indeed, de Noailles was well aware of the orthodoxy of Irish clerics in Paris.[58]

Some early biographers attributed a fifth publication to Moore providing another, rather more tenuous, link to Jansenism. According to a 1727 biography, Moore produced 'une traduction Latine de la morale de Grenoble faite à Montefiascone, et dédiée au Pape Clement XI en 1702.'[59] This was originally published in French: *Theologie morale ou résolution des cas-de-conscience, selon l'ecriture sainte, les canons et les saintes pères* (Paris, 1679) and quickly went into multiple editions and enlargements until well into the eighteenth century.[60] The author was

52 J.M. Gres-Gayer, *Théologie et pouvoir en Sorbonne: la faculté de théologie de Paris et la bulle Unigenitus, 1714–21* (Paris, 1991), pp 21–5. **53** Ibid.; *Histoire du Cas-de-Conscience, signé par quarante docteurs de Sorbonne* (1705–11). **54** AN, Le secretariat d'état de la Maison du Roi, O1 47, f. 45. **55** *Histoire du Cas-de-Conscience*, iv, p. 333. On Dupin's exile, vi, pp 332–6. **56** *Histoire du Cas-de-Conscience* vi, pp 54–8. **57** On this complex issue see: P. O'Connor, 'Irish students in Paris faculty of theology: aspects of doctrinal controversy in the *ancien régime*, 1730–60' (1998); idem, 'Irish clerics and French politics of grace: the reception of Nicholas Madgett's doctoral theses, 1732' (2003); Thomas O'Connor, 'The role of Irish clerics in Paris University politics, 1730–40' (1997–9). **58** Clark, *Strangers and sojourners*, p. 215, note 4. **59** Desmolets, *Continuation des mémoires*, ii, p. 204. The attribution is repeated by Walter Harris in *The whole works*, ii, p. 290, which claims the book was published in London in 1687. **60** *Catalogue général des livres imprimés de la Bibliotheque Nationale*, lviii, 105G.

François Genet (1640–1702), who wrote the multi-volume work at the behest of Etienne le Camus, bishop of Grenoble. Genet was created bishop of Vaison in 1685, but three years later he was arrested for Jansenism and imprisoned for fifteen months.[61] The Latin translation of the work appeared in Cologne in 1706, but was the work of Genet's brother, Joseph François.[62]

The connection with Moore was explained in Moreri's *Dictionnaire*:

> Voici l'histoire de cette traduction. M. Durant, ex-doctrinaire, étant Prof de théologie morale au séminaire de Montefiascone dont M. Morus étoit superieur sous l'épiscopat de Monseigneur Barbarigo, traduisit en Latin plusieurs endroits choisis de cette théologie qu'il dicta à ses disciples. On ne sait si son dessein était de la traduire en entier, il est sur que n'ayant point achevé cette traduction, elle le fut par M. Genet, Bénéficier à Vaison, frère de l'eveque de laditte ville. Cette traduction ainsi finie et mise en état d'etre imprimée parut d'abord à Venise et ensuite à Montefiascone en 1702, dédiée au Pape Clément XI. Cette meme traduction a été imprimée depuis à Paris.[63]

M. Durant was almost certainly the Montefiascone professor Giovanni Battista Duranti. If the translation was published in Paris in 1702, it is possible that Michael Moore was responsible for taking the work from Montefiascone to Paris for publication when he returned in 1701.

More revealing of Moore's links with Jansenism was his very close relationship to one of the most ardent Irish-born Jansenists of the early eighteenth century, Matthew Barnewall.[64] Joseph O'Leary noted the connection and commented that: 'A slight shadow may be cast on his [Moore's] reputation as an ardent anti-Jansenist in these years by the friendship he showed to … Matthew Barnewall.'[65] Barnewall was a member of the Kingsland branch of the Barnewall family, and claimed to be from Grace Dieu in Ireland. According to one commentator: 'Il est frere de Milord Barnewall qui fut martyrifé par les heretiques en ayant été pris les

61 *Dictionnaire de Biographie Française*, xv 1985), p. 1016. 62 Ibid., p. 1016; *Catalogue général*, lviii, 105G. 63 Moreri, *Le grand dictionnaire*, vi, p. 467. 'Here is the history of this translation. Mr Durant, former Doctrinaire, being professor of moral theology at the seminary of Montefiascone of which Mr Moore was superior under the episcopate of Mr Barbarigo, translated some chosen passages of this *Theology* into Latin, which he dictated to his students. It is not known if his purpose was to translate the whole work, [but] it is certain that he had not achieved this translation, it was done by Mr Genet of the Benefice of Vaison, brother to the bishop of the said city. This translation, thus finished and put in the state to be printed appeared first in Venice and then at Montefiascone in 1702, dedicated to Pope Clement XI. This same translation was later printed in Paris.' 64 Information on Barnewall is available in: Material relating to Jean de Padriac, deacon, and Matthieu de Barneville, priest, Bastille, 21 May 1712 and following (Bibliothèque de l'Arsenal, Archives de la Bastille, MS 10602, ff 87–183); F. Ravaisson-Mollien, *Archives de la Bastille* (1866–1904), xiii, pp 24–6; xv, pp 81–2; M.F. Funck-Bretano, *Les lettres de cachet à Paris étude suivie d'une liste des prisonniers de la Bastille (1659–1789)* (1903), pp 167, 275–6. 65 O'Leary, 'The Irish and Jansenism in the seventeenth century', p. 40.

armes à la main en combattant pour la religion.'⁶⁶ Barnewall was born around 1659 (he used the name Mattieu de Barneville in France) and arrived in France when he was fifteen, around 1674. He was educated at the University of Paris, where he studied philosophy at the Collège des Grassins and must have encountered Michael Moore. He arrived in Dublin in 1685 or 1686, around the same time as Moore, where he was ordained a priest, but later returned to France and occupied a number of ecclesiastical positions, including the rectorship of a seminary in Grenoble, the diocese of Etienne le Camus (mentioned above). Around 1703, Barnewall decided to return to Ireland but after four months waiting in Paris 'Le sieur Mauruir [Michael Moore] Irlandoise, le principal des Artiers du College de Navarre l'engager de demeurer avec luy en attendant … pour retourner en Irlande.'⁶⁷ Barnewall remained at the college for three years, where he had 'le soin de la conduitte des Boursiers'.⁶⁸ Moore evidently felt that he would make a capable assistant during his reform of the Collège de Navarre. Barnewall later travelled to Rome, before returning to Paris where he was arrested in June 1712, with Father St Jean de Pardiac, and lodged in the Bastille, charged with the distribution of suspect Jansenist literature.⁶⁹ He remained incarcerated until 27 November 1713. During this time he corresponded with the principal of his residence at the Collège de Boncourt, Mr Huré. On 30 June he wrote:

> Je vous prie d'envoier a Mr Morus Maldonat sur les evangiles qu'il m'a presté avec mes remerciments et de me faire tenir une imitation Latine avec une Bible Angloise in octavo couvert de noir pour chercher les passages dont les Protestants abuse pour les combattre.⁷⁰

Like Moore, Barnewall lived into his eighties and obviously continued to frequent Jansenist circles, though one commentator who noted his 'grande pieté et son zéle' stated that: 'Il observoit un grand silence et travailloit beaucoup à la concorde des ecritures.'⁷¹ However, Barnewall spent a second spell in confinement after becoming involved in extremist popular Jansenism around 1731. The group

---

66 Manuscrit à la Bastille, huitième lettre (BHVP, MS C.P. 3509, ff 87–8): 'He is the brother of Lord Barnewall, who was martyred by the heretics, having taken up arms to fight for his religion.' Matthew Barnewall must have been the brother of Henry Barnewall, Viscount Kingsland, who died in 1688, though he was not 'martyred', nor was his heir, Nicholas (1668–1725). See: *The complete peerage*, i (I), pp 427–30.   67 'Interrogatoire de Sr Barneville, 14 Juillet 1712' (Bibliothèque de l'Arsenal, Archives de la Bastille, MS 10602, f. 137): 'Mr Moore, Irish, principal of arts students at the Collège de Navarre engaged him to live with him while waiting … to return to Ireland.'   68 Ibid., f. 137v.   69 Ravaisson-Mollien, *Archives de la Bastille*, xiii, p. 25; O'Leary, 'The Irish and Jansenism in the seventeenth century', p. 42.   70 De Barneville à Mr Huré, 30 Juin [1712] (Bibliothèque de l'Arsenal, Archives de la Bastille, MS 10602, ff 130–1): 'Please send Maldonado on the evangelists to Mr Moore, which he lent me, with my thanks, and obtain for me a Latin *Imitation* [*of Christ*, by Thomas à Kempis] with an English bible in octavo, covered in black, to look for the passages that the Protestants abuse, so as to combat them.' Barnewall later produced a translation of the New Testament: L'Abbé M. de Barneville, *Le Nouveau Testament de Notre Seigneur Jésus-Christ* (1719).   71 Manuscrit à la Bastille, huitième lettre (BHVP, MS C.P. 3509, ff 87–8).

known as the convulsionnaires had its origins in the cult surrounding the death and burial of the Jansenist deacon François de Pâris at St Metard cemetery in 1729. By 1731 large crowds were gathering in the area in expectation of miraculous happenings. As Kreiser put it: 'From the relatively calm and simple scene of pious devotions and occasional miracles, the situation at the cemetery had progressed – or degenerated – to the wilder, often frenzied spectacle of people in convulsions, people who claimed to be inspired by the Holy Spirit through the intercession of M. Pâris.'[72] Given the deacon's credentials, the situation was obviously exploited by the remaining Jansenists in the city. Barnewall was linked to one of the more radical groups, led by 'Frère Augustin' or Jean Robert Cosse, who adopted an increasingly extra-legal attitude to his activities and unwittingly assisted the authorities by helping to split the movement.[73]

On 12 January 1736 Barnewall and a group of 'Augustinistes' were arrested while on a pilgrimage to the old Jansenist haven at Port Royal. In prison he penned a remarkable *Profession de Foy*, which firmly outlined his trenchant Jansenist opinions and rejected the recantation of Jansenism forced out of him at the Bastille during his previous incarceration. In the midst of his multiple denunciations, he praised the memory of the Irish Jansenist John Sinnich. The self-described 'prisonier pour J.C. et pour son evangile à la conciergerie' died in 1738.[74] Barnewall had a profound influence on at least one relation, for his niece Marie Anne de Barneville was imprisoned from September 1740 until March 1741 for involvement in another convulsionnaire affair centred on Monsieur Frion.[75] Barnewall's sincere and increasingly extreme Jansenism must have been apparent to Moore, but there is no evidence to indicate that Moore sympathised with theological Jansenism. The most suspicious incident was Moore's recruitment of Barnewall as an under-principal at the Collège de Navarre between 1703 and 1706. However, it is possible to read the Barnewall connection as another example of the network of Pale families ensconced on the continent. This is underlined by Barnewall's reappearance as Nicholas Wogan's representative in August 1726 when Moore's will was being executed.[76] Moore, like many of his contemporaries, avoided serious involvement in the theological Jansenism, but he could act as patron to Barnewall, a fellow Irish migrant. This Irish connection brings us to Michael Moore's other Irish associations during the early eighteenth century, when he became more involved in the Irish community at the Collège des Lombards.

72 B.R. Kreiser, *Miracles, convulsions and ecclesiastical politics in early eighteenth century Paris* (1978), p. ix. 73 Ibid., pp 309–39. 74 *Profession de Foy de M. De Barneville, Prêtre, Grand-Chantre de l'Eglise Cathédrale de la Sainte Trinité de Dublin en Irlande mort à la conciergerie au Palais à Paris le 16 Décembre 1738* (n.d.) (Bibliotheque de la Société de Port Royal, L.P. 197 Recueil des pièces (1651–1732) 25 bis); O'Leary, 'The Irish and Jansenism in the seventeenth century', p. 43; Material relating to the affair of Sr Frion etc., September 1740 (Bibliotheque de l'Arsenal, Archives de la Bastille, MS 11,462, ff 54–150, see ff 105–6). 75 Material relating to the affair of Sr Frion etc., September 1740 (Bibliotheque de l'Arsenal, Archives de la Bastille, MS 11,462, ff 54–150). One Marie Fizgerald from Dublin was also arrested (f. 134); Funck-Bretano, *Les lettres de cachet*, pp 275–6. 76 'Inventaire, Aoust 1726' (AN, MC, ET XVII/647).

Given the fact that Michael Moore had been appointed vicar-general to the archbishop of Dublin, Patrick Russell, during his stay in Ireland, he must have been a candidate for an episcopal see. The obvious explanation for the absence of a mitre is his quarrel with James II, who remained in control of nominations to vacant Irish sees until his death. Moreover, as Irish sees were refilled during the late seventeenth and early eighteenth centuries both the Roman authorities and personnel on the ground in Ireland preferred to have resident bishops in the country.[77] On the death of Patrick Russell in July 1692, Moore probably lost his position as the deceased's vicar-general and was in no position to challenge for the vacant post. Russell was succeeded by Piers (or Peter) Creagh, who held the post from 1693 until his death in July 1705.[78] Creagh resided on the continent, from 1694 in Strasbourg, which resulted in some Irish opposition, most notably from Bishop John O'Molony of Limerick.[79] Creagh managed the archdiocese through his vicar-general, Edmund Murphy, himself archbishop from 1724 to 1728, and the bishop of Kildare and Leighlin, John Dempsey, who resided in Dublin.[80] A 1698 report on the Irish sees noted that Creagh was absent and went on to outline the most prominent episcopal candidates in the Leinster province:

> Inter ecclesiasticos istius provinciae, cunctis anteferendus foret dominus Michael Morus; in absens est actuque occupans cathedram moralium Sorbonae. Post quem idoniores existentes in Hibernia videntur dominus Edmundus Murphy, olim vicarius generalis Dublinensis, nunc Ossoriensis, sacrae theologiae doctor Salmanticensis ...[81]

While the author was unaware that Moore was in Montefiascone in 1698, not Paris, and incorrectly connected him with the Sorbonne, it is clear that he remained one of Dublin's most prominent ecclesiastics.

Moore's continued high profile within the Irish church is further underlined by the use of his name and status in the debate about an oath of abjuration for Irish Catholics in the early eighteenth century. After 25 March 1710 Catholic priests in Ireland were required to take the oath, which denied James III's kingship.[82] In theory, by accepting the legitimacy of the reigning dynasty, Catholics

---

77 Giblin, 'The Stuart nomination of Irish bishops 1687–1765' (1966). 78 Fenning, 'The archbishops of Dublin, 1693–1786', pp 175–8; McCarthy (ed.), *Collections on Irish church history*, i, pp 329–33. A succession list of Dublin bishops is available in T.W. Moody, F.X. Martin and F.J. Byrne (eds), *A new history of Ireland*, x (1984), pp 370–1. 79 C. Mooney, 'The library of Archbishop Piers Creagh' (1955), pp 120–1. 80 W.M. O'Riordan, 'A list of the priests, secular and regular, of the diocese of Dublin in the year 1697' (1955), p. 141. 81 Cathaldus Giblin (ed.), 'Miscellaneous papers' (1951), p. 67. The document is held in the Vatican Archives, Fondo Albani, vol. 163, ff 260–61v: 'Among the priests of that province Master Michael Moore would have been placed first of all, he is away occupying the chair of morality at the Sorbonne. After whom Edmund Murphy seems the most suitable [candidate] living in Ireland, [he is] the former vicar general of Dublin, now Ossory, doctor of sacred theology at Salamanca ...' 82 P. Fagan, *Divided loyalties: the question of an oath for Irish Catholics in*

could hope to overturn their civil disabilities. However, in 1709 the internuncio at Brussels, Grimaldi, wrote to the archbishop of Dublin condemning the oath and ordering Catholics to ignore it. Cornelius Nary later estimated that only thirty priests had sworn.[83] By March 1710 Grimaldi's advice had penetrated Ireland, as is clear from a letter written by the bishop of Clogher:

> The mind of the pope on the resolution taken by the Irish parliament was made clear to MacMahon in a letter he received from Grimaldi, and he passed on the knowledge to others; this has produced a good effect, as the faithful would prefer to risk all than go against the directions set forth in the letter from the internuncio; it is true that fifteen or twenty priests, mostly men of little knowledge and experience, have been led to take the oath by a letter which was circulating in Ireland, *and which was said to have been sent by Mr Moore, a doctor of Paris university*; there are some who think that the bishop of Waterford composed the letter, but the more enlightened believe it to be the work of some mischief-maker in Ireland.[84]

MacMahon felt that the 'superficial and somewhat unchristian reasoning of the letter' ruled out Moore as the author. In fact, what appears to have been the same circular letter was printed in Dublin in 1713. The printer stated that: 'The following paper was intended by a popish priest of great repute amongst those of his own profession, to have been sent in the manner of a circular letter, to persuade his brethren to take speedily the oath of abjuration.'[85] The letter was discovered by a protestant supporter of the government and published to illustrate that Jacobitism, not religion, was the reason for the widespread opposition to the oath. The unidentified author argued that the 'powers that are ordained of God' should be obeyed and that opposition to the oath endangered the faith.[86] Moreover, it suggested that an attachment to 'that poor exil'd man' [James III] should not prevent acceptance of the oath. Indeed, the document went on to question the absolute rights of monarchs.[87] Only one element of the argument suggests that Moore could have been the author, the apathy to the Jacobite cause.[88] However, it is highly unlikely that Moore was such an ardent anti-Jacobite in 1710 or that he wanted to parade his opinions in such a public manner. Ultimately, what is interesting about this episode, is that some clerics in Ireland were willing to attach Moore's name to the letter, in order to boost its legitimacy and status.

the eighteenth century (1997), pp 29, 33.   83 Ibid., pp 34–46. The faculty of theology at Louvain, whose advice was sought by Grimaldi, were unable to decide on the oath's standing.   84 MacMahon, bishop of Clogher, Drogheda, to Grimaldi, 4 March 1710 (new style) in C. Giblin (ed.), 'Catalogue of material of Irish interest in the collection *Nunziatura di Fiandra*, Vatican Archives' (1962), pp 13–14 (Giblin's summary, my italics).   85 *Advice of the Romish Catholick priests of Ireland to take speedily the oath of abjuration* (1713), p. 2.   86 Ibid., pp 4, 6–7.   87 Ibid., pp 14–15.   88 The author also mentioned that he was in 'Paris and Charenton' with other Irish priests during the Huguenot exodus in 1685, which, in Moore's case, was very probable (*Advice*, p. 6).

Exiles in European universities could provide authoritative testimony for clerics in Ireland. For example, in 1715 Moore penned an 'approbatio doctorum' for
the English translation of the New Testament published by his fellow diocesan
priest Cornelius Nary in 1718.[89] Nary's methodology reflected Moore's own ideas
as outlined in his *Hortatio*: 'I was always of the opinion that it was morally impossible to succeed in translating the New Testament into any vulgar language out of
the Latin, without being read in the Hebrew and in the Greek.'[90] Despite Moore's
background as a censor, the work was ordered withdrawn and condemned in
1720, though it avoided the ultimate disgrace of a place on the Index.[91] These
small incidents indicate that Moore was held in quite high regard by Irish clerics.

Moore was also closely associated with the Irish community in Paris. It has
already been noted that he persuaded Matthew Barnewall to accept the position of
under-principal at the Collège de Navarre. Barnewall was not the only Irishman at
the institution during the early eighteenth-century. Masters Calahan and MacNa-
mara both resided at the college around 1710. One Dillon was a senior figure at the
college at the same time.[92] Moore also retained his position as doyen of the Nation
d'Allemagne during his absences from Paris between 1686 and 1701 and continued
to play a full role in the institution during the first two decades of the eighteenth
century. He served as procurator from October 1708 to April 1709 and again from
August to December 1717.[93] He appears to have retired from the nation on 10
October 1720.[94] Moore was also closely involved with the Irish Collège des Lombards in the early eighteenth-century. At the election of Hugh Coffy as Leinster
proviseur of the college in 1718, de Noailles nominated Moore presiding official in
the absence of the college's French supervisors.[95] Moore also donated money to the
College, for instance 250 livres in March 1721, as well as investing in property for
the college in 1720.[96] He also ensured that monies entrusted to him assisted the college, for instance the 6,000 livres testament of Lieutenant-General William Dor-
rington was invested for the Collège des Lombards in 1720, underlining the important role of Irish clerics in the exile community in Paris.[97] Most notably, perhaps,
he left a considerable portion of his testament to the college and his executors were
the four proviseurs who administered the college.[98] Moore was also granted power

89 [Nary], *The New Testament,* unpaginated. Two other approbations were provided by John Farrely
and Michael Fogarty. 90 Ibid., p. 3. Moore's *Hortatio* argued the same point, see chapter four. 91
Fagan, *Dublin's turbulent priest,* pp 79–99; H. Poe, 'A Dublin priest translates the Latin New Testament into English' (1939). 92 Jourdain, *Histoire de l'Université de Paris,* pp 156–7; Conclusions des
Assemblés de Messieurs les Deputés de Collège Royal de Navarre, 1709–1774 (AN, MM 469). 93
Livres des conclusion. Nation d'Allemagne de l'an 1698 à l'an 1730 (AUP, Registre 38, ff 114–18,
185). The post was rendered legally annual in 1719 (see the arrêt of Parlement, f. 197). 94 Ibid., f.
203v. The rector's obituary was copied into the register in 1726 (ff 250–252). 95 Swords (ed.), 'Calendar of Irish material ... part 2, 1716–1730', p. 95. A new set of rules had been drawn up for the college the previous year in an attempt to settle intermittent disputes, see: Swords, 'Collège des Lombards', p. 47. 96 Swords (ed.), 'History of the Irish College, Paris, 1578–1800', pp 51–2. 97 Swords
(ed.), 'Calendar of Irish material ... part 2, 1716–1730', p. 104. 98 P. O'Connor, 'Irish clerics and
Jacobites in early eighteenth-century Paris, 1700–1730' (2001). See also: F. Éliot, 'L'émigration

of attorney for members of the exiled Luttrell family from Dublin in 1716 and 1717.[99] In other words, Moore became an important member of the Irish community in Paris in the early eighteenth century.

It is clear from the important positions Moore held in the early eighteenth century that his contemporaries held him in high esteem. Le Grys Norgate, the author of Moore's *Dictionary of National Biography* entry, published in 1894, believed that Cardinal de Noailles was a 'friend' of Moore's and that 'He [Moore] helped to remodel the university for Louis XIV, who founded for him the college of Cambray.'[1] The Collège de Cambrai's original foundation actually dates to the fourteenth century, and Moore had no connection with the college.[2] But appointments to both Collège Royaux in Paris suggests that de Noailles became an important patron to Moore (possibly after Bossuet's death in April 1704). Perhaps he admired Moore's constancy and thought of him as a safe appointee who could be trusted both to reform the Collège de Navarre and continue the battle for Aristotelianism at the Collège de France. A meeting of the Nation d'Allemagne in 1708 recorded a telling description of Moore in this context:

> Then Michael Moore, dean of the Most Constant Nation and one of the deputies, always consistent, not as a little one swayed by the wind of every doctrine nor as a reed moving to and fro, but imperturbable as a rock in the midst of storms, declared that, if what had been for so many years agreed upon by the tacit consent of all the Nations, and even expressly sanctioned, were set aside, there would remain nothing certain nor fixed in the University.[3]

Irlandaise et les prêtres Irlandais en France' (1978); M. Walsh, 'Irish soldiers and Father Charles O'Neill of the Irish College in Paris' (1978).   **99** Swords (ed.), 'Calendar of Irish material … part 2, 1716–1730', pp 89–90.   **1** *DNB*, xxxviii, 336. This must have been a garbled reference to Moore's reforms at the Collège de Navarre.   **2** Inventaire des titres et papiers du Collège de Cambray autrement dit des Trois Eveques et Bourgogne réunis à celui de Louis-le-Grand, n.d. (AN, MM 372); Papers relating to the college in S.6390A.   **3** Translated and cited in Boyle, 'Dr Michael Moore', p. 12.

6

The last scholastic: the Collège de France,
1703–20

During the 1690s, when Moore was absent from Paris, Cartesian mechanism became increasingly dominant in the philosophy curricula of French universities. For the first four decades of the eighteenth century it formed the basis of natural philosophy courses, before succumbing in turn to the challenge of Newtonianism. However, aspects of Aristotelianism continued to co-exist with Cartesian physics and the criticisms of late Aristotelians meant that mechanism did not enter the universities in undiluted form.[1] Moore provides a striking example of the longevity of Aristotelian natural philosophy at the Collège de France. He was appointed 'Professeur en Physique' in June 1703, though the chair had traditionally borne the title 'Greek and Latin philosophy'.[2] One of the last prominent advocates of a qualitative Aristotelian physics, Moore continued to emphasise core tenets such as hylomorphism, 'anima' and final cause. Two courses he delivered to students between 1703 and 1720 were published. *Vera sciendi methodus* appeared in 1716, while *De principiis physicis* was published shortly before Moore's death in 1726. These courses reached to the heart of the Aristotelian-Cartesian debate. Continuing fears that mechanism would lead to radical materialism meant that Aristotelian concerns were taken seriously and Cartesian professors were forced to respond. Concerns about the metaphysical implications of mechanism were widely held in Europe among natural philosophers of all hues. Many natural

---

1 L.W.B. Brockliss, 'Aristotle, Descartes and the new sciences: natural philosophy at the University of Paris 1600–1740' (1981), p. 52; idem, 'The scientific revolution in France' (1992), pp 68–79; idem, 'Descartes, Gassendi and the reception of the mechanical philosophy in the French *collèges de plein exercice* 1640–1730', (1995). The latter stresses the accommadatory nature of the Cartesian physics that was accepted by the university professors. See also: Gilson, *Études sur le role de la pensée médiévale dans la formation du systéme Cartésien*, pp 316–33.   2 Provision de Professeur en Physique au Collège Royal pour Sr Morus à Versailles le 4 Juin 1703 (AN, Secretariat du Maison du Roi, O1 f. 47). Another copy exists in Moore's 'Dossier des Professeurs' (C-XII) at the Archives du Collège de France, which also contains a summarised version of Goujet's brief biography (see below), a partial summary of his course titles, and an 'Eloge de Michel Morus', which is a copy of Desmolets' mini-biography (*Continuation des mémoires*, iii, pp 202–4). See also: A.P. Goujet, *Mémoire historique et littéraire sur le Collège Royal de France* (1758), ii, pp 308–10; L. Am. Sédillot, *Les professeurs de mathématiques et de physique générale au Collège de France* (1869), p. 140; Y. Laissus et J. Torlais, *Le Jardin du Roi et le Collège Royal dans l'enseignement des sciences au XVIIIᵉ siècle* (1986), p. 277. On the chair's title see: A. LeFranc, *Histoire du Collège de France, depuis ses origines jusqu'à la fin du premier empire* (1893), p. 381.

philosophers retained 'souls and spirits' and even final causes to prevent mechanism becoming materialism or deism.[3] This concern with the relationship between physics and metaphysics was strongly reflected in Moore's writings.

The chair at the Collège de France provided Moore with a platform from which to expound his ideas to generations of students. The college developed from a series of royal professorships founded by Francis I in 1530, at the prompting of the humanist scholar Guillaume Budé, and was completely independent from the University of Paris in order to facilitate the development of a humanist curriculum unfettered by the Scholastic establishment. While autonomy afforded a general sense of intellectual independence, by the late seventeenth century the college was directly controlled by the monarch and his representative, the 'Grand Aumonier', Archbishop de Noailles. By the early eighteenth century it offered a broad range of subjects taught by twenty royal professors in Hebrew, Greek, Mathematics, Greek and Latin Philosophy, Rhetoric, Medicine, Surgery, Pharmacy, Botany, Arabic, Canon Law and Syrian.[4]

Moore formally took up his royal professorship on 1 July 1703 and regularly attended meetings of the college's governing council over the subsequent two decades.[5] Each professor was paid an annual salary; by 1714 the sum was 600 livres.[6] In addition professors were entitled to an 'augmentation' on account of their work at the college. Around 1709 an unknown patron suggested that Moore should receive an 'augmentation':

> Je vous suplie, aussi, monsieur, de me permettre de vous faire souvenir qu'il y a six ans et plus que M. Morus est professeur royal et qu'il n'a encore augmentation. Il ne m'en a parlé. Je pres neanmoins la liberté de vous en avertir, parceque je crois qu'il y a de mon devoir de faire.[7]

Moore was later granted the minimum 'augmentation' for his work – 50 livres. At the same time the other professor of Greek and Latin philosophy, Pierre

3 S. Schaffer, 'Godly men and mechanical philosophers: souls and spirits in restoration natural philosophy' (1987): M.J. Osler, 'Whose ends: teleology in early modern natural philosophy' (2001). 4 LeFranc, *Histoire du Collège de France*, pp 244–52; Laissus et Torlais, *Le Jardin du Roi et le Collège*, p. 266. 5 Registre des délibérations du conseil des lecteurs royaux, Collège de France 1674–1731 (ACF), ff 74v, 76v–87. The council drew up the 'affiches des cours' at the start of each semester, dealt with new appointments, the election of officers and the celebration of certain feast days. 6 'Estat de la depense que le Roy veut et ordonne estre faite par l'orde de son tresor Royal M. Pierre Pruin pour le payment des gages des professeurs royaux pendant l'année 1714' in Recueil de mémoires lettres, règlements etc., relatif au Collège de France (1710–1757) et projet d'union du Collège de France avec la Bibliothèque du Roi (BN, MS Francais n.a. 5395, ff 10–12). 7 Untitled note, no date but another part of the letter makes reference to deaths in 1708 and 1709 (BN, MS Francais n.a. 5395, f. 7): 'I implore you, also, sir, to permit me to remind you that Mr Moore is royal professor for six years and more, and that he has still not [received] an *augmentation*. He has not spoken to me about it. Nevertheless I am taking the liberty to inform you, because I believe it is my duty to do so.' It appears likely that the note was written by someone connected with the Collège de France, to an official of the Royal Treasury.

Varignon, was in receipt of 350 livres, in addition to his salary. Obviously the experimental physics expounded by Varignon was deemed of greater benefit to the state than Moore's speculative natural philosophy.[8] Nevertheless, the above letter indicates that Moore continued to enjoy the support of some members of the academic establishment in Paris. He taught his final course in spring 1720 and was replaced by Jean Terrasson, a member of the 'modern' literary and scientific circles in early eighteenth-century Paris, especially those based around Fontanelle and Madame Lambert.[9]

It is possible to reconstruct a list of courses taught by Moore at the Collège de France between 1711 and 1720 from the extant Affiches des Cours. At the start of every academic term a list of the courses offered by each professor was compiled and printed. For instance, on the earliest surviving affiche for November 1711 the following was announced:

> Graecae et Latinae Philosophiae … Michel Morus, in collegio Navarrico Gymnasiarcha, brevi de Vera Scientia Methodo tres Aristotelis de anima libros perleget debus Martis, Jovis et Veneris hora post meridiem prima. Incipet die XXIV Novembris.[10]

Moore taught the following courses between 1711 and 1720:

Autumn 1711	A short course on the true scientific method
	Three books of Aristotle's *De anima*
Spring 1712	Books II and III of *De anima*
Autumn 1712	A short course on the straightforward method of investigation
	On the principles of physics
Spring 1713	On the principles of physics, concluded
Autumn 1713	A short course on the true scientific method
	Three books of Aristotle's *De anima*

---

8 'Augmentation en consideration du travail pendant la d[it] anneé, 1714' (B.N., MS Francais n.a. 5395, f.12). 9 Registre des délibérations du conseil des lecteurs Royaux, Collège de France 1674–1731 (ACF, ff 87–87v). Abbé Jean Terrasson (1670–1750) published extensively on classical literature, including the widely read historical novel, *Sethos, histoire, ou vie tirée des monumens anecdotes de l'ancienne Egypte, traduit d'un manuscrit Grec* (1731). Terrasson's novel introduced the idea of an 'Egyptian mystery system' as a basis for Greek and Roman civilisation, and influenced the ritual of eighteenth-century freemasonry. *La philosophie applicable à tous les objets de l'esprit et de la raison, ouvrage en réflexions détachées* was published in Paris in 1754 with 'réflections' penned by D'Alembert. See: R. Marchal, *Madame Lambert et son milieu* (1991); A. Niderst, *Fontanelle* (1991); M. Lefkowitz, *Not out of Africa: how afrocentrism became an excuse to teach myth as history* (1997). My thanks to Dr J.B. Shank, for information on Terrasson. 10 Affiche des Cours, November 1711 (ACF): 'Of Greek and Latin philosophy … Michael Moore, principal in the Collège de Navarre, will give a brief course on the true method of "knowledge" followed by the three books of Aristotle's *De anima*, on Tuesday, Thursday and Friday at 1 p.m. Beginning on 24 November.'

Spring 1714	The nature of the soul and its different faculties
	Books II and III of *De anima*
Autumn 1714	A short course on the scientific method
	General physics
Spring 1715	Natural bodies
	Their species
Autumn 1715	On meteors and the inanimate genus [mixtis]
Spring 1716	The animate body
Autumn 1716	A short course on the scientific method
	Physics
Spring 1717	Physics, concluded
Autumn 1717	On the world, sky and elements
Spring 1718	On the soul and animate body
Autumn 1718	A short course on the scientific method
	Physics
Spring 1719	Physics, concluded
Autumn 1719	Heavenly bodies, elements and firm bodies
Spring 1720	On the soul and animate body[11]

This list highlights three significant themes: method, physics and the soul. Though there are no surviving affiches from the period 1703–10, the fact that Moore regularly repeated a number of core courses suggests that his two early eighteenth-century texts resulted from courses given during his entire career at the Collège de France.

The professorships of Greek and Latin philosophy were increasingly filled with thinkers attracted to, or even central to, the development of mechanism, such as Jean Baptiste Du Hamel, Pierre Varignon, Jean Terrasson or Joseph Privat de Molières.[12] The other royal professor of Greek and Latin philosophy in the early eighteenth century was Pierre Varignon, a priest from Caen, who had been a professor of mathematics at the Collège de Mazarin and was a member of the Académie des Sciences. He became a royal professor in 1704, a post he held until his death in 1722.[13] Varignon was an important figure in the spread of new mathematical and mechanical ideas in France as outlined in his *Projet d'une nouvelle méchanique* (Paris, 1687). He was also responsible for the early diffusion of calculus in France, and was a correspondent of both Newton and Leibniz.[14] Varignon's courses stood in sharp contrast to those offered by Moore. He lectured on the movements of animals, light and colour, mechanical philosophy, muscles, elastic, the movement of water, meteors, and in 1722 he taught a course on infinitesimal

11 Affiches des Cours, 1711–20 (ACF). 12 LeFranc, *Histoire du Collège de France*, pp 383–7. 13 Laissus et Torlais, *Le Jardin du Roi et le Collège Royal*, p. 277; *Dictionary of Scientific Biography* (1970–80), xiii, pp 584–7. 14 R. Gowing, 'A study of spirals: Cotes and Varignon' (1992); M. Blay, 'Varignon, ou la théorie du mouvement des projectiles "comprise en une proposition générale"' (1988); idem, 'Varignon et le statut de la loi de Torricelli' (1985).

calculus and 'superior' physics.[15] Much of his work appeared posthumously in his *Eclaircissimens* (Paris, 1725) and *Élémens de mathematiques de M. Varignon* (Paris, 1731). There may even have been some rivalry between the two royal professors of Greek and Latin philosophy. While Moore was teaching a course on 'Heavenly bodies, elements and firm bodies' in autumn 1719, Varignon was lecturing on meteors.[16]

The attitudes of Moore and Varignon illustrate the difficulty in demonstrating clear patterns of intellectual change in institutions under royal patronage. Both men were Catholic priests and spent their professional lives working at third-level educational institutions, largely in Paris, but were polar opposites in terms of natural philosophy. The differences between them reflect the diversity of opinion concerning the role of natural philosophy in early-modern France. While an appointment to the Collège de France was attractive because of the intellectual freedom it offered, lecturers were expected to reflect royal policy. Royal and church fears concerning the implications of new natural philosophies permitted the co-existence of experimental and qualitative physics until the second decade of the eighteenth century.

Varignon represented the success of mechanist natural philosophy in Paris during the late seventeenth and early eighteenth centuries. However, there was strong support for Aristotelianism among some sections of the academic élite. The archbishop of Paris, who was responsible for both Moore's positions at the collèges royaux, and some Paris-based theologians actively opposed Cartesianism.[17] In 1704 four Sorbonne doctors accused the former rector, de Montempuys, of teaching Cartesian philosophy at the Collège de Plessis. This resulted in the signing of the 1691 anti-Cartesian formulary by Parisian philosophy professors in October 1704 and again the following year.[18] Moore's own work contains plenty of evidence of concern regarding the success of Cartesian physics. In *De principiis physicis* he admitted the failure of the college and university, as well as the secular authorities, to protect the pre-eminence of Aristotle.[19] Brockliss has used Moore's comments in the preface of *Vera sciendi methodus* to suggest that Aristotelian natural philosophy had practically disappeared from the university curriculum by 1716:

> Truly in our schools of physics you will hear of nothing but subtle, spherical and fluted matter, fanciful illusions which have no connections with the nature of things; nor in most cases is our physics anything more than a commentary on Descartes' fanatical fable of the origins of the world.[20]

---

15 Affiches des Cours, 1711–22 (ACF).   **16** Affiche des Cours, Autumn 1719 (ACF).   **17** Brockliss, 'Aristotle, Descartes and the new sciences: natural philosophy at the University of Paris, 1600–1740', p. 53   **18** Michael Moore, a royal professor, was outside university jurisdiction, and therefore was not required to sign. Jourdain, *Histoire de l'Université de Paris*, p. 286. See also de Montempuys' defence: 'Journal des contradictions que j'ai eu a soutenir sur ma philosophie de la part des personnes de la maison de Sorbonne depuis l'année 1704 jusqu'en 1707' in ibid., pièces justificatives, pp 129–53.   **19** *DPP*, pp i–iv.   **20** Cited in Brockliss, 'Aristotle, Descartes and the new sciences', p.

However, *Vera sciendi methodus* also evidences continued support for Moore's viewpoint in the faculty of theology at the University of Paris and was dedicated to Pierre de Pardailhan de Gondrin d'Antin (1692–1733), a nobleman who was studying at the Sorbonne around the time the text was published. He received his doctorate in 1718 and was appointed bishop of Langres in 1724.[21]

Moore's other text, *De principiis physicis*, was probably the last course of Aristotelian natural philosophy to appear on the market in France.[22] Nevertheless, many newly converted mechanists continued to regard themselves as Aristotelians, and hence had no difficulty in signing the anti-Cartesian declarations of 1704 and 1705. They largely retained the notion of substantial forms, at least until 1720, and rejected the idea of plant and animal 'machines'. Furthermore, the Eucharistic problem, raised by Moore in 1700, put many off accepting completely the definition of matter as extension alone.[23] Aristotelianism was not replaced by an orthodox Cartesian alternative and Cartesians were much more likely to attack different elements of their founder's theories. Moreover, some elements of Cartesian science were regarded as highly probabilist, notably the idea of 'subtle matter', which Moore rejected on just such grounds. All this led to a range of competing alternatives.[24]

Moore's courses reflected the pedagogical elasticity possible for professors at the Collège de France, who were not expected to provide the full courses taught at the collèges de plein exercise under the university's umbrella. Seventeenth-century textbooks in natural philosophy aimed at a comprehensive understanding of nature. But Moore's natural philosophy dispensed with significant portions of the Aristotelian universe, such as the four elements or astronomical bodies.[25] Moore explored the convergence of the understanding of nature and the requirements of a Christian philosophy. He stands squarely within the tradition of 'text-book natural philosophy', but his presentation reflected the criticisms of the 'new science' and the reduction of Aristotelianism to a fundamental core under the impetus of Cartesian mechanism.[26]

53. 21 *VSM*, unpaginated; J. Armand, *Les évêques et les archévêques de France depuis 1682 jusqu'à 1801* (1891), p. 228. It is also likely that Moore's two late texts were published for very specific reasons. *VSM* may have been an attempt to promote Aristotelianism after the death of Louis XIV. *DPP* could have been a response or alternative to the mathematical physics textbook published by the royal professor Privat de Molières, *Leçons de mathématique nécessaires pour l'intelligence des principes de physique qui s'enseignent actuellement au Collège Royal* (1725).   22 Brockliss suggested that the last published course of qualitative physics was G. Buhon's *Philosophia ad monem gymnastiorum, finemque accomodata* (1723). The last full course published by a Paris professor was J. du Hamel's *Philosophia universalis, sive commentarius in universam Aristotelis philosophiam ad usum scholarum comparatam* (1705). It was published at the 'promptings' of an anti-Cartesian faction within the faculty of theology, possibly in the wake of the de Montempuys affair. See: *French higher education*, p. 350.   23 *Hortatio*, pp 15–16; Brockliss, *French higher education*, pp 352–4, 357; Azouvi, *Descartes et la France*, pp 82–5.   24 Brockliss, *French higher education*, p. 377. Newtonianism did not make a direct impact on French universities, until around 1740. (ibid., pp 360–71); Israel, *Radical Enlightenment*, pp 477–85.   25 See P. Reif, 'The textbook tradition in natural philosophy, 1600–1650' (1969), pp 23–4. As she notes, hylomorphism was the basic constituent of natural philosophy text books (ibid., p. 26).   26 *VSM* used the traditional question and answer technique between 'disciple' and 'master', which had

One of these core elements was method, a traditional part of any logic course, which took on increased significance in early eighteenth-century Paris.[27] Descartes' *Discourse on Method*, first published in 1637, and Moore's *Vera sciendi methodus*, both dealt with how knowledge is accumulated by providing the logical tools necessary for the production of sure knowledge and the investigation of nature. Indeed, it has been argued that Cartesian and Aristotelian conceptions of method were not as radically different as sometimes suggested, for example both put much faith in a priori explanations.[28] Essentially, there were two kinds of method: 'The first conception of method focused on transmitting existing bodies of knowledge, while the second considered the problem of acquiring new knowledge, whether of causes or theorems.'[29] Method was central to any early modern philosophical system, as Dear has commented:

> As a term designating a way of reasoning and a way of discovering things unknown from things known, method was understood to be the appropriate heading under which to validate claims to possession of efficacious approaches to knowledge. It therefore played a significant role in the arguments of the [seventeenth] century's philosophical innovators, paradoxically structuring their arguments along lines well established in orthodox pedagogy.[30]

But while the proximity of Aristotelian and Cartesian conceptions of method may be noted, there were enough differences to engender considerable debate, as Moore's work suggests.

For an Aristotelian, like Moore, knowledge was obtained through the senses.[31] We do not have innate ideas, as Descartes suggested, indeed the presence of atheists in Asia, Africa and America, or among the ancients, proved that we do not have an innate idea of God's existence.[32] The mind was literally a 'tabula rasa', which was filled with ideas derived from sense experience. The problem was deciding how something was true, for our imagination and our opinions could lead us to false assumptions if they were not rigorously subordinated to 'thought' and, ultimately, method.[33] One could produce reliable knowledge from sense experience by applying 'method', by arranging and dividing ideas and forming them into logical constructs.[34] Some knowledge could be achieved through immediate propositions that were intelligible in themselves.[35] These were first principles, such as the standard

been the mainstay of scholastic pedagogy.   **27** Brockliss, *French higher education*, p. 203. On 'method' in the early seventeenth century: L. Brockliss, 'Discoursing on method in the university world of Descartes's France' (1995).   **28** Reif, 'The textbook tradition in natural philosophy, 1600–1650', pp 28–9; M. Hunter, 'The debate over science' (1995), p. 103.   **29** That is, pedagogy and discovery. P. Dear, 'Method and the study of nature' (1998), p. 148. Dear specifically points out that the study of 'methodology' must be distinguished from the contemporary concept of 'method' as 'a logical and philosophical category' (ibid., p. 147). This latter category is the one that pertains to Moore.   **30** Dear, 'Method and the study of nature', p. 150.   **31** *VSM*, p. 9.   **32** Ibid., p. 15.   **33** Ibid., pp 9–10.   **34** Ibid., pp 37–42   **35** Ibid., pp 49–50.

Scholastic example: 'Impossibile est idem simul esse et non esse'.[36] But for other knowledge, the method of demonstration, definition and division was necessary, with demonstration based on the use of a 'perfect syllogism'.[37]

Moore had raised the logical flaws in Cartesian philosophy in *De existentia Dei*.[38] *Vera sciendi methodus* presented a more forthright attack on Cartesian logic. His earlier book had set out to prove that Cartesian metaphysics was inadequate; Moore now asserted that Cartesian logic was riddled with problems and could not be relied upon to produce 'sure knowledge'.[39] The fundamental problem was Descartes' appeal to mathematics as a basis for the study of nature. It was the rise of the 'mathematical discipline', Moore argued, that corrupted rational scientia and replaced it with a quantitative and mechanical natural philosophy.[40] Moore objected that there was a clear distinction between physics and geometry, that change and motion were not the same thing and that geometric bodies, unlike natural ones, had no principle of motion.[41] In his confusion of mathematical and physical principles, Descartes had ignored the fundamental logical principles of definition, division and demonstration.[42] This allowed Descartes and his followers to reject the first principles of the natural body, matter and form, and as a direct result the soul, the form of the human body, was ignored in philosophy classrooms.[43]

To the philosophical considerations Moore added a series of religious and linguistic objections to Cartesianism. He argued that that the Cartesian 'fable' of creation could not be squared with the Book of Genesis and conflicted with basic Christian doctrines.[44] Thus the world was created almost by chance, the earth was but one more planet and the sun one more star. Moore felt that the religious implications of Cartesianism had been ignored because the discipline of physics was not considered as important as theology.[45] But the new mechanical theories of nature had profound metaphysical and religious implications and this convergence of metaphysics and physics is a recurring theme in Moore's eighteenth-century courses. He also echoed objections raised in his *Hortatio*, that the decline of Greek had been instrumental in the move away from Aristotle and that the use of vernacular language only added confusion to the debate.[46]

A renewal of Aristotelian method and natural philosophy was required.[47] But at the root of the discipline of philosophy was a fundamental problem. Moore believed that one had to consider the origin and duration of the world:

36 *VSM*, pp 51–2. Moore provides two other examples: 'Totum est majus sua parte', and 'Omnis numerus est unitatum multitudo' 37 Ibid., p. 86, and in general, pp 86–98. 38 For example, *DED*, pp 7–12, where he tackles Descartes' use of definitions. 39 See the useful, but brief, summary of the overall argument in *VSM*, [pp 25–8]. The preface is unpaginated, therefore the page number references in square brackets refer to the numbers which would naturally follow the letter of dedication (ibid., [pp 5–8]). The text proper begins on p. 1. 40 *VSM* [pp 10–11]. 41 Ibid. [pp 17–25] 42 Ibid. [pp 11, 17]. On logic see: Gabriel Nuchelmans, 'Logic in the seventeenth century: preliminary remarks and the constituents of the proposition' (1998). 43 *VSM*, pp 156–8, 208–22. 44 Ibid. [pp 12–16], 179–82, 195–200. 45 Ibid. [pp 16–17] 46 Ibid., pp 159–66. 47 Ibid. [p. 25].

... in which all philosophers, Plato, Aristotle, Anaxagoras, Epicurus, Dem-
ocritus and also the most disgraceful Descartes made a mistake, because
nothing could be known to them, but conjecturing and foreseeing as much
as [is] easily understood, truly to us ... the world was created from nothing by God.[48]

Philosophy had a boundary, for there was more truth than that which was available through scientia.[49] For Moore, Aristotle was the first thinker to write accurately about what could be known. But supernatural truths, concerning the Trinity or the Word Incarnate, were only known through revelation. The poverty of
philosophy was evident even where a rigorous logic or method produced water-
tight demonstrations.[50]

De principiis physicis underlined many of the points made in *Vera sciendi methodus* regarding the logical inadequacy of Cartesianism. Moore argued that the new
physics was based on 'these corpuscles and particles, which they do not see'.[51] The
magnitude and other properties assigned to particles were imagined and therefore
could not produce scientia, only probable opinion, which resulted in uncertain
principles. Moore also reiterated the traditional distinction between physics and
mathematics, arguing that geometry was different (and exact) precisely because it
existed only in the human imagination; it was universal but not applicable to sin-
gular things. Moreover, if mathematics became the basis of physics, there was no
room for a final cause or divine providence.[52]

Moore's final text vividly illustrates the religious importance of natural philosophy in the early eighteenth century. From the start, he argued that from visible things (the world), the mind was led to invisible things (God).[53] Cartesians
claimed that by directly connecting the human mind to knowledge of God's existence they avoided the imperfections of the world.[54] Natural philosophers, of
both hues, promoted the religious benefits of their respective systems. Moore
argued that the mechanical philosophy discarded the notion of a final end in
physics and could thereby encourage the development of atheism. This is an
important point, but it is also crucial to recognise that Moore did not believe that
Cartesians were necessarily atheists: 'Non quod ego Cartesium aut eius Discipu-
los Athoes esse credam, sed quod eius doctrina, finem negligendo, in vehere
videatur Atheiam.'[55]

As in his other texts, Moore argued here that the fundamental error in the new
physics rested on first principles. Just as in grammar, which he thought had
become rooted in an 'inchoate literature'[56], or in geometry, so in physics the prin-

---

48 *VSM*, p. 215.   49 Ibid., p. 216   50 Ibid., pp 233–4.   51 *DPP*, p. iv.   52 Ibid., pp iv-xi   53 Ibid.,
p. ii. On scholastic physics see: R. Ariew and A. Gabbey, 'The Scholastic background' (1998) and S.
Nadler, 'Doctrines of explanation in late scholasticism and in the mechanical philosophy' (1998),
especially pp 513–18.   54 Kors, *Atheism in France, 1650–1729*, especially pp 325–40.   55 *DPP*, p.
xii: 'I do not believe that Descartes or his disciples are atheists, but that their doctrine seems to carry
atheism.' He later makes a similar point, but stops short of labelling Cartesians heretics (p. 112).   56
Ibid., p. 1.

ciples of nature, matter and form, were ignored. The importance of hylomorphism for natural philosophy was the core point of the text.[57] For a Scholastic like Moore there were different types of 'scientiae', each with their own first principles. Thus, arithmetic dealt with numbers, geometry with plain figures and solids, while physics dealt with the natural body.[58] Moore devoted much space to the discussion of form in this book for three reasons. First, the Aristotelian conception of substantial forms had been severely attacked by the new philosophers.[59] Second, hylomorphism formed the basis of a counter-attack, which Moore thought fundamentally undermined the metaphysical underpinnings of Cartesian physics. Third, the discussion of form led Moore to the theory of souls and, in particular, the immortality of the human soul.

In line with orthodox Aristotelianism Moore viewed matter as a passive potentiality that could be actualised. The actualising force was form, which gave the natural body its functions. Substance was therefore composed of matter and form. But one type of form, what Moore called 'metaphysical form' was separable from all matter, and held for all minds (mens), whether divine, angelic or human.[60] It was therefore possible to argue that the human soul was immortal. Moore reiterated the threefold nature of the soul: vegetative, sensitive and rational. All living things have 'anima', which created the impression of a kind of life force in the universe. The operations of the vegetative soul were nutrition, growth and generation. Included in this category were magnets, which is revealing about the scholastic mindset in the creation of a systematic understanding of nature.[61] Moore argued that magnets appeared to be located between plants and metals, just as 'plantanimals' were somewhere between plants and animals, or man between animals and angels, 'For nature progresses in a certain continuity, without being used to any interruption interceding, thus between two extreme kinds there is usually a medium.'[62] The operations of the sensitive soul necessarily included the vegetative, but also included perception, the external senses in animals and motion.[63] The operations of the rational soul obviously included the former two, for it could not function without them. This meant that the human soul

---

57 *DPP*, pp 1–7. The comments below are largely based on the lengthy summary and conclusion of the book (ibid., pp 92–117). The book also contained a long series of appendices (ibid., pp 117–44). It is important to note that while it was the product of Moore's teaching between 1703–20, the published version did not appear until 1726. This may account for the somewhat disjointed nature of the ten appendices. A very terse 'approbatio' penned by C. Leulliet was dated 11 December 1725, while the privilege du roy was granted on 1 February 1726, less than seven months before Moore's death in August. The preface was addressed 'ad professores academicos philosophiae'. 58 *DPP*, p. 92. 59 On the competing range of theories of souls in the seventeenth-century see: D. Garber, 'Soul and mind: life and thought in the seventeenth century' (1998); C. McCracken, 'Knowledge of the soul' (1998); Fowler, *Descartes on the human soul,* passim. 60 *DPP*, pp 93–100. 61 *DPP*, pp 101–2. 62 Ibid., p. 55. The text devotes a section to the discussion of magnets: pp 55–6. 63 Ibid., pp 102–4. The denial of an animal or sensitive 'anima' generated huge debate in early-modern France: L.C. Rosenfield, *From beast-machine to man-machine: animal soul in French letters from Descates to La Mettrie* (1968), especially pp 79–92, which discusses the peripatetic arguments of the Jesuits Pardies, Daniel and Regnault.

was part material, and the intellectual part of the soul was immaterial. This spiritual part of the soul was the mens properly speaking; it was incorporeal, inorganic and form subsisting through itself. It was distinct from the natural body. Thus the mens could be separated from the body but not from existence, just as 'roundness' was inseparable from a circle.[64]

To this core argument Moore added a number of other points. He repeated that Cartesians could not account for the Catholic Eucharist, for if the bread was extension alone no change could be explained rationally. Moore cleverly pointed out that this permitted only something like Lutheran consubstantiation. However, he stopped short of accusing Descartes of outright heterodoxy.[65] Moore also suggested that the conception of ideas in Descartes and Malebranche amounted to a confusion of Platonic ideas with the real world. In an attack on the influential Cartesian philosophy of Malebranche, which Moore did not mention in any previous publications, he argued that our ideas could not be a participation in the mind of God, because we simply cannot know the divine essence. Angels on the other hand do not have to rationalise, they 'infuse' ideas directly from God. Human ideas are based on reason; they are the definitions of things collected from their proper principles or operations.[66]

Moore's *De principiis physicis* presents an interesting picture of the late scholastic natural philosopher. The problem was not experimental physics per se but the denial of concepts such as final cause and 'anima'.[67] French and Cunningham have argued that Dominican and Franciscan friars created natural philosophy in the twelfth and thirteenth centuries in their fight against heresy, particularly to combat the materialistic theories of the Cathars and Averroists.[68] Thus, 'Dominican natural philosophy in Aquinas' hands was partly shaped by the use it had been put to in defending the faith.'[69] Natural philosophy sought to understand 'what a thing was in itself',[70] the essence of a thing, and Aristotelian essence or form was directly related to the concept of 'anima'. Natural philosophy clearly had religious implications. Medieval thinkers, trained in natural philosophy and theology, were adept at utilising both tools in their understanding of the natural world.[71] Moore believed he was upholding a long natural philosophy tradition that opposed materialist heterodoxy. Indeed his opposition to a 'mathematical' philosophy of nature was equally in accord with the principles of natural philosophy which he outlined; causes of things were rooted in substantial forms, not mathematical proportions.[72]

---

64 *DPP*, pp 106–8. To underline the importance of Aristotle, he cited *De anima* in favour of his argument.   **65** *DPP*, p. 112.   **66** Ibid., pp 113–16. Just as in *VSM*, Moore finished by noting the imperfection of our knowledge because of our mortality (ibid., pp 116, 143).   **67** Moore discussed topics similar to those treated in Du Hamel's popular scholastic text *Philosophia universalis*. See: Rosenfield, 'Peripatetic adversaries of Cartesianism in 17th century France', p. 29.   **68** R. French and A. Cunningham, *Before science: the invention of the friars' natural philosophy* (1996).   **69** Ibid., p. 191.   **70** Johns, 'Identity, practice and trust in early modern natural philosophy', p. 1130.   **71** For an overview see: E. Grant, 'Science and theology in the middle ages' (1986).   **72** Johns, 'Identity, practice and trust in early modern natural philosophy', p. 1131; Brockliss, *French higher education*, p. 380, note 97.

Moore's courses reflected widely held concerns that mechanism, whether Cartesian or otherwise, would open the door to materialism, and ultimately atheism.[73] The Cambridge Platonist Henry Moore, the Irish philosopher George Berkeley, and the English physicist Isaac Newton were all likewise concerned about the implications of mechanism.[74] Berkeley commented that: 'The doctrine of matter, or corporeal substance, [is] the main pillar and support of scepticism, [and] upon the same foundation have been raised all the impious schemes of atheism and irreligion.'[75] Berkeley was concerned, like Moore, by apparent lack of room for God in the mechanical universe, and went on to provide an alternative in his radical theory of immaterialism.[76] Advocates of mechanistic philosophies invested much time in dispelling the fears that mechanism introduced materialism, and with it the possibility of religious heterodoxy.[77] French Cartesians argued that their philosophy was far superior to the Aristotelians precisely because it provided a more congenial approach to the divine. Descartes had avoided the imperfections of the senses, they suggested, and placed the intellectual ascent to God in the mind. There was a close link between the early acceptance of Cartesian theories of the natural world in France and the perceived benefits of Cartesian epistemology for the Christian. As presented in *De principiis physicis*, the scholastic interpretation of nature was based on a journey from the physical world, via the senses, to God. At the root was a belief that the explanation lay in the essences of things, their forms. Remove forms and the edifice crumbles. For Cartesians, their theories were not only compatible with Christianity, they were far superior. A host of pious French Cartesians defended Descartes from accusations of heterodoxy: Adrian Baillet (his early biographer), Nicholas Poisson, Bernard Lamy, Rene Le Bossu, Robert Desgabets, Antoine Le Grand and many others.[78] As Kors puts it: 'It was precisely this perceived spirituality of Cartesian philosophy, its presumed reliance upon divine illumination of the soul, that made it seem so exquisitely superior to Aristotelian sensationalism in the judgement of many theological and religious minds.'[79]

But during the last decades of the seventeenth century French Cartesians came under sustained pressure to expand on the metaphysical implications of Cartesian natural philosophy, reflecting the fear that Cartesianism represented the thin end of a Spinozist and materialist stick.[80] Indeed, Jonathan Israel has recently argued

73 W.B. Ashworth, 'Catholicism and early modern science' (1986), pp 139–40; R.S. Westfall, 'The rise of science and the decline of orthodox Christianity: a study of Kepler, Descartes and Newton' (1986), pp 224–8.   74 M. Hunter, 'Science and heterodoxy: an early modern problem reconsidered' (1995), p. 242; P. McGuinness, '"Perpetual flux": Newton, Toland, science and the status quo' (1997).   75 Cited in D. Attis, 'The ascendancy of mathematics: mathematics and Irish society from Cromwell to the Celtic Tiger' (2000), chapter 2, pp 31–2.   76 Ibid., chapter 2, pp 30–41; D. Garber, 'Locke, Berkeley and corpuscular scepticism' (1982), pp 174–93.   77 Gary Hatfield has discussed the relationship between metaphysics (assumed or otherwise) and the canonical figures of the scientific revolution: 'Metaphysics and the new science' (1986).   78 Kors, *Atheism in France, 1650–1729*, pp 323–56.   79 Ibid., p. 332.   80 See: Israel, *Radical Enlightenment*, pp 477–501; M.C. Jacob, *The cultural meaning of the scientific revolution* (1988), pp 61–9.

that *L'usage de la raison et de la foy* (Paris, 1704) by the Cartesian Pierre-Sylvain Régis 'is a notable landmark in the French intellectual crisis of Louis XIV's reign, above all because it marks the virtual withdrawal of Cartesianism from the battle to establish the core elements of religion philosophically, by means of reason'.[81] In short, the spectre of atheism and heterodoxy forced proponents of mechanist philosophies to prove their Christian intellectual credentials, whether to distinguish themselves from the threat of a radical pantheism suggested by the controversial Irish thinker John Toland or others, or from what Michael Hunter has suggested was 'a confident unintellectual, commonsensical scepticism, which flourished among the fashionable leaders of society and was felt to encourage the decline of traditional values'.[82]

Moore argued that Aristotelians continued to fulfil the duties of the Christian philosopher based on the scholastic method and a sensationalist natural philosophy. *De principiis physicis*, with its emphasis on hylomorphism and sensationalism, retained the fundamental principles necessary to preserve the concept of 'anima', and with it the Christian soul. The problem of the immortality of the human soul was one of the major stumbling blocks to a complete acceptance of Cartesianism at the University of Paris during the first two decades of the eighteenth century. Moreover, as an educationalist, the unity of knowledge inherent in the Aristotelian system, for example, in the classification of nature outlined in *De principiis physicis*, was important for Moore. To reject the contemporary validity of Michael Moore's arguments is to misconceive the practice of natural philosophy and the politico-religious nature of the debate about the new mechanistic philosophy in all its manifestations. Indeed, even Moore was associated with non-Scholastic thinkers. *Vera sciendi methodus* carried an approbation from Moore's colleague at the Collège de Navarre, Bernard Marion, who held a 'private academy' at the Hôtel de Beligan, where physicists of differing philosophical positions met to discuss new ideas.[83]

By the early eighteenth century Moore hoped, not so much to maintain the status quo, but rather to encourage a renewal in Aristotelian Scholasticism. In the preface to *Vera sciendi methodus*, he commented that the triumph of Cartesianism had meant the loss of real 'scientia', the loss of the work of great thinkers against Pyrrhonism. Moore saw his project as an attempt 'to recover and restore' the traditional scholastic philosophy.[84] Linked to his career at Montefiascone and the Collège de Navarre, *Vera sciendi methodus* and *De principiis physicis* were part of an intellectual outlook which stressed the authority of the ancients and Catholicism. The educational structures instituted at the Collège de Navarre, and Montefias-

---

81 Israel, *Radical Enlightenment*, p. 492.   82 Hunter, 'Science and heterodoxy: an early modern problem reconsidered', p. 243; M.C. Jacob, *The radical Enlightenment: pantheists, freemasons and republicans* (1981), pp 29–62.   83 *VSM*, 'approbatio', unpaginated; Spink, *French free-thought from Gassendi to Voltaire*, p. 206. Indeed, Spink notes that Marion's reputation lasted well into the eighteenth-century, when he was mentioned in the work of the Enlightenment thinker Helvétius.   84 *VSM* [p. 25].

cone, and the courses delivered at the Collège de France were part of a programme designed to produce the orthodox and rounded Christian citizens which the ancien régime demanded of its educational institutions.

French and Cunningham have argued that 'Traditional and theocentric natural philosophy died only when the heat went out of the religious quarrels, and this did not happen until after the seventeenth century.'[85] For Moore, as a self-consciously Irish scholar[86], the religious battles did not end in the seventeenth century. The main point of his *Hortatio* was the need to defend against heterodoxy, and its milder relation, Cartesian materialism. The French state and church required an orthodox metaphysics and ethics in the seventeenth and eighteenth centuries in order to maintain a status quo within the political and religious spheres. But they felt confident that the growing 'scientific' revolution was not a threat, allowing a more independent spirit to emerge in a subject like physics. In Moore's mind this dichotomy was flawed, since traditional natural philosophy was a key component of the broader philosophical approach based on Aristotle. As an Irish scholar he was perhaps more keenly aware of the potential damage inherent in mechanistic physics and its latent materialism.[87] Moore's project was not successful in the long term, but his endeavours were responsible for the kind of Cartesian physics that entered the university curricula in France. As Brockliss has commented: 'It is unsurprising that it was in … [a] probabilist, inorganic, neo-Aristotelian form that Cartesian mechanism was introduced into the collège curriculum at the turn of the eighteenth century.'[88]

85 French and Cunningham, *Before science*, p. 272. Admittedly these views become rather tentative when stretched beyond the thirteenth century, but the case of Michael Moore tends to support their argument at the other end of the history of natural philosophy. 86 This is demonstrated, for instance, by his use of the signature 'Michaelis Morus Hibernus', though one contemporary list of royal professors mistakenly labelled Moore as 'escossois' (Scottish): Professeurs royaux depuis la fondation du Collège Royal par Francois Ier par Martin Billet-de-Fanière, Parisien, 1709 avec notes … [par] Abbé Mercier de Saint Leger (BN, MS Francais 15,274, f.13). 87 Brockliss, *French higher education*, pp 444–6. 88 Brockliss, 'Descartes, Gassendi and the reception of the mechanical philosophy in the French *collèges de plein exercise*, 1640–1740', p. 470.

Conclusion

Moore retired from his positions in both royal colleges in 1720, when he was about eighty years old, though he remained active among the Irish community in Paris. He was also working on his course material from the Collège de France, some of which appeared as *De principis physiciis* in 1726. After his retirement Moore continued to reside in his apartment in the Collège de Navarre and had become something of an institution in his own lifetime. In his oration following Moore's death, the rector M. Delaval described Moore:

> He was gracious to all, affable to all, and, although his age was very great and his health broken, as soon as day broke he used to give everyone the opportunity of having an audience with him. He loved his fatherland, nor was he sparing either of his counsel or of his firmness so that he might help with all resource and effort those of the common people whom he knew who were in genuine need. Likewise he loved our university, and established at his own house a meeting hall, so to speak, of academicians, in which nothing was more diligently considered than the regulations of the university and the chronicles of our predecessors.[1]

Michael Moore died in his lodgings at the Collège de Navarre on 22 August 1726. In his will he expressed a desire to be buried in the chapel of the Collège des Lombards:

> 1. Je recommande mon ame a la misericorde de mon Dieu et de mon sauveur et seigneur Jesus Christ a l'intercession de la tres sainte vierge et de tous les saints.
> 2. Je souhaite que mon corps sont enterre simplement et pauvrement sans trouble sans sonnerie comme celuy d'un pauvre dans le cemitiere de la paroisse et qu'on dise la messe le meme jour ou le lendemain a la paroisse si mes executeurs testamentaires ne souhaitent pas qu'il soit enterre dans la chappelle du College des Lombards en cas que je meurs à Paris.[2]

---

1 Cited in Boyle, 'Dr Michael Moore', p. 16. The translation was made by G. Deighan for the late Fr Colm Connellan, some of whose notes were kindly lent to me by Dr John Cleary. 2 Michael Moore's will, 10 April 1721 (AN, MC, ET XVII/632, Novembre-Decembre 1723): '1. I recommend

However, there is no other evidence to agree, with Walter Harris, that his remains were interred in the Collège des Lombards.[3] He is listed on a plaque in the near-by parish chapel of St Etienne du Mont, a stone's throw from the location of the Collège de Navarre.

Moore left his property (*bien*) in Ireland to 'mon beau frere Wogan et ses her-itiers males' and money to other members of his family.[4] A number of small bequests were made in favour of Irish friends and associates in Paris. He left his red robe to the Nation d'Allemagne. He intended his servant, Louis Dammen-valle, to receive his furniture and clothes or eighty francs. The executors were the four proviseurs of the Collège des Lombards. The original will was made on 10 April 1721. Two codicils were added over the following two and a half years. The first codicil, dated 1 May 1721, was related specifically to a life pension which was left to Michael Moore by his patron Alexis de Barjot, who had died 'il y a quinze ou se[i]ze ans'. The late marquis de Moussy had left Moore an annual pension of two hundred livres and Moore had been forced to engage in a legal action with the guardian of Alexis de Barjot's heir to obtain the bequest. He had won the case but 'Je ne l'ay pas conclu faire par respect a la maison de Mons L'Abbe de Moussy.' The codicil recommended that the judgement should be enforced and the pen-sion of about 1,600 livres bequeathed to the Collège des Lombards. A second cod-icil was drawn up in December 1723, which increased Louis Dammenvalle's bequest and dealt with the arrears of three institutional life pensions of which Moore was in receipt. Moore requested that money due from the pension owed by the Collège de Navarre should be given to the principal of arts, Jacques Vraye, to be distributed in 100 livres portions to the college's boursiers. The arrears of his two other life pensions, from the university and the Collège de France, were to go to the proviseurs of the Collège des Lombards.

Moore also left behind a large private library, containing over 1,200 volumes, which he bequeathed to the Collège des Lombards. A record of about one third of the books was made just after his death and provides an insight into his read-ing habits and intellectual tastes, though the notary who was responsible for the record was primarily interested in those books which were most valuable, largely because of their age. The library contained a collection of bibles (Latin, Greek and Hebrew versions were all present), biblical commentaries, the writings of the fathers of the church, theology and philosophy, classical writers and grammars,

my soul to the mercy of God and of my saviour and lord Jesus Christ at the intercession of the most holy virgin and all the saints. 2. I wish that my body is buried simply and poorly without trouble and ceremony as that of a poor person in the cemetery of the parish and that one says mass the same day or the day after at the parish, if my testamentary executors do not wish it to be buried in the chapel of the Collège de Lombards, in case that I die in Paris'. 3 Ware, *The whole works*, ed. Harris, ii, p. 289. 4 Michael Moore's will, 10 April 1721, codicil to the will, 1 May 1721, second codicil to the will, 7 December 1723 (AN, MC, ET XVII/632, Novembre-Decembre 1723). Summarised in Swords (ed.), 'Calendar of Irish material in the files of Jean Fromont … part 2, 1716–1730', pp 111–13. The following comments are based on these sources.

and history. That theology, loosely defined, and history were the most significant categories conformed to general patterns of clerical book ownership during the period, but Moore's library also throws up some surprises. His history books were predominately 'national' studies, rather than the aristocratic or ecclesiastical works to be found in other libraries. He also possessed the works of the major, and some minor, Protestant theologians, which was still quite rare into the early eighteenth century. The library contained a small number of books dealing with geography, travel and civil and canon law, as well as the writings of prominent European humanists. He had few books by Irish authors, but the selection criteria of the notary would have excluded the recently, and probably cheaply, published writings of Moore's compatriots.[5]

What conclusions can we draw from this study of Moore's experience of Irish clerical migration? First, his case underlines the importance of patronage networks in the lives of the Irish abroad. Establishing oneself in a foreign country was not easy and migrants relied on assistance at least in the early stages of their careers. Moore was fortunate in the patrons he acquired. While we know relatively little about his relationship with Alexis de Barjot, it is clear that it was a long lasting friendship and one that was probably very beneficial to Moore. His links with the Talbots were crucial to his, initially successful, career in Dublin in the late 1680s. The patronage of two senior clergy, Barbarigo in Italy and de Noailles in France, allowed him to resurrect his career after he so acrimoniously placed himself outside the ambit of Jacobite patronage in 1690. Patronage was not a unidirectional phenomenon and Moore became an important benefactor to various Irish groups on the continent. In the 1670s and 1680s his position at the Collège des Grassins meant that he could take charge of the exiled Fleminge children. He was obviously an important patron for Matthew Barnewall, though the two men did not share theological outlooks, as well as the Collège des Lombards. Even in Montefiascone, Moore was able to provide assistance to Irish students who went there to study after he took charge of the seminary in 1696.

Second, two themes emerge from Moore's intellectual and educational experiences: orthodoxy *and* reform. It was on these twin pillars that Moore successfully built his career in France and Italy. The Aristotelianism that Moore championed was an important element of the intellectual patrimony of the Irish Catholic elite until well into the eighteenth century and therefore deserves much more attention than it usually receives. Intellectual orthodoxy, of the Aristotelian variety, did not mean backwardness or inflexibility. Moore engaged critically with Cartesianism and addressed the most pressing issues of the period, such as the search for a method which would guarantee 'sure knowledge' and the debate about the implications of the mechanical philosophy for theories of non-human

5 'Inventaire, Aoust, 1726' (AN, MC ET/XVII/647). On the library see: L. Chambers, 'The library of an Irish clerical migrant: Michael Moore's Bibliothèque, 1726' (forthcoming).

and human souls.[6] The intellectual orthodoxy of Irish exiles was expressed differently in other contexts, as suggested by the role of Irish Franciscans like Luke Wadding or John Punch in the revival of Scotism in the mid-seventeenth century.[7] Moore's philosophical orthodoxy was accompanied by a belief in the necessity of educational reform. His experience of the model Tridentine seminary at Montefiascone provided a blueprint for later reforms carried out at the Collège de Navarre. Common to both was the centralisation and regularisation of student activities designed to instil 'civility' and produce model Christian citizens. How students learned was as important as what they learned, captured in his maxim: '*Science* is a vain ornament if it is not accompanied by a solid piety.'[8]

Moore's emphasis on orthodoxy *and* reform was suited to his position as an Irish clerical exile. In part it was a response to the lingering threat of Protestantism, manifested most clearly in the collapse of Jacobite Ireland in 1689–91. The wars of religion may have been over for many Europeans by the late seventeenth and early eighteenth centuries, but the emergence of the Protestant Ascendancy in Ireland suggested otherwise to people like Moore. Their position as migrants and exiles created insecurity which made intellectual orthodoxy all the more appealing and the need for reform all the more urgent. In any case, Moore's orthodoxy was predicated on the prevailing attitudes of the French church and state authorities to philosophical debates. It was only in the early eighteenth century, when Cartesian natural philosophy was considered less suspect, that Moore was forced to fight a rearguard defence of Aristotelianism. Both opportunism and conviction played a role in fashioning the intellectual outlook of the Irish in exile.

Third, the Irish were more than mere receptors and disseminators of ideas; they reacted to and shaped ideas to suit their own circumstances. Edward Said wrote that: 'There is a popular but wholly mistaken assumption that being exiled is to be totally cut off, isolated, hopelessly separated from your place of origin.' Instead, he pointed out that: 'Because the exile sees things both in terms of what has been left behind and what is actually here and now, there is a double perspective that never sees things in isolation.'[9] Irish clerical migrants like Moore operated with this 'double perspective', within a complex dual set of social, political and intellectual contexts. Moore's position on Gallicanism, the quasi-independence of the French Catholic church, is instructive in this regard. He opposed trenchantly the attempts by the Jacobite court in Ireland to nominate clergy to vacant benefices and sees in the Irish Catholic church in 1689–90. However, he was quick to point out to a French correspondent that this was by no means an attack on Gallicanism in principle. In other words, Moore was content to accept Gallicanism in France but simultaneously reject its mirror image in Ireland.[10] Moore also

---

6 Mercer, 'The vitality and importance of early modern Aristotelianism' (1993). 7 Millet, 'Irish Scotists at St Isodore's College, Rome in the seventeenth century' (1968). 8 Untitled petition, Michael Moore to Cardinal de Noailles, July 1705 (A.N., MM 243, pièce 54). 9 E. Said, 'Intellectual exile: expatriates and marginals' (2000), pp 370, 378. See also E. Said, *Reflections on exile and other literary and cultural essays* (2001). 10 'Letter of a Catholick priest in Ireland containing the grevences [*sic*] of the Irish clergy of the Romish faith under James II 1691' (TCD, MS 1184).

provides a good example of the role of migrants in the transmission of ideas. For instance, he used the experience of Tridentine reform in Montefiascone to good advantage when undertaking the reform of the Collège de Navarre in Paris in the face of strong internal resistance.

The intellectual and educational history of the Irish in early modern Europe is a complex phenomenon. Opportunism, individuality and conviction affected the career choices and intellectual positions of the Irish in exile. The mentality of the Irish clergy abroad was neither homogenous nor straightforward, for local conditions and political concerns also influenced attitudes. Indeed, as the eighteenth century progressed and the pressures on Irish Catholicism diminished the nature of the intellectual engagement of the Irish abroad changed. Moore's case illustrates the increasing abilities of Irish exiles in the late seventeenth and early eighteenth centuries to attain promotion within the French and Italian educational systems. Election as rector of the University of Paris in 1701 was a remarkable achievement for an obscure Irish clerical migrant. Above all, Moore's case underlines the importance of the universities and colleges of Europe for the survival and invigoration of Irish Catholicism in the early-modern period.

Bibliography

PRIMARY SOURCES: MANUSCRIPT

Archives de l'Université de Paris
Registre 28, Liber procurationum Constantissimae Germanorum Nationis (1660–98).
Registre 33, Conclusions de l'Université, 1677–1682.
Registre 35, Conclusions de l'Université, 1683–1689.
Registre 38, Livre des conclusions, Nation d'Allemagne de l'an 1698 à l'an 1730.
Registre 101, Répetoire général ou table méthodique des matières contenus dans les registres des conclusions de 1612 à 1728.
Carton 10, 7e liasse, Serments à presenter à Mr le Recteur (1450–1727).
Carton 13, E21, Arrest de continuation en faveur de Mr Morus, 17 Mars 1702.
Carton 14D, Papiers de la Nation d'Allemagne.

Archives Nationales, Paris
Fonds Divers
Minutier Central: Études XI, XVII.
Anciens Fonds
H³ 2561B, Collège des Lombards (1623–1763).
M73, pièce 67, Registre des papiers et livres impruntés des coffres des Archives de la Nation d'Allemagne, Mai 1722–Aout 1751.
M 147, Collège des Lombards, sixteenth-eighteenth centuries.
MM 242, pièce 23, *Contrat de la ville de Paris avec l'Université pour faire un eloge du Roy le 15 May de chaque année, jour de l'avenement de sa majesté de la couronne* (Paris, 1685)
MM 242 à 246, Recueil des pièces concernant l'université, XVIIᵉ à XVIIIᵉ siècles.
MM 372, Inventaire des titres et papiers du Collège de Cambray autrement dit des Trois Eveques et Bourgogne réunis à celui de Louis-le-Grand, n.d.
MM 447, Collège des Grassins, Annales XVIIᵉ siècle (*c.* 1665–72).
MM 469, Conclusions des Assemblés de Messieurs les Deputés de Collège Royal de Navarre, 1709–1774.
O¹ 30, 46, 47, Le secretariat d'état de la Maison du Roi, various papers
S. 6181/8, Vitus, memoires, réglements concernant le Collège de Navarre, 1567–1767.
S.6546, Collège de Navarre où de Champagne, 1304–An. X.
S.6390ᴬ, Papers relating to the Collège de Cambrai.

Bibliothèque Nationale, Paris
MS Latin 9371, Catalogue des livres de la Bibliothèque du Collège de Navarre, 1743.
MS Latin 9962, Notes et documents sur l'histoire du Collège de Navarre, n.d. [seventeenth- and eighteenth-centuries]
MS Francais n.a. 5395, Recueil de mémoires, lettres, règlements etc., relatif au Collège de France (1710–1757) et projet d'union du Collège de France avec la Bibliothèque du Roi.
MS Francais 15,274, Professeurs Royaux depuis la fondation de Collège de France par Francois 1er par Martin Billet-de-Fanière, 1709.

MS Francais 18827–8, Pièces concernant l'Université de Paris XVIIe-XVIIIe siècles.
MS Joly de Fleury, tome 268, ff 178–258, Bourses du Sr Jacobini.

Archives de Paris
DC6 1, ff. 11v-12, [Michel Morus], Naturalisation, 1702.
DC6 218, ff. 74v-75, Michel Morus, Testament, 1721.

Bibliothèque Sainte-Geneviève, Paris
MS 987 (34–35), J.B.L. Crevier (?), 'Estat de la faculté des arts' in Receuil des pièces concernant l'Université de Paris XVIe-XVIIIe siècles, n.d. [late 17th cent.].
MS 2566, Recueil des lettres originales relatives aux affaires religieuses de l'Irlande et plus particulièrement au prieuré de ChristChurch, à Dublin, 1542–1689.

Archives du Collège des Irlandais
See: Liam Swords (ed.), 'History of the Irish College, Paris, 1578–1800. Calendar of the papers of the Irish College, Paris' in *Archiv. Hib.*, xxxv (1980).

Archives du Collège de France
Registre des délibérations du conseil des lecteurs royaux, Collège de France, 1674–1731.
Printed 'Affiches des Cours', Collège de France, 1711–20.
Dossiers des Professeurs (Michel Morus).

Bibliothèque Historique de la Ville de Paris
MS C.P. 3509, Manuscrit à la Bastille, huitième lettre.

Bibliothèque de l'Arsenal
Archives de la Bastille MS 10602, ff 87–183, Material relating to Jean de Padriac, deacon and Matthieu de Barneville, priest, Bastille, 21 May 1712 and following.
Archives de la Bastille MS 11,462, ff 54–150, Material relating to the affair of Sr Frion and others, September 1740.

Bibliotheque de la Société de Port Royal
L.P. 197 Recueil des pièces (1651–1732) 25 bis, *Profession de Foy de M. De Barneville, Prètre, Grand-Chantre de l'Eglise Cathédrale de la Sainte Trinité de Dublin en Irlande mort à la conciergerie au Palais à Paris le 16 Décembre 1738* (n.p., n.d.).

National Library of Ireland, Dublin
P.C. 231, unsorted, Verschoyle-Campbell [Dowdall] papers.
Reports on private collections, No. 354, Wogan Browne papers.
G.O. MS 169, pp 356–61, MS 177, pp 105–12, Dowdall pedigree.
G.O. MS 173, pp 140–3, Talbot of Malahide pedigree.

Examined on microfilm, National Library of Ireland:
Archivio della Sacra Congregazione di Propaganda Fide, Acta, volume 67 (1697), volume 68 (1698).
Public Record Office, London, State Papers, Ireland, Elizabeth I-George III, S.P. 63, vol. 340.

Trinity College, Dublin
MS 1184 Collection of papers relative to Great Britain and Ireland copied from Pieresch's MSS in the hands of the President Mazagues at Aix in Provence (*c.*1736).
MSS 1774, 1774a, 1774b, John Hely Hutchinson, 'An essay towards a history of Trinity College Dublin' n.d. (he was provost between 1774 and 1794).
MUN/V/5/2, 'General registry from 1640' [1640–1740].
MUN/V/23/1, Entrance book of students/matriculation records (1637–1725).

MUN/P/1/521–57, Muniments: papers, general and miscellaneous (1686–90).
MUN/P/2/434/1–7, Papers relating to the 1937 reading room and the planned war memorial.

Representative Church Body Library, Dublin
MS C6.1.26.6.32 'Some papers of Stafford, pretended Dean of this church and his chapter in 1689'.

Registry of Deeds, Dublin
11/166/4259, Deed relating to John Wogan and Judith Moore, 17 September 1713.

British Library, London
Add. MSS 34,727, ff 159–62, Cormac comharba Ciarain to Mileadh o Morro, *c.*1691.

Archivio Segreto Vaticano, Vatican City
Congregazione del Concilio, Relationes Diocesium, 541A, ff 306–58, Diocesan reports of Cardinal Marco Antonio Barbarigo for the years 1689, 1694, 1696, 1699, 1702, 1706.
Congreg. Concilio, Relat. Dioec., 541A ff 359–92, Diocesan report of Sebastianus Pompilius Bonaventura, 20 November 1710.

Seminario Barbarigo, Archivio, Montefiascone
A.D., 1692–1701, Libro Mastro del Ven Seminario di Montefiascone.
MS 57, Residui debitori à denaro di Ven. Semin°.
MS 140, Alunni e convitti del Ven. Semin° di Montefiascone 1700–1701.
MSS 162–7, Correspondence, late seventeenth and eighteenth centuries.

PRIMARY SOURCES: PUBLICATIONS BY MICHAEL MOORE

Illustrissimo nobilissimoque adolescenti D.D. Alexio Barjot de Moussy de Roncée theses sustinenti carmen ['Offerebat Michael Morus Hibernus'] (Paris, 1663).
Eminentissimo principi domino D. Antonio Barberino, sanctae Romanae ecclesiae cardinali camerario magno Franciae eleemosynario, Archepiscopi Duci Rhemensi designato Primo Franciae Pari etc. Dum sub eius auspiciis theses philosophicas sustineret illustrissimus ac nobilissimus adolescans Alexis Barjot de Moussy de Roncée ['Ita vouet et precatur Eminentiae tuae addictissimus et humillimus cliens Michael Morus Hibernus'] (Paris, 1663).
De existentia Dei et humanae mentis immortalitate secundum Cartesii et Aristotelis docrinam disputatio (Paris, 1692).
Hortatio ad studium linguae Graecae et Hebraicae, recitata coram eminentissimo D.D. Marco Antonio Barbadico ... a Michaele Moro sacerdote Hiberno (Montefiascone, 1700).
Vera sciendi methodus (Paris, 1716).
De principiis physicis, seu corporum naturalium disputatio (Paris, 1726).

PRIMARY SOURCES: CONTEMPORARY PUBLICATIONS, JOURNALS
AND SOURCE COLLECTIONS

Anon., *Conclusion de la faculté de théologie de Paris pour les Hybernois. Contre le décret de Monsieur le Recteur de l'Université du 4 Mars 1651 et contre les Jansenistes* (Paris, 1651).
——., *Memoires apologetiques pour les Recteur, Doyens, Procureurs et Supposts de l'Université de Paris. Contre l'entreprise de quelques Hibernois, la plupart estudians en l'Université* (Paris, s.d. [1651]).

——., *Vetera acta et instrumenta sacrae facultatis theologiae Parisiensis adversus Rectorem et facultatem artium* (Paris, 1668).

——., *A full and impartial account of all the secret consults, negotiations, stratagems, and intriegues* [*sic*] *of the Romish party in Ireland* (London, 1690).

——., *Synodus dioecesana I, Montis Falisci et Corneti, quam Marcus Antonius Barbadicus S.R.E. presbyter Cardinalis Tit. S. Susannae supradictarum civitatum episcopus habuit anno MDCXCII. Innocentio XII Pont.* (Rome, 1693).

——., *Secundus synodus dioecesana Montefalisci et Corneti. Ab eminentissimo et reverendissimo D. Marco Antonio tit. S. Marci Cardinali Barbarigo episcopo in ecclesia Cathedrali Montefalisci celebrata Anno Domini MDCXCVI. Die 20.21 et 22 Mensis Maii* (Montefiascone, 1700).

——., *Histoire du Cas-de-Conscience, signée par quarante docteurs de Sorbonne* (8 vols, Nancy, 1705–11).

——., *Advice to the Romish Catholick priests of Ireland to take speedily the oath of abjuration* (Dublin, 1713).

——., *Regole per il Seminario di Montefiascone, cavate degli atti di S. Carlo Borromeo e tradotte dal Latino d'ordine Dell'Eminentissi, e Reverendissi Sig. Cardinale Barbarigo vescovo di Montefiascone e Corneto, e preseritte allo stresso suo seminario deccate al medismo santo* (Montefiascone, 1742).

Thomas Aquinas, *Summa theologiae: Latin text and English translation*, ed. Blackfriars (61 vols, New York, 1964–81).

Caroli Du Plessis D'Argentré, *Collectio judiciorum de novis erroribus* (3 vols, Paris, 1728–36).

Aristotle, *The complete works of Aristotle*, ed. Jonathan Barnes (2 vols, Princeton, 1991).

Matthieu de Barneville, *Le Nouveau Testament de Notre Seigneur Jésus-Christ* (Paris, 1719).

J.R. Bloxam (ed.), *Magdalen College and King James II, 1686–1688* (Oxford, 1886).

César Egasse du Boulay, *Remarques sur la dignité, rang, préséance, autorité et jurisdiction du Recteur de l'Université de Paris* (Paris, 1668).

Nicholas Boileau, *Oeuvres complètes*, ed. Antoine Adam (Paris, 1966).

John Brenan, *An Irish bishop of penal times being the letters and reports of John Brenan, bishop of Waterford (1671–93) and archbishop of Cashel (1677–93)*, ed. Patrick Power (Cork, 1932).

Germain Brice, *Description de la ville de Paris*, sixth edn (3 vols, Paris, 1713).

Gaspard Buhon, *Philosophia ad monem gymnastiorum, finemque accomodata* (4 vols, Lyon, 1723).

Calendar of state papers preserved in the Public Record Office, domestic series (81 vols, London, 1856–1972).

Calendar of treasury books 1660–[1718] preserved in the Public Record Office (32 vols, London, 1904–69).

Calendar of treasury papers, 1556–[1728] preserved in the Public Record Office (6 vols, London, 1868–89).

Neal Carolan, *Motives of conversion to the Catholick faith, as it is professed in the reformed church of England* (Dublin, 1688).

William Carrigan, 'Catholic episcopal wills in the Public Record Office, Dublin 1683–1812' in *Archiv. Hib.*, iv (1915), pp 66–95.

Patrick J. Corish (ed.), 'Bishop Wadding's Notebook' in *Archiv. Hib.*, xxix (1970), pp 49–114.

René Descartes, *The philosophical writings of Descartes*, ed. John Cottingham, Robert Stoothoff and Dugald Murdoch (2 vols, Cambridge, 1984).

Pierre Nicolas Desmolets (contin. A.H. de Salengre), *Continuation des mémoires de litterature et d'histoire* (11 vols, Paris, 1726–31).

Nicholas Donnelly (ed.), 'The "per obitum" volumes in the Vatican Archivio' in *Archiv. Hib.*, i (1912), pp 29–38.

Dublin Magazine (1762).

Jean Du Hamel, *Philosophia universalis, sive commentarius in universam Aristotelis philosophiam ad usum scholarum comparatam quaedam recentiorum philosophorum ac praesertim Cartesii propositiones damnatae et prohibitae* (Paris, 1705).

Edmund Everard, *The depositions and examinations of Mr Edmund Everard (who was four years close prisoner in the Tower of London) concerning the horrid popish plot* (London, 1679).

Patrick Fagan (ed.), *Ireland in the Stuart papers: correspondence and documents of Irish interest from the Stuart Papers in the Royal Archives, Windsor* (2 vols, Dublin, 1995).

M. Frantz Funck-Bretano, *Les lettres de cachet à Paris étude suivie d'une liste des prisonniers de la Bastille (1659–1789)* (Paris, 1903).

François Genet, *Theologie morale ou résolution des cas-de-conscience, selon l'ecriture sainte, les canons et les saintes pères* (Paris, 1679).

Cathaldus Giblin (ed.), 'Miscellaneous papers' in *Archiv. Hib.*, xvi (1951), pp 62–98.

——, 'Catalogue of material of Irish interest in the collection *Nunziatura di Fiandra*, Vatican Archives' in *Collect. Hib.*, 5 (1962), pp 7–125.

John Gilbert (ed.), *History of the Irish Confederation and the war in Ireland, 1641–1643* (7 vols, Dublin, 1882–9).

John Hanly (ed.), *The letters of Saint Oliver Plunkett, 1625–1681* (Dublin, 1979).

Richard Hayes (ed.), 'Reflections of an Irish brigade officer' in *Irish Sword*, i, 2 (1950–1), pp 68–74.

HMC, *Seventh report, part i* (London, 1879).

——, *Eleventh report, appendix, part i: the manuscripts of the House of Lords, 1678–88* (London, 1887).

——, *Thirteenth report, appendix, part vi: The manuscripts of Sir William Fitzherbert, Bart., and others* (London, 1893).

——, *Report on the manuscripts of his grace the duke of Portland K.G., preserved at Welbeck Abbey* (9 vols, London, 1891–1931).

——, *Manuscripts of the earl of Egmont* (London, 1893).

——, *Calendar of the manuscripts of the marquess of Ormonde K.P. preserved at Kilkenny Castle*, new series (8 vols, London, 1902–20).

——, *Calendar of the Stuart papers belonging to his majesty the king preserved at Windsor Castle* (7 vols, London, 1904–23).

C.T. Lambert (ed.), *Some funeral entries of Ireland* ([Dublin], [1907–12]).

C.E. Lart (ed.), *The parochial registers of Saint Germain-en-Laye: Jacobite extracts of births, marriages and deaths* (2 vols, London, 1910–12).

Le Journal des Sçavans, 1692, 1693.

William King, 'Diary of William King, D.D., archbishop of Dublin, during his imprisonment in Dublin Castle' ed. Hugh Jackson Lawlor in *Journal of the Royal Society of Antiquaries of Ireland*, xxxiii (1903), pp 119–52, 255–83, 389–415, 439–41.

——, *The state of the Protestants of Ireland under the late King James's government* (London, 1691).

François Ledieu, *Les dernières années de Bassuet: journal de Ledieu*, ed. C. Urban and E. Levesque (2 vols, Paris, 1928).

Daniel McCarthy (ed.), *Collections on Irish church history from the MSS of the late V. Rev. Laurence Renehan D.D.* (Dublin, 1861).

Charles McNeill (ed.), 'Reports on the Rawlinson collection of manuscripts preserved in the Bodleian Library, Oxford', in *Anal. Hib.*, 1 (1930), pp 12–178.

—— (ed.), 'Rawlinson manuscripts Class C. and D.' in *Anal. Hib.*, 2 (1931), pp 1–92.

—— and A.J Otway-Ruthven (ed.), *Dowdall Deeds* (Dublin, 1960).

Giovani Marangoni, *Vita del servo di Dio Card. Marco Antonio Barbarigo vescovo di Montefiascone e Corneto. Manoscritto del sec. XVIII con introduzione e note del sac. Enrico Chierichetti vicario generale e pro rettore del Seminario Barbarigo* (Montefiascone, 1930).

Joseph Privat de Molières, *Leçons de mathématique nécessaires pour l'intelligence des principes de physique qui s'enseignent actuellement au Collège Royal* (Paris, 1725).

Canice Mooney (ed.), 'The library of Archbishop Piers Creagh' in *Reportorium Novum*, i, 1 (1955), pp 117–139.

P.F. Moran, *Spicilegium Ossoriense: being a collection of original letters and papers illustrative of the history of the Irish church from the Reformation to the year 1800* (3 vols, Dublin, 1874, 1878 and 1884).

Louis Moreri, *Le grand dictionnaire historique ou le mélange curieux de l'histoire sacrée et profane*, eighteenth edn (7 vols, Amsterdam, 1740).

[Cornelius Nary] (trans.), *The New Testament of Our Lord and Saviour Jesus Christ newly translated out of the Latin vulgar and with the original Greek, and divers translations in vulgar translations diligently compared and revised* ([Dublin], 1718).

Richard O'Ferrall and Robert O'Connell (eds), *Commentarius Rinuccinianus, de sedis apostolicae legatione ad foederatos Hiberniae catholicos per annos 1645–9*, ed. Stanislaus Kavanagh (6 vols, Dublin, 1932–49).

Seán Ó Gallchóir (ed.), *Séamus Dall MacCuarta dánta* (Baile Átha Cliath, 1971).

Jane Ohlmeyer and Éamonn Ó Ciardha (eds), *The Irish statute staple books, 1596–1687* (Dublin, 1998).

W.M. O'Riordan, 'On two documents in the *Liber Decanatus I*, in the Dublin Diocesan Archives' in *Reportorium Novum*, i, 2 (1956), pp 369–80.

Paul Perdrizet (ed.), *Le calendrier de la Nation d'Allemagne de l'ancienne Université de Paris* (Paris, 1937).

Pietro Pomponazzi, 'On the immortality of the soul', introduced by J. Herman Randall Jr, in E. Cassirer, P.O. Kristeller and J.H. Randall (eds), *The Renaissance philosophy of man: selections in translation* (Chicago, 1967), pp 257–381.

Edmond Pourchot, *Institutio philosophica ad faciliorem veterum ac recentiorum philosophorum lectionem comparata* (4 vols, Paris, 1695).

Francois Ravaisson-Mollien, *Archives de la Bastille* (17 vols, Paris, 1866–1904, reprinted 1975).

David Rothe, *Brigida thaumaturga* (Paris, 1620).

[Patrick Russell?], *An address given in to the late King James, by the titular archbishop of Dublin: from the general meeting of the Romish bishops and clergy of Ireland, held in May last, by that King's order* (London, 1690).

Robert C. Simington (ed.), *The civil survey A.D. 1654–1656 vol. vii County of Dublin* (Dublin, 1945).

—— (ed.), *The civil survey A.D. 1654–1656 vol. v County of Meath* (Dublin, 1940).

J.G. Simms (ed.), 'Irish Jacobites: lists from TCD MS N.1.3.' in *Anal. Hib.*, 22 (1960), pp 11–230.

Liam Swords (ed.), 'Calendar of Irish material in the files of Jean Fromont, notary at Paris, May 1701–24 Jan. 1730, in the Archives Nationales, Paris: part 1, 1701–15' in *Collect. Hib.*, 34–5 (1992–3), pp 77–115.

—— (ed.), 'Calendar of Irish material in the files of Jean Fromont, notary at Paris, May 1701–24 Jan. 1730, in the Archives Nationales, Paris: part 2, 1716–1730' in *Collect. Hib.*, 36–7 (1994–5), pp 85–139.

Lilian Tate (ed.), 'The letterbook of Richard Talbot' in *Anal. Hib.*, iv (1932), pp 99–138.

The fifty seventh report of the keeper of public records and keeper of the state papers in Ireland (Dublin, 1936).

John Toland, *John Toland's Christianity not mysterious: text, associated works and critical essays*, ed. Philip McGuinness, Alan Harrison and Richard Kearney (Dublin, 1997).

Luke Wadding, *A pious garland being the December letter and Christmas carols of Luke Wadding, bishop of Ferns, 1683–1688* (first published in 1684; Dublin, 1960).

Sir Robert Walsh, *A true narrative and manifest, set forth by Sir Robert Walsh* (n.p., 1679).

Sir James Ware, *The whole works of Sir James Ware concerning Ireland, revised and improved*, ed. Walter Harris (2 vols, Dublin, 1739–45).

PUBLISHED SECONDARY SOURCES

Anon., *Laudatio funebris Benedicti Bonelli nobilis Tyrolensis in seminario et collegio Falisco theologiae dogmaticae lect.* (Montefiascone, 1787).

——., 'The Wogans of Rathcoffey' in *Journal of the Royal Society of Antiquaries of Ireland*, fifth series, i, 1 (1890), p. 320.

David Allan, '"An ancient sage philosopher": Alexander Ross and the defence of philosophy' in *The Seventeenth-Century*, xvi, 1 (Spring 2001), pp 68–94.

Robert Amadou, 'Saint-Ephrem Des Syriens du Collège des Lombards à nos jours' in *Mémoires de la Féderation des sociétés historiques et archéologiques de Paris et l'Ile de France*, 37 (1986), pp 6–152.

Roger Ariew, 'Theory of comets at Paris during the seventeenth century' in *Journal of the History of Ideas*, 52, 3 (1992), pp 355–72.

——, 'Damned if you do: Cartesians and censorship, 1663–1706' in *Perspectives on Science*, 2 (1994), pp 255–74.

——, 'Critiques Scholastiques de Descartes: *le cogito*' in *Laval Théologique et Philosophique*, 53, 3 (Oct 1997), pp 587–603.

——, 'Aristotelianism in the 17th century' in Edward Craig (ed.), *Routledge encyclopaedia of philosophy* (10 vols, London, 1998), i, pp 386–93.

—— and Alan Gabbey, 'The Scholastic background' in Garber and Ayers, *The Cambridge history of seventeenth-century philosophy*, pp 425–53.

——, *Descartes and the last scholastics* (Ithaca, 1999).

Jean Armand, *Les évêques et les archévêques de France depuis 1682 jusqu'à 1801* (Paris, 1891).

L.J. Arnold, *The Restoration land settlement in County Dublin, 1660–1688: a history of the administration of the acts of settlement and explanation* (Dublin, 1993).

William B. Ashworth Jr., 'Catholicism and early modern science' in Lindberg and Numbers (eds), *God and nature: historical essays on the encounter between Christianity and science*, pp 136–66.

François Azouvi, *Descartes et la France: histoire d'une passion nationale* (Paris, 2002).

T.C. Barnard, 'The Hartlib Circle and the origins of the Dublin Philosophical Society' in *IHS*, xix (1974–5), pp 56–71.

——, 'Reading in eighteenth century Ireland' in Bernadette Cunningham and Márie Kennedy (eds), *The experience of reading: Irish historical perspectives* (Dublin, 1999), pp 60–77.

J.C. Beckett, *The making of modern Ireland 1603–1923* (Belfast, 1966).

Alphons Bellesheim, *Geschichte der Katholischen kirche in Irland* (3 vols, Mainz, 1890–1).

Pietro Bergamaschi, *Vita di Lucia Filippini* (2 vols, Bagnorea, 1916).

——, *Vita del servo di Dio Card. Marc'Antonio Barbarigo vescovo di Montefiascone e Corneto* (2 vols, Roma, 1919).

David Berman, 'Enlightenment and counter-enlightenment in Irish philosophy' in *Archiv fur gestichte der philosophie*, 64 (1982), pp 148–65.

——, 'The culmination and causation of Irish philosophy' in *Archiv fur gestichte der philosophie*, 64 (1982), pp 257–79.

——, 'The Irish counter enlightenment' in Richard Kearney (ed.), *The Irish mind: exploring intellectual traditions* (Dublin, 1985), pp 119–40.

Sir William Betham, *Historical and genealogical memoir of the family of Slane in the county palatine of Meath, Ireland*, ed. George A. Birdsall (published by Betham in 1829; revised edn, Virginia, 1969).

Jean-Marie Beyssade, 'The idea of God and the proofs of his existence' in John Cottingham (ed.), *The Cambridge companion to Descartes* (Cambridge, 1992), 174–99.

Robert Bireley, *The refashioning of Catholicism, 1450–1700: a reassessment of the counter reformation* (Basingstoke, 1999).

Ann Blair, 'The teaching of natural philosophy in early seventeenth century Paris: the case of Jean Cécile Frey' in *History of Universities*, xii (1993), pp 95–158.

Michael Blay, 'Varignon et le statut de la loi de Torricelli' in *Archives Internationale d'Histoire des Sciences*, 35 (1985), pp 330–45.

——, 'Varignon, ou la théorie du mouvement des projectiles "comprise en une proposition générale"' in *Annales of Science*, 45 (1988), pp 591–618.

Elizabethanne Boran, 'The foundation of Jesuit colleges in seventeenth century Ireland' in Gian Carlo Brizzi and Jacques Verger (eds), *Le università minori in Europa (secoli xv-xix)* (Rubbertino, 1998), pp 273–88.

Francisque Bouillier, *Histoire de la philosophie Cartésienne*, third edition (2 vols, Paris, 1868).

Patrick Boyle, 'Lord Iveagh and other Irish officers, students at the Collège des Grassins, in Paris, from 1684–1710' in *IER*, 4th series, x (1901), pp 385–94.

——, *The Irish College in Paris from 1578–1901* (London, 1901).

——, 'Glimpses of Irish Collegiate life in Paris in the seventeenth and eighteenth centuries' in *IER*, 4th series, xi (1902), pp 432–50.

——, 'The Irish College in Paris 1578–1901' in *IER*, 4th series, xi (1902), pp 193–210.

——, 'Irishmen in the University of Paris in the 17th and 18th centuries' in *IER*, 4th series, xiv (1903), pp 24–45.

——, 'Brigida thaumaturga' in *IER*, 4th series, xxix (1911), pp 225–34.

——, 'Dr Michael Moore, sometime provost of Trinity College and rector of the University of Paris (A.D. 1640–1726)' in *Archiv. Hib.*, v (1916), pp 7–16.

——, 'The Abbe' John Baptist Walsh, D.D., Administrator of the Irish Foundation in France from 1787–1815' in *IER*, 4th series, xviii (1905), pp 431–54.

——, '"The Abbé" Charles Kearney, D.D. (1762–1824). His life and sufferings during the French Revolution' in *IER*, 4th series, xxiii (1908), pp 454–66.

David Bracken, 'Piracy and poverty: aspects of the Irish Jacobite experience in France, 1691–1720' in O'Connor (ed.), *The Irish in Europe, 1580–1815*, pp 127–42.

John Brady, 'Oliver Plunkett and the popish plot' in *IER*, 89 (1958), pp 1–13, 340–54; 90 (1958), pp 12–27.

——, 'Dr Michael Moore' in *Reportorium Novum*, ii, 1 (1958), pp 207–8.

——, 'Dr Michael Moore' in *Reportorium Novum*, ii, 2 (1960), pp 377–8.

——, 'Archdeacon Luke Rochford and his circle' in *Reportorium Novum*, i, 3 (1962), pp 108–20.

Catherine Breathnach, 'Archbishop John Brenan (1625–1693): his life and work' in *Tipperary Historical Journal* (1993), pp 148–59.

Robin Briggs, *Communities of belief: cultural and social tensions in early modern France* (Oxford, 1989, republished 1995).

——, *Early modern France, 1560–1715*, second edn (Oxford, 1998).

L.W.B. Brockliss, 'Philosophy teaching in France 1600–1740' in *History of Universities*, i (1981), pp 131–68.

——, 'Aristotle, Descartes and the new sciences: natural philosophy at the University of Paris, 1600–1740' in *Annals of Science*, 38 (1981), pp 33–69.

—— and P. Ferté, 'Irish clerics in France in the seventeenth and eighteenth centuries: a statistical study' in *Proc. RIA*, 87C, 9 (1987), pp 527–72.

——, *French higher education in the seventeenth and eighteenth centuries: a cultural history* (Oxford, 1987).

——, 'The 'Intruded' president and fellows' in Brockliss, Harriss and Macintyre (eds), *Magdalen College and the crown*, pp 83–106.

——, 'The University of Paris and the maintenance of Catholicism in the British Isles, 1426–1789: a study in clerical recruitment' in Dominique Julia, Roger Chartier et Jacques Revel (eds), *Les universites Européenes du XVIe au XVIIe siècles: Histoire sociale des populations étudiants* (2 vols, Paris, 1986–9), pp 577–616.

——, 'Copernicus in the university: the French experience' in John Henry and Sarah Hutton (ed.), *New perspectives on Renaissance thought: essays in the history of science, education and philosophy in memory of Charles B. Schmitt* (London, 1990), pp 190–213.

——, 'The scientific revolution in France' in Roy Porter and Mikulás Teich (eds), *The scientific revolution in national context* (Cambridge, 1992), pp 55–89.

——, 'Descartes, Gassendi and the reception of the mechanical philosophy in the French collèges de plein exercise, 1640–1730' in *Perspectives on Science*, 3, 4 (1995), pp 450–79.

——, 'Curricula' in Hilde de Ridder-Symoens, (ed.), *A history of the university in Europe*, pp 563–620.

Laurence Brockliss, Gerald Harriss and Angus Macintyre (eds), *Magdalen College and the crown: essays for the tercentenary of the restoration of the college 1688* (Oxford, 1988).

Michael J. Buckley, *At the origins of modern atheism* (Yale, 1987).

Bernard Burke, *A genealogical and heraldic history of the landed gentry of Ireland*, new edn (London, 1912).

Burke's peerage and baronetage, 105th edn (London, 1970, reprinted 1976).

W.P. Burke, *The Irish priests in the penal times (1660–1670)* (Waterford, 1914).

Luigi Pieri Buti, *Storia di Montefiascone scritta e corredata di molti inediti documenti dal cavaliere* (Montefiascone, 1870).

J.B. Buzy, *Notice historique sur le Collège des Grassins* (Sens, 1881).

Andrew Carpenter, 'William King and the threats to the Church of Ireland during the reign of James II' in *IHS*, 18 (1972), pp 22–8.

J.L. Carr, *Le Collège des Ecossais à Paris (1662–1962)* (Paris, 1963).

W.O. Cavenagh, 'The Wogans of Rathcoffey, Co. Kildare – a correction' in *Journal of the County Kildare Archaeological Society*, v (1906–8), pp 109–113.

Liam Chambers, 'Defying Descartes: Michael Moore (1639–1726) and Aristotelian philosophy in France and Ireland' in Michael Brown and Stephen Harrison (eds), *The medieval world and the modern mind* (Dublin, 2000), pp 11–26.

——, 'A displaced intelligentsia: aspects of Irish Catholic thought in *ancien régime* France' in Thomas O'Connor (ed.), *The Irish in Europe, 1580–1815* (Dublin, 2001), pp 157–74.

——, 'Knowledge and Piety: Michael Moore's career at the University of Paris and *Collège de France*, 1701–20' in *Eighteenth-Century Ireland*, 17 (2002), pp 9–25.

—— (ed.), 'The library of an Irish clerical migrant: Michael Moore's *Bibliothèque*, 1726' in *Archiv. Hib.* (forthcoming).

——, 'Irish Catholics, French Cartesians: Irish reactions to Cartesianism in France, 1671–1726' in Eamon Maher and Grace Neville (eds), *Ireland and France: anatomy of a relationship* (Frankfurt-am-main, 2004), pp 133–45.

Ruth Clark, *Strangers and sojourners at Port Royal: being an account of the connections between the British Isles and the Jansenists of France and Holland* (Cambridge, 1932).

Aidan Clarke, *The Old English in Ireland, 1625–42* (London, 1966).

Desmond Clarke, 'An outline of the history of science in Ireland' in *Studies*, 62 (1973), pp 287–302.

——, 'Cartesian science in France, 1660–1700' in A.J. Holland (ed.), *Philosophy: its history and historiography* (Dordrecht, 1985), pp 165–78.

——, *Occult powers and hypotheses: Cartesian natural philosophy under Louis XIV* (Oxford, 1989).

J.S. Clarke, *The life of James II* (2 vols, London, 1816).

George C. Cockayne, *The complete peerage of England, Scotland, Ireland, Great Britain and the United Kingdom: extant, extinct or dormant* (8 vols, London, 1887–98; revised microprint edn, Gloucester, 1987).

Anthony Cogan, *The diocese of Meath: ancient and modern* (3 vols, Dublin, 1867).

Louis Cognet, *Le Jansénisme* (Paris, 1961).

Leonora Cohen Rosenfield, 'Peripatetic adversaries of Cartesianism in 17th century France' in *Review of Religion*, 22 (1957), pp 14–40.

——, *From beast-machine to man-machine: animal soul in French letters from Descates to La Mettrie* (New York, 1968).

Marie-Madeleine Compère, *Du collège au lycée (1500–1800)* (Paris, 1985).

—— et Dominique Julia, *Les collèges français, 16e–18e siècles* (2 vols, Paris, 1988).

James Corboy, 'Father Christopher Holywood S.J., 1559–1626' in *Studies*, xxxiii, 132 (Dec 1944), pp 543–9.

Patrick J. Corish, 'John Callaghan and the controversies among the Irish in Paris, 1648–54' in *Irish Theological Quarterly*, 21 (1954), pp 32–50.

——, 'The beginnings of the Irish college, Rome' in Franciscan Fathers (ed.), *Father Luke Wadding*, pp 284–94.

——, *The Catholic community in the seventeenth and eighteenth centuries* (Dublin, 1981).

Edward Corp, 'The Irish at the Jacobite court of Saint Germain-en-Laye' in O'Connor (ed.), *The Irish in Europe, 1580–1815*, pp 143–56.

P. Costabel, 'Pierre Varignon et la diffusion en France du calcul differentiel et integral' in *Conférences du Palais de la Découverte*, 108 (1965).

Martin J. Counihan, 'Ireland and the scientific tradition' in Patrick O'Sullivan (ed.), *The Irish world wide: history, heritage, identity, volume three: the creative migrant* (Leicester, 1997), pp 28–43.

Donal Cregan, 'The social and cultural background of a counter-reformation episcopate, 1618–60' in Art Cosgrove and Donal McCartney (eds), *Studies on Irish history presented to R. Dudley Edwards* (Dublin, 1979), pp 85–117.

Eveline Cruickshanks and Edward Corp, *The Stuart court in exile and the Jacobites* (London, 1995).

Louis Cullen, 'Galway merchants in the outside world, 1650–1800' in Diarmuid Ó Cearbhaill (ed.), *Galway: town and gown, 1484–1984* (Dublin, 1984), pp 63–89.

——, 'The Irish Diaspora of the seventeenth and eighteenth centuries' in Nicholas Canny (ed.), *Europeans on the move: studies on European migration, 1500–1800* (Oxford, 1994), pp 113–49.

Bernadette Cunningham and Máire Kennedy (eds.), *The experience of reading: Irish historical perspectives* (Dublin, 1999).

John D'Alton, *Illustrations, historical and genealogical of King James' Irish army list, 1689*, second edition (2 vols, London, 1801).

——, *Memoirs of the archbishops of Dublin* (Dublin, 1838).

Frank D'Arcy, 'Exiles and strangers: the case of the Wogans' in Gerard O'Brien (ed.), *Parliament, politics and people: essays in eighteenth-century Irish history* (Dublin, 1989), pp 171–85.

Seamus Deane (ed.), *The Field Day anthology of Irish writing* (3 vols, Derry, 1991).

Peter Dear, 'Method and the study of nature' in Garber and Ayers, *The Cambridge history of seventeenth-century philosophy*, pp 147–77.

J. Delteil, 'Le Collège des Grassins à Paris' in *La vie urbaine, urbanism – habitation aménagement du territoire*, nouvelle série, 4 (Oct-Dec 1967), pp 241–66.

Matthew Devitt, 'Rathcoffey' in *Journal of the County Kildare Archaeological Society*, iii (1900), pp 79–87.

David Dickson, *New foundations: Ireland 1660–1800*, second edn (Dublin, 2000).

Dictionary of National Biography (63 vols, London, 1885–1901).

Dictionary of Scientific Biography (10 vols, New York, 1970–80).

Dictionnaire de Biographie Française (Paris, 1933–).

Dizionario Biografico degli Italiano (Florence, 1960–).

N[icholas] D[onnelly], 'The diocese of Dublin in the eighteenth century' in *IER*, third series, xi (1888), pp 837–49.

Nicholas Donnelly, *Short histories of Dublin parishes* (17 parts, Dublin, 1904–17).

Thomas Doyle, 'Jacobitism, Catholicism and the Irish protestant elite, 1700–1710' in *Eighteenth-Century Ireland*, 12 (1997), pp 28–59.

William Doyle, *Jansenism: Catholic resistance to authority from the reformation to the French revolution* (New York, 2000).

Thomas Duddy, *A history of Irish thought* (London, 2002).

—— (ed.), *Dictionary of Irish philosophers* (Bristol, 2004).

Richard H.A.J. Everard, 'The family of Everard: part iii Everard of Fethard, Co. Tipperary' in *Irish Genealogist*, 8, 2 (1991), pp 175–206.

Patrick Fagan, *Dublin's turbulent priest: Cornelius Nary (1658–1738)* (Dublin, 1991).

——, *Divided loyalties: the question of an oath for Irish Catholics in the eighteenth century* (Dublin, 1991).

——, *An Irish bishop in penal times: the chequered career of Sylvester Lloyd OFM, 1680–1747* (Dublin, 1995).

Mordechai Feingold, 'Aristotle and the English universities in the seventeenth century: a re-evaluation' in Robinson-Hammerstein (ed.), *European universities in the age of reformation and counter-reformation*, pp 135–48.

Hugh Fenning, 'Dublin imprints of Catholic interest, 1701–39' in *Collect. Hib.*, 39–40 (1997–8), 106–54.

——, 'The archbishops of Dublin, 1693–1786' in Kelly and Keogh (eds), *History of the Catholic diocese of Dublin*, pp 175–214.

——, 'Dominic Maguire, O.P., Archbishop of Armagh: 1684–1707' in *Seanchas Ard Mhacha*, 18, 1 (1999–2000), pp 30–48.

David Fitzpatrick, 'Eamon de Valera at Trinity College' in *Hermathena*, cxxxiii (Winter, 1982), pp 7–14.

Francis Finegan, 'The Irish College at Poiters: 1674–1762' in *IER*, civ (1965), pp 18–35.

——, 'The Jesuits in Dublin (1660–1760)' in *Reportorium Novum*, iv (1971), pp 43–100.

J.M. Flood, *The life of Chevalier Charles Wogan: an Irish soldier of fortune* (Dublin, 1922).

H. Floris Cohen, *The scientific revolution: a historiographical inquiry* (Chicago, 1994).

Laurence J. Flynn, 'Hugh MacMahon, bishop of Clogher 1707–15 and archbishop of Armagh 1715–37' in *Seanchas Ard Mhacha*, 7, 1 (1973), pp 108–75.

Alison Forrestal, *Catholic synods in Ireland, 1600–1690* (Dublin, 1998).

C.F. Fowler, *Descartes on the human soul: philosophy and the demands of Christian doctrine* (Dordrecht, 2000).

Franciscan Fathers (ed.), *Father Luke Wadding commemorative volume* (Dublin, 1957).

Roger French and Andrew Cunningham, *Before science: the invention of the friars' natural philosophy* (Aldershot, 1996).

Willem Frijhoff, 'Patterns' in Hilde de Ridder-Symoens, (ed.), *A history of the university in Europe*, pp 43–110.

Daniel Garber, 'Locke, Berkeley and corpuscular scepticism' in Colin Turbayne (ed.), *Berkeley: critical and interpretative essays* (Manchester, 1982), pp 174–94.

——, 'Descartes, the Aristotelians and the revolution that did not happen in 1637' in *The Monist*, 71, 4 (Oct 1988), pp 47–86.

——, *Descartes' metaphysical physics* (Chicago, 1992).

—— and Michael Ayers, *The Cambridge history of seventeenth-century philosophy* (Cambridge, 1998).

John Gascoigne, 'A reappraisal of the role of the universities in the scientific revolution' in Lindberg and Westman, *Reappraisals of the scientific revolution*, pp 207–60.

Stephen Gaukroger, *Descartes: an intellectual biography* (Oxford, 1995).

Nathalie Genet-Rouffiac, 'Jacobites in Paris and Saint-Germain-en-Laye' in Cruickshanks and Corp (eds), *The Stuart court in exile and the Jacobites*, pp 15–38.

Cathaldus Giblin, 'The *Processus Datariae* and the appointment of Irish bishops in the seventeenth century' in Franciscan Fathers (ed.), *Father Luke Wadding*, pp 508–616.

——, 'The Stuart nomination of Irish bishops, 1687–1765' in *IER*, fifth series, cv (1966), pp 35–47.

——, 'Hugh MacCaghwell O.F.M. and Scotism at St Anthony's College, Louvain' in *De doctrina Ioannis Duns Scotus*, iv (Rome, 1968), pp 375–97.

——, 'Irish exiles in Catholic Europe' in P.J. Corish (ed.), *A history of Irish Catholicism*, iv, 3 (Dublin, 1971).

John T. Gilbert, *A history of the city of Dublin*, (3 vols, Dublin 1854–9).

Raymond Gillespie, 'Church, state and education in early modern Ireland' in Maurice O'Connell (ed.), *O'Connell: education, church and state* (Dublin, 1992).

——, 'The circulation of print in seventeenth-century Ireland' in *Studia Hibernica*, 29 (1995–7), pp 31–58.

——, 'Reading the bible in seventeenth century Ireland' in Cunningham and Kennedy (eds.), *The experience of reading*, pp 10–38.

——, 'Catholic religious cultures in the diocese of Dublin, 1614–97' in Kelly and Keogh (eds), *History of the Catholic diocese of Dublin*, pp 127–43.

——, 'The coming of reform, 1500–58' in Milne (ed.), *Christ Church Cathedral Dublin*, pp 151–173.

——, 'The shaping of reform, 1558–1625' in Milne (ed.), *Christ Church Cathedral Dublin*, pp 174–194.

——, 'The crisis of reform, 1625–60' in Milne (ed.), *Christ Church Cathedral Dublin*, pp 195–217.

Étienne Gilson, *Études sur le role de la pensée médiévale dans la formation du systéme Cartésien* (Paris, 1930).

——, *Index Scholastico-Cartésien*, second edn (Paris, 1979).

A.P. Goujet, *Memoire historique et littéraire sur le Collège Royal de France* (2 vols, Paris, 1758).

Ronald Gowing, 'A study of spirals: Cotes and Varignon' in P.M. Harman and Alan E. Shapiro (eds), *Investigation of difficult things: essays on Newton and the history of exact sciences in honour of D.T. Whiteside* (Cambridge, 1992), pp 371–81.

Anthony Grafton, 'Teacher, text and pupil in the Renaissance classroom: a case study from a Parisian college', *History of Universities*, i (1981), pp 37–70.

——, *Defenders of the text: the traditions of scholarship in an age of science, 1450–1800* (Harvard, 1991).

——, 'The new science and the traditions of humanism' in Kraye (ed.), *The Cambridge companion to Renaissance Humanism* (Cambridge, 1996), pp 203–23.

Edward Grant, 'Aristotelianism and the longevity of the medieval world view' in *History of Science*, 16 (1978), pp 93–106.

——, 'Science and theology in the middle ages' in Lindberg and Numbers (eds), *God and nature*, pp 49–75.

Jacques M. Gres-Gayer, 'Un théologian Gallican témoin de son temps, Louis Ellies Du Pin (1657–1719)' in *Revue d'histoire de l'Église de France*, 72 (1986), pp 67–121.

——, 'Le Gallicanisme de Louis Ellies Du Pin' in *Lias*, 18 (1991), pp 37–82.

——, *Théologie et pouvoir en Sorbonne: la faculté de théologie de Paris et la bulle* Unigenitus, *1714–21* (Paris, 1991).

——, *Jansénisme en Sorbonne, 1643–1656* (Paris, 1996).

Brian M. Halloran, *The Scots College Paris, 1603–1792* (Edinburgh, 1997).

Alastair Hamilton, 'Humanists and the Bible' in Jill Kraye (ed.), *The Cambridge companion to Renaissance Humanism* (Cambridge, 1996), pp 100–17.

Gary Hatfield, 'Metaphysics and the new science' in Lindberg and Westman, *Reappraisals of the scientific revolution*, pp 93–166.

Richard Hayes, 'Irish associations with Nantes' in *Studies*, 28 (1939), pp 115–26.

——, *A biographical dictionary of Irishmen in France* (Dublin, 1949).

Gráinne Henry, *The Irish military community in Spanish Flanders, 1586–1621* (Dublin, 1992).

Nora M. Hickey, 'The Cromwellian settlement in Balyna parish, 1641–1688' in *Journal of the County Kildare Archaeological Society*, xvi, 5 (1985–6), pp 496–509.

C.H. Holland (ed.), *Trinity College Dublin and the idea of a university* (Dublin, 1991).

K.T. Hoppen, *The common scientist in the seventeenth century: a study of the Dublin Philosophical Society, 1683–1708* (London, 1970).

——, 'The papers of the Dublin Philosophical Society, 1683–1708: introductory material and index' in *Anal. Hib.*, 30 (1982), pp 151–248.

Michael Hunter, *Science and shape of orthodoxy: intellectual change in late seventeenth-century Britain* (Woodbridge, 1995).

John Ingamells, *A dictionary of British and Irish travellers in Italy, 1701–1800* (London, 1997).

Jonathan Israel, *Radical Enlightenment: philosophy and the making of modernity, 1650–1750* (Oxford, 2001).

James R. Jacob and Margaret C. Jacob, 'The Anglican origins of modern science: the metaphysical foundations of the Whig constitution' in *Isis*, 71 (1980), pp 251–67.

Margaret C. Jacob, *The radical enlightenment: pantheists, freemasons and republicans* (London, 1981).

——, *The cultural meaning of the scientific revolution* (New York, 1988).

Adrian Johns, 'Identity, practice and trust in early modern natural philosophy' in *The History Journal*, 42, 4 (1999), pp 1125–45.

Charles Jourdain, *Histoire de l'Université de Paris au XVIIe et au XVIIIe siècles* (Paris, 1862).

Dominique Julia, 'Les institutions et les hommes' in Jacques Verger (ed.), *Histoire des universités en France* (Toulouse, 1986), pp 141–98.

James Kelly and Dáire Keogh (eds), *History of the Catholic diocese of Dublin* (Dublin, 2000).

——, 'The impact of the penal laws' in Kelly and Keogh (eds), *History of the Catholic diocese of Dublin*, pp 144–73.

Joseph P. Kelly, 'The parish of Johnstown' in *Riocht na Midhe*, iii, 3 (1965), pp 205–9.

Patrick Kelly, '"A light to the blind": the voice of the dispossessed élite in the generation after the defeat at Limerick' in *IHS*, xxiv, 96 (1985), pp 431–62.

——, 'Nationalism and the contemporary historians of the Jacobite war in Ireland' in Michael O'Dea and Kevin Whelan (eds), *Nations and nationalisms: France, Britain, Ireland and the eighteenth-century context* (Oxford, 1995), pp 89–102.

John Kingson, 'Catholic families of the Pale' in *Reportorium Novum*, i, 1 (1955), pp 76–90, i, 2 (1956), pp 323–350, ii, 2 (1960), pp 88–108.

Vincent Kinnane and Anne Walsh (eds), *Essays on the history of Trinity College Library Dublin* (Dublin, 2000).

Stuart Kinsella, 'From Hiberno-Norse to Anglo-Norman, *c.*1030–1300' in Milne (ed.), *Christ Church Cathedral Dublin*, pp 25–52.

Charles Alan Kors, *Atheism in France 1650–1729, volume 1: the orthodox sources of disbelief* (Princeton, 1990).

——, 'Theology and atheism in early modern France' in Anthony Grafton and Ann Blair (eds), *The transmission of culture in early modern Europe* (Philadelphia, 1990).

B. Robert Kreiser, *Miracles, convulsions and ecclesiastical politics in early eighteenth century Paris* (Princeton, 1978).

Paul Oskar Kristeller, 'The myth of Renaissance atheism and the French tradition of free thought' in *Journal of the History of Philosophy*, 6 (1968), pp 233–43.

Dorothea Krook, *John Sergeant and his circle: a study of three seventeenth-century English Aristotelians*, ed. Beverley C. Southgate (Leiden, 1993).

Yves Laissus et Jean Torlais, *Le Jardin du Roi et le Collège Royal dans l'enseignement des sciences au XVIIIᵉ siècle* (Paris, 1986, first published in Taton, *Enseignement*).

Paul Lallemand, *Histoire de l'éducation dans l'ancien Oratoire de France* (Paris, 1888; reprinted Geneva, 1976).

Hugh Law, 'Sir Charles Wogan' in *Journal of the Royal Society of Antiquaries of Ireland*, lxvii (1937), pp 253–64.

Joep Leerssen, *Mere Irish and Fíor Ghael: studies in the idea of Irish nationality, its development and literary expression prior to the nineteenth century*, second edn (Cork, 1996).

Mary Lefkowitz, *Not out of Africa: how afrocentrism became an excuse to teach myth as history* (New York, 1997).

Abel LeFranc, *Histoire du Collège de France, depuis ses origines jusqu'à la fin du premier empire* (Paris, 1893).

Pádraig Lenihan, *Confederate Catholics at war, 1641–49* (Cork, 2001).

Colm Lennon, 'Primate Richard Creagh and the beginnings of the Irish counter-reformation' in *Archiv. Hib.*, li (1997), pp 74–86.

——, *The urban patriciate of early-modern Ireland: a case study of Limerick* (Dublin, 1999).

——, *An Irish prisoner of conscience of the Tudor era: Archbishop Richard Creagh of Armagh, 1523–86* (Dublin, 2000).

——, 'Mass in the manor house: the counter-reformation in Dublin, 1560–1630' in Kelly and Keogh (eds), *History of the Catholic diocese of Dublin*, pp 112–26.

John Leonard, 'Kilkenny's short-lived university (Feb–Jul 1690)' in *Archiv. Hib.*, xliii (1988), pp 65–84.

——, *A university for Kilkenny: plans for a royal college in the seventeenth century* (Dublin, 1996).

Thomas M. Lennon, *The battle of gods and giants: the legacies of Descartes and Gassendi: 1655–1715* (Princeton, 1993).

Emmanuel LeRoy Ladurie, *L'ancien régime, I: 1610–1715* (Paris, 1991).

David Lindberg and Ronald Numbers (eds), *God and nature: historical essays on the encounter between Christianity and science* (London, 1986).

—— and Robert Westman (eds), *Reappraisals of the scientific revolution* (Cambridge, 1991).

James Lydon, 'The silent sister: Trinity College and Catholic Ireland' in C.H. Holland (ed.), *Trinity College Dublin and the idea of a university* (Dublin, 1991), pp 29–53.

Mary Ann Lyons, '"Vagabonds", "Mendicants", "Gueux": French reactions to Irish immigration in the early seventeenth century' in *French History*, 14, 4 (2000), pp 363–82.

Prioncias MacCana, *Collège des Irlandais Paris and Irish studies* (Dublin, 2001).

Hector McDonnell, *The wild geese of the Antrim MacDonnells* (Dublin, 1996).

R.B. McDowell and D.A. Webb, *Trinity College, Dublin, 1592–1952: an academic history* (Cambridge, 1982).

James MacGeoghegan, *The history of Ireland, ancient and modern*, trans. Patrick O'Kelly (first published Paris, 1759–62; Dublin, 1844).

Bríd McGrath, 'Meath members of parliament 1634–1641' in *Ríocht na Midhe*, xii (2001), pp 90–107.

Philip McGuinness, '"Perpetual flux": Newton, Toland, science and the status quo' in McGuinness, Harrison and Kearney (eds), *John Toland's Christianity not mysterious*, pp 313–27.

James McGuire, 'Richard Talbot, earl of Tyrconnell (1630–91) and the Catholic counter-revolution' in Ciaran Brady (ed.), *Worsted in the game: losers in Irish history* (Dublin, 1989), pp 73–83.

——, 'James II and Ireland, 1685–90' in W.A. Maguire (ed.), *Kings in conflict: the revolutionary war in Ireland and its aftermath, 1689–1750* (Belfast, 1990), pp 45–57.

Angus Macintyre, 'The college, King James II and the revolution, 1687–1688' in Brockliss, Harriss and Macintyre (eds), *Magdalen College and the crown*, pp 31–82.

Thomas McLoughlin, 'Censorship and defenders of the Cartesian faith in mid-seventeenth century France' in *Journal of the History of Ideas*, 40, 4 (1979), pp 563–82.

John McManners, *Church and society in eighteenth century France*, (2 vols, Oxford, 1999).

W. Macneile Dixon, *Trinity College Dublin* (London, 1902).

The Marquis McSwiney of Mashanaglass, 'Notes on the history of the Book of Lecan' in *Proc. RIA*, section C, xxxviii (1928–9), pp 31–50.

W.A. Maguire (ed.), *Kings in conflict: the revolutionary war in Ireland and its aftermath, 1689–1750* (Belfast, 1990).

J. Malthorez, 'Notes sur les prêtres Irlandais réfugiés à Nantes aux XVIIe et XVIIIe siècles' in *Revue d'Histoire de l'Église de France*, 3e année (1912), pp 164–73.

Roger Marchal, *Madame Lambert et son milieu* (Oxford, 1991).

Margherita Marchione (trans. and adaptation), *From the land of the Etruscans: the life of Lucy Filippini by Pietro Bergamaschi* (Rome, 1986).

C.L. Marie, *Les convulsionnaires de Saint-Médard: miracles, convulsions et prophéties à Paris au XVIIIe siècle* (Paris, 1985).

Constantia Maxwell, *A history of Trinity College Dublin, 1591–1892* (Dublin, 1946).

Christiana Mercer, 'The vitality and importance of early modern Aristotelianism' in Tom Sorrell (ed.), *The rise of modern philosophy: the tension between the new and traditional philosophies from Machiavelli to Leibnitz* (Oxford, 1993), pp 33–67.

Jean Meyer, *La France moderne de 1515 à 1789* (Paris, 1985).

John Miller, *Popery and politics in England, 1660–1688* (Cambridge, 1973).

——, 'Thomas Sheridan and his Narrative' in *IHS*, xx, 78 (1976), pp 105–28.

——, 'The earl of Tyrconnell and James II's Irish policy' in *Historical Journal*, xx, 4 (1977), pp 803–23.

Benignus Millet, 'Archbishop Edmund O'Reilly's report on the state of the church in Ireland, 1662' in *Collect. Hib.*, 2 (1959), pp 105–14.

——, 'Irish Scotists at St Isodore's College, Rome in the seventeenth century', in *De doctrina Ioannis Duns Scotus*, 4 (1968), pp 399–419.

——, 'Survival and reorganisation 1650–95' in Patrick J. Corish (ed.), *A history of Irish Catholicism*, iii, 7 (1968).

——, 'Irish literature in Latin 1550–1700' in T.W. Moody, F.X. Martin and F.J. Byrne (eds), *A new history of Ireland: iii, early modern Ireland 1534–1691* (Oxford, 1976), pp 561–86.

Kenneth Milne (ed.), *Christ Church Cathedral Dublin: a history* (Dublin, 2000).

——, 'Restoration and reorganisation, 1660–1830' in idem (ed.), *Christ Church Cathedral Dublin*, pp 255–97.

Sean Moran, 'Michael Moore of Paris. Commentary on a summer scheme staged within Trinity College' in *Catholic Bulletin*, xxvii (Aug. 1937), pp 609–15.

James More, 'The O'More family of Balyna in the County Kildare, by James More of Balyna, circa 1774', ed. Rev E. O'Leary and Lord Walter Fitzgerald, in *Journal of the County Kildare Archaeological Society*, ix (1918–21), pp 277–91, 318–330.

Hiram Morgan (ed.), *Political ideology in Ireland, 1541–1641* (Dublin, 1999).

Thomas Morrissey, *James Archer of Kilkenny: an Elizabethan Jesuit* (Dublin, 1979).

Rainer A. Muller, 'Student education, student life', Hilde de Ridder-Symoens (ed.), *A history of the university in Europe, volume two*, pp 326–54.

Daniel Murphy, *A history of Irish emigrant and missionary education* (Dublin, 2000).

H.L. Murphy, *A history of Trinity College Dublin from its foundation to 1702* (Dublin, 1951).

Steven Nadler, 'Arnauld, Descartes and transubstantiation: reconciling Cartesian metaphysics and the real presence' in *Journal of the History of Ideas*, 49, 2 (1998), pp 229–46.

——, 'Doctrines of explanation in late scholasticism and in the mechanical philosophy' in Garber and Ayers, *The Cambridge history of seventeenth-century philosophy*, pp 513–54.

Alain Niderst, *Fontanelle* (Paris, 1991).

Jeroen Nilis (and Joseph Laenen), 'The Irish College Antwerp' in *Clogher Record*, xv, 3 (1996), pp 1–86.

Gabriel Nuchelmans, 'Logic in the seventeenth century: preliminary remarks and the constituents of the proposition' in Garber and Ayers, *The Cambridge history of seventeenth-century philosophy*, pp 103–17.

James O'Boyle, *The Irish colleges on the continent: their origin and history* (Belfast, 1935).

Éamonn Ó Ciardha, 'The Stuarts and deliverance in Irish and Scots-Gaelic poetry 1690–1760' in S.J. Connolly (ed.), *Kingdoms united? Great Britain and Ireland since 1500: integration and diversity* (Dublin, 1999), pp 78–94.

——, *Ireland and the Jacobite cause, 1685–1766: a fatal attachment* (Dublin, 2002).

Éamon Ó Ciosáin, 'Les Irlandais en Bretagne 1603–1780: "invasion", accueil, intégration' in Catherine Laurent et Helen Davis (eds), *Irlande et Bretagne vingt siècles d'histoire* (Rennes, 1994), pp 152–66.

——, 'Attitudes towards Ireland and the Irish in Enlightenment France' in Graham Gargett and Geraldine Sheridan (eds), *Ireland and the French Enlightenment, 1700–1800* (London, 1999), pp 129–51.

——, 'A hundred years of Irish migration to France, 1590–1688' in O'Connor (ed.), *The Irish in Europe 1580–1815*, pp 93–106.

Patricia O Connell, *The Irish College at Alcalá de Henares, 1649–1785* (Dublin, 1997).

——, 'The early-modern Irish college network in Iberia, 1590–1800' in O'Connor (ed.), *The Irish in Europe*, pp 49–64.

Priscilla O'Connor, 'Irish students in Paris faculty of theology: aspects of doctrinal controversy in the *ancien régime*, 1730–60' in *Archiv. Hib.*, liii (1998), pp 85–97.

——, 'Irish clerics and Jacobites in early eighteenth-century Paris, 1700–1730' in O'Connor (ed.), *The Irish in Europe*, pp 175–190.

——, 'Irish clerics and French politics of grace: the reception of Nicholas Madgett's doctoral theses, 1732' in O'Connor and Lyons (eds), *Irish migrants in Europe after Kinsale, 1602–1820*, pp 182–202.

Thomas O'Connor, *An Irish theologian in Enlightenment France: Luke Joseph Hooke, 1714–96* (Dublin, 1995).

——, 'Surviving the civil constitution of the clergy: Luke Joseph Hooke's revolutionary experiences' in *Eighteenth-Century Ireland*, 2 (1996), pp 129–45.

——, 'The role of Irish clerics in Paris University politics, 1730–40' in *History of Universities*, xv (1997–9), pp 193–225.

——, 'Towards the invention of the Irish Catholic *Natio:* Thomas Messingham's *Florilegium*' in *Irish Theological Quarterly*, 64 (1999), pp 157–77.

——, 'Custom, authority and tolerance in Irish political thought: David Rothe's *Analecta*, 1616' in *Irish Theological Quarterly*, 65, 2 (2000), pp 133–56.

——, 'Thomas Messingham (*c.*1575–1638?) and the seventeenth-century church' in *Ríocht na Midhe*, xi (2000), pp 88–105.

—— (ed.), *The Irish in Europe 1580–1815* (Dublin, 2001).

—— and Mary Ann Lyons (eds), *Irish migrants in Europe after Kinsale, 1602–1820* (Dublin, 2003).

——, 'A justification for foreign intervention in early modern Ireland: Peter Lombard's Commentarius (1600)' in O'Connor and Lyons (eds), *Irish migrants in Europe after Kinsale*, pp 14–31.

Thomas Ó Fiaich, 'The appointment of Bishop Tyrrell and its consequences' in *Clogher Record*, 1, 3 (1955), pp 1–14.

Standish O'Grady and Robin Flower (eds), *Catalogue of Irish manuscripts in the British Museum* (3 vols, London, 1926–53).

Eoghan Ó hAnnracháin, 'Irish veterans at the Hotel Royal des Invalides (1692–1769)' in *Irish Sword*, xxi, 83 (1999), pp 5–39.

Tadhg Ó hAnnracháin, '"Though hereticks and politicians should misinterpret their good zeal": political ideology and Catholicism in early modern Ireland' in Ohlmeyer (ed.), *Political thought in seventeenth-century Ireland*, pp 155–75.

——, *Catholic reformation in Ireland: the mission of Rinuccini, 1645–1649* (Oxford, 2002).

Jane Ohlmeyer, 'Seventeenth-century Ireland and the New British and Atlantic Histories' in *American Historical Review*, 104, 2 (April 1999), pp 446–62.

—— (ed.), *Political thought in seventeenth-century Ireland: kingdom or colony* (Cambridge, 2000).

Joseph O'Leary, 'The Irish and Jansenism in the seventeenth century' in Swords (ed.), *The Irish-French connection*, pp 21–43.

T.F. O'Rahilly, 'Irish scholars in Dublin in the early eighteenth century' in *Gadelica*, i (1912–13), pp 156–62.

W.M. O'Riordan, 'A list of the priests, secular and regular, of the diocese of Dublin in the year 1697' in *Reportorium Novum*, i, 1 (1955), pp 140–53.

Ciaran O'Scea, 'The devotional world of the Irish Catholic exile in early-modern Galicia, 1598–1666' in O'Connor (ed.), *The Irish in Europe*, pp 27–48.

Micheál Ó Siochrú, (ed.), *Kingdoms in crisis: Ireland in the 1640s* (Dublin, 2001).

Margaret J. Osler, 'Whose ends: teleology in early modern natural philosophy' in *Osiris*, 16 (2001), pp 151–168.

Antonio Patrizi, *Storia del seminario di Montefiascone* (Bolsena, 1990).

Juan José Pérez-Camacho, 'Late renaissance humanism and the Dublin scientific tradition (1592–1641)' Norman McMillan (ed.), *Prometheus's fire: a history of scientific and technological education in Ireland* (Carlow, 2000), pp 51–73.

René Pillorget, 'Louis XIV et L'Irlande' in *Revue d'Histoire Diplomatique*, cvii (1992), pp 7–28.

Martin L. Pine, 'Pomponazzi, Pietro (1462–1525)' in Edward Craig (ed.), *Routledge encyclopaedia of philosophy* (10 vols, London, 1998), vii, pp 529–33.

Hugh Poe, 'A Dublin priest translates the Latin New Testament into English' in *IER*, 54 (1939), pp 235–43.

Roy Porter, 'The scientific revolution in the universities' in Hilde de Ridder-Symoens, (ed.), *A history of the university in Europe, volume two*, pp 531–62.

E. Preclin et E. Jarry, *Les luttes politiques et doctrinales aux XVIIᵉ et XVIIIᵉ siècles* (2 parties, Paris, 1955–6).

Thomas L. Prendergast, 'Descartes: immortality, human bodies and God's absolute freedom' in *Modern Schoolman*, lxxi (Nov 1993), pp 17–46.

Pietro Redondi, *Galileo heretic (Galileo eretico)*, trans. Raymond Rosenthal (London, 1988).

Patricia Reif, 'The textbook tradition in natural philosophy, 1600–1650' in *Journal of the History of Ideas*, 30 1 (1969), pp 17–32.

Hilde de Ridder-Symoens, (ed.), *A history of the university in Europe, volume two: universities in early modern Europe (1500–1800)* (Cambridge, 1996).

Helga Robinson-Hammerstein (ed.), *European universities in the age of reformation and counter-reformation* (Dublin, 1998).

Mafaldina Rocca, *Cardinal Mark Anthony Barbarigo*, ed. and trans. Margherita Marchione (Rome, 1992).

Richard Roche, 'Alexius Stafford: "the popish dean of Christ's Church"' in *History Ireland*, 8, 3 (Autumn 2000), pp 32–4.

Edward Rogan, *Synods and catechesis in Ireland, c.445–1962* (Rome, 1987).

Wolfgang Rother, 'The teaching of philosophy at seventeenth century Zurich' in *History of Universities*, xi (1992), pp 59–74.

Guy Rowlands, 'An army in exile: Louis XIV and the Irish forces of James II in France, 1691–1698' in *Royal Stuart Papers*, 60 (2001), pp 1–29.

Simon Schaffer, 'Godly men and mechanical philosophers: souls and spirits in restoration natural philosophy' in *Science in Context*, 1, 1 (1987), pp 55–85.

Tad M. Schmaltz 'What has Cartesianism to do with Jansenism?' in *Journal of the History of Ideas*, 60, 1 (1999), pp 37–56.

Charles B. Schmitt, *Aristotle and the Renaissance* (Harvard, 1983).

Jorge Secada, *Cartesian metaphysics: the late scholastic origins of modern philosophy* (Cambridge, 2000).

A. Sedgwick, *Jansenism in seventeenth century France: voices in the wilderness* (Charlottesville, 1977).

L. Am. Sédillot, *Les professeurs de mathématiques et de physique générale au Collège de France* (Rome, 1869).

Domenico Sella, *Italy in the seventeenth century* (London, 1987).

Sebastiano Serena (ed.), *L'opera data dal Cardinale Beato Gregorio Barbarigo nel seminario di Padova agli studi della lingua e della litteratura Latina* (Padova, 1938).

Philip W. Sergeant, *Little Jennings and fighting Dick Talbot: a life of the duke and duchess of Tyrconnell* (2 vols, London, 1913).

John J. Silke, 'The Irish abroad, 1534–1691' in *A new history of Ireland: iii, early modern Ireland, 1534–1691* (Oxford, 1976), pp 587–633.

J.G. Simms, 'Dublin in 1685' in *IHS*, xiv, 55 (March 1965), pp 212–226.

——, *Jacobite Ireland, 1685–91* (London, 1969).

——, *The Jacobite Parliament of 1689* (Dundalk, 1974).

——, 'The Irish on the continent, 1691–1800' in *A new history of Ireland: iv, eighteenth-century Ireland, 1691–1800* (Oxford, 1986), pp 629–56.

William Smyth, 'Exploring the social and cultural topographies of sixteenth and seventeenth century County Dublin' in F.H.A. Aalen and Kevin Whelan (eds), *Dublin city and county: from prehistory to the present: studies in honour of J.H. Andrews* (Dublin, 1992), pp 121–79.

J.S. Spink, *French free-thought from Gassendi to Voltaire* (New York, 1960).

W.B. Stanford, *Ireland and the classical tradition*, second edn (Dublin, 1984).

Alice Stroup, 'The political theory and practice of technology under Louis XIV' in Bruce T. Moran (ed.), *Patronage and institutions: science, technology and medicine at the European court, 1500–1700* (London, 1991), pp 211–34.

J.W. Stubbs, *The history of the University of Dublin from its foundation to the end of the eighteenth century* (Dublin, 1889).

Liam Swords (ed.), *The Irish-French connection, 1578/1978* (Paris, 1978).

——, 'Collège des Lombards' in Swords (ed.), *The Irish-French connection 1578/1978*, pp 44–62.

Maxime Targe, *Professeurs et régents de Collège dans l'ancienne université de Paris (XVIIᵉ et XVIIᵉ siècles)* (Paris, 1902).

Rene Taton (ed.), *Enseignement et diffusion des sciences en France du dix huitième siècle*, second edn (Paris, 1986).

Lynn Thorndike, 'Censorship by the Sorbonne of science and superstition in the first half of the seventeenth century' in *Journal of the History of Ideas*, 16, 1 (1955), pp 119–25.

Andre Tuilier, *Histoire de l'Université de Paris et de la Sorbonne* (2 vols, Paris, 1994).

Alexandro Volpini, *De vita et moribus M. Antonii Barbadici Card. Pontificis Faliscodunensium et Cornetanorum* (Faventiae, 1877).

Thomas Wall, 'Seventeenth-century Irish theologians in exile' in *IER*, fifth series, lii (1939), pp 501–15.

——, 'Irish enterprise in the University of Paris (1651–1653)' in *IER*, fifth series, lxiv (1944), pp 94–106.

A. Walsh, 'Irish exiles in Brittany' in *IER*, fourth series, i (1897), pp 311–22, ii (1897), pp 125–38, iii (1898), 323–45, iv (1898), pp 354–65.

T.J. Walsh, *The Irish continental college movement* (Cork, 1973).

Michael Ward, 'The Dowdall crosses in County Meath' in *Annala Dhamhliag (Annals of Duleek)*, i, (1971), pp 9–14.

Norman Wells, 'Jean du Hamel, the Cartesians and Arnauld on idea' in *Modern Schoolman*, 74, 4 (1999), pp 245–71.

Richard S. Westfall, 'The rise of science and the decline of orthodox Christianity: a study of Kepler, Descartes and Newton' in Lindberg and Numbers (eds), *God and nature*, pp 218–37.

Fred Wilson, 'The rationalist response to Aristotle in Descartes and Arnauld' in Elmar J. Kremer (ed.), *The Great Arnauld and some of his philosophical contemporaries* (Toronto, 1994), pp 28–65.

C.E. Wright and Ruth Wright, *The diary of Humfrey Wanley, 1715–1726* (2 vols, London, 1966).

UNPUBLISHED SECONDARY SOURCES

David Attis, 'The ascendancy of mathematics: mathematics and Irish society from Cromwell to the Celtic Tiger' (Ph.D., Princeton, 2000).

A. Bachelier, 'Essai sur l'Oratoire à Nantes au XVIIᵉ et au XVIIIᵉ siècles' (Thèse complémentaire pour le doctorat es lettres, Angers, 1934).

L.W.B. Brockliss, 'The University of Paris in the sixteenth and seventeenth centuries' (Ph.D., Cambridge, 1976).

—— and P. Ferté, 'A prosopography of Irish clerics who studied in France in the seventeenth and eighteenth centuries, in particular at the universities of Paris and Toulouse', unpublished, 1987 (Typescript copy, Russell Library, N.U.I., Maynooth).

Vincent P. Carey, 'Gaelic reaction to plantation: the case of the O'More and O'Connor Lordships of Laois and Offaly, 1570–1603' (M.A., Maynooth, 1985).

Liam Chambers, 'The life and writings of Michael Moore, c.1639–1726' (Ph.D., N.U.I., Maynooth, 2001).

Ann de Valera, 'Antiquarian and historical investigations in Ireland in the eighteenth-century' (M.A., UCD, 1978).

Mary Elizabeth Kennedy, 'French language books in eighteenth-century Ireland: dissemination and readership' (2 vols, Ph.D., UCD, 1994).

David Murphy, 'Christ Church Cathedral, Dublin: 1660–1760' (M.A., UCD, 1995).

Priscilla O'Connor, 'Les Irlandais et la faculté de théologie de Paris: la condamnation des thèses, 1730–1760' (Mémoire de D.E.A., L'École Pratique des Hautes Études, 1995).

Index